Adversity *to* Adaptability

Turn Life's Greatest Challenges into Your Greatest Opportunities

CERTIFIED COACHES FEDERATION™

ADVERSITY TO ADAPTABILITY
TURN LIFE'S GREATEST CHALLENGES INTO
YOUR GREATEST OPPORTUNITIES

iUniverse books may be ordered through booksellers or by contacting:

iUniverse
1663 Liberty Drive
Bloomington, IN 47403
www.iuniverse.com
1-800-Authors (1-800-288-4677)

Because of the dynamic nature of the Internet, any web addresses or links contained in this book may have changed since publication and may no longer be valid. The views expressed in this work are solely those of the author and do not necessarily reflect the views of the publisher, and the publisher hereby disclaims any responsibility for them.

Any people depicted in stock imagery provided by Getty Images are models, and such images are being used for illustrative purposes only. Certain stock imagery © Getty Images.

ISBN: 978-1-5320-9594-8 (sc)
ISBN: 978-1-5320-9596-2 (hc)
ISBN: 978-1-5320-9595-5 (e)

Library of Congress Control Number: 2020905620

Print information available on the last page.

iUniverse rev. date: 04/16/2020

Contents

Dedication

To Matthew, Maleia, and Makai,

When you face adversity, keep going, and you will always find a way through. As the Japanese proverb suggests, "fall down seven times, get up eight."

About Us

Founded in 2006 by Derrick Sweet, the Certified Coaches Federation has certified more than 14,000 Life Coaches and Executive Coaches. We are now one of the leading coach education programs in the world.

The Certified Coaches Federation believes that the primary criteria to be a coach is your ability to leverage your life experience. We embrace the truth and authenticity of the human condition, with its bright lights and dark shadows. We believe that every human being is unique, therefore you are exceptional in your own way.

Rather than shy away from vulnerability, we teach coaches to move towards it. It is in our vulnerability that we can discover our greatest strengths. We believe that acknowledging and embracing vulnerability is a core component of coaching and is part of how we educate and certify coaches.

Our hope in publishing this book is that you too may be inspired to hire a coach so you can evolve into the person you wish to be or perhaps become a coach so you can join us in making the world a better place.

Preface

Everyone faces adversity at some point in their lives, and in some cases, several times in their lives. It often helps to know that others have faced challenges and found ways to overcome them. It is part of our human nature to "borrow hope" from someone else's example of overcoming adversity.

In this book, you will discover stories shared by fifteen coaches whose lives have been far from easy. You will benefit from their stories and the processes they used to overcome their adversities and eventually become coaches themselves.

Each author was carefully selected for their story or philosophy and their ability to convey it. They have shared what they accomplished, but also how you may learn from them. Their greatest wish is that their stories may help you.

As the editor, and one of the authors, the act of collecting these stories was akin to collecting sacred memories and burgeoning philosophies to be shared as a celebration of human life. I hope the stories both inspire and inform you in a variety of ways and help you overcome adversity in your life. I am grateful that the authors let us into their lives, and equally, that you, the readers, will open your hearts to their stories.

Rod Macdonald,
CEO Certified Coaches Federation, Editor, Author

Acknowledgments

This book would not exist without the ongoing support of my coach, and founder of the Certified Coaches Federation and Healthy Wealthy and Wise® Corporation, Derrick Sweet. Along with his wife, and Certified Coaches Federation COO, Marsha Staton-Sweet, they have had a profound impact on my life and the lives of tens of thousands of others.

I also appreciate the authors of this book for their contributions and powerful vulnerability in sharing their stories. Their willingness to help others by revealing sometimes intense, always authentic personal accounts of their challenges is inspiring. This project has been a labor of love for all of us involved. I genuinely appreciate everyone's dedication, bravery, and patience as it grew from an idea to its full presentation.

I am eternally grateful to my mother for being my first hero and role-model and helping shape the person I am today. Finally, I thank my wife, Jubette, for her love and support in completing this and countless other projects.

Rod Macdonald,
CEO Certified Coaches Federation, Editor, Author

Introduction

Whatever adversity you face, you can overcome it.

When a person receives the calling to be a coach, it comes from deep within, often awoken by adversity. While adversity is an inevitable aspect of life, what one does with the aftermath of adversity is often lost, rather than learned. Many people target "resilience" as the best response to adversity. In this book, we look to adaptability, so that we may not only return to how and where we were but be better than when we started.

We often internalize the pain of adversity accumulated over many years, when we could let the pain go and allow the lesson to remain. Coaches learn this and then support others in discovering this.

Adversity can take many forms, including, but not limited to, loss of a loved one, abuse, abandonment, neglect, manipulation, anxiety, depression, and more. Some people experience adversity for short periods and others for years or decades.

If this sounds familiar, then you know there is a desire for resolution. As you read this book, you will learn from the adversities the authors experienced and the lessons they've unearthed from those adversities. You are encouraged to read every chapter, but you may also treat it like a recipe book, from which you can extract whatever you need for whatever you are facing.

Our hope is you will be inspired, not just by the stories of overcoming adversity, but also the mindset and strategies used. Our wish is that you get past the things that no longer serve you, get through the challenges you are currently facing, and get to the opportunities that lay ahead.

We wish you health, wealth, and wisdom on your journey,

The Certified Coaches Federation
Making the World a Better Place through Coaching

Beginning Anew

by Jennifer Albrecht

Illustration by Adrianna Harder

I was waiting for the sign. Waiting is often the most challenging part of any process; however, wait, I did. The sign was eventually revealed to me. It was a late afternoon in January. An owl was perched atop a leafless, frost-covered poplar tree. She was majestic—a great grey, and she appeared to me three days in succession. Day one, I stopped my vehicle to observe her. She didn't move or even so much as look my way. I didn't think much of this initial encounter, other than to appreciate the owl's natural beauty and feel blessed to have experienced the moment. It was a time in my life that I did not want to make the trip along that road where I lived. It had stopped feeling like a "home" and was more like a strange, altered reality where no one was content or comfortable, least of all me.

Day two, I traveled the same pathway at nearly the same time of day. It was dusk, approaching darkness. The owl was there again, perched on what seemed to be the same limb as the day before. I rolled down my passenger window and opened the sunroof to get a better view, hoping I'd see her move. I waited to see if she would spin her curious beak toward me, or ruffle her feathers in the cold, winter air; she did! She twisted her head in my direction, and then away again just as quickly; in a blink, it was over. It was as if she had heard my inner voice yearning to see her move, to prove she was real and not a mirage or an illusion— so strange it was to see her a second time! Owls in the wild are silent, sentient, elusive beings. Having a close-up sighting two days in a row was a true gift. I whispered aloud, "what are you doing up there again today?" I looked at the back of her smooth, feathered head for some time. She gave no indication that she was any longer aware of my presence or that she had heard my soft inquiry. I drove on and marveled that she was there two days in a row. The hunting must have been a sure bet from the vantage point of that sturdy treetop. I intuitively knew that it was the same owl. I felt she was there to greet me twice.

Day three felt surreal, and upon revisiting this memory many years later, I scarcely believe it unfolded as it did. As I made that same trek home that third day, I saw her sitting on what seemed to be the same, sturdy branch. I knew it was the same tree and the same, confident owl. Some experiences are undeniable. This time there was no hesitation. I unbuckled my seatbelt, propped myself up on the console of my vehicle, and slid open my sunroof, so my head poked out. We regarded one another with awareness and with what I would describe a silent greeting that sometimes happens when human meets one of God's feral creatures. I then whispered aloud, "what are you trying to tell me?" Some people pray for guidance, an answer, a circumstance to alter, an issue to resolve, someone or something to appear; I was looking for, praying for, "the sign." At that moment, she seemed to have been expecting this question that was embedded deep within my heart. She stretched upwards from her perch, unfurled her expansive wings, and ascended into the crisp, grey afternoon sky. She flapped her wings to gain height, circled once in the waning afternoon light, and dove for a farmer's field, encrusted with deep, lilac-tinged snow. Her talons grasped her prey: an unsuspecting mouse. She then ascended from the earth and in what seemed like a single, fluid motion, returned to the tree, her meal firmly in her grip. With a brisk shiver, she settled her feathers into place and observed me again with a stern, strong, look of conviction. She then turned her head away from me, staring at the spot she flew down to moments ago. I had never witnessed anything so swift and silent, so beautiful yet so visceral. At that moment, despite my fear, self-doubt, and indecisiveness, I had the sign; I knew what to do.

Not unlike a majestic owl lifting off and leaving the comfort and familiarity of a sturdy, safe branch, we humans have our unique ways of lifting off and "leaving." Leaving is a universal experience. We arrive in the lives of those with whom we have a connection, and sometimes we leave those relationships. Many life circumstances culminate in departure. Positive, life-changing, personal growth experiences can cause us to lift off from a sturdy, familiar branch and take flight toward an exciting future. We hope to land somewhere safe with a solid foundation, and even more robust than the last branch we took flight from. Circumstances such as growing up and "leaving the nest" to attend post-secondary school, entering the world of work, accepting a promotion, and moving up the proverbial corporate ladder. Or even entering a committed relationship or marriage which may require a departure to begin anew. These are but a few examples of positive, life-affirming events that may require leaving.

Conversely, there are troubling, sad, and contentious reasons people choose to leave behind all they know and the lives they have built. Some circumstances resulting in departure are the result of negative situations that may be unhealthy, personally stagnating, or even harmful. People leave jobs, partnerships, organizations, faith communities, marriages, and friendships (to name but a few circumstances) when they have come to the realization that to stay would mean remaining broken or continuing to fracture further. Most people lean toward where they naturally experience the greatest measure of hope, light, and possibility. For some, this will mean staying where they are, and for others, departure is probable.

Most often, we cannot foresee all that will come to replace what was once so central to our identity. There is a phrase that I often recite to myself when trying to make sense of situations that arise in my life, "I Plan, God Laughs." There is some truth in this simple statement, regardless of one's faith. Sometimes, despite all our ideas about how leaving will play out, even if our departure is sudden and unfolds quickly, it never entirely goes as planned. It is in the valleys—the low, dark places—where it can become apparent that our carefully planned departure (or hastily executed one) is not going to unfold as we'd hoped it would. It is in these difficult and often lonely places, that the deepest and most profound moments of learning and personal growth occur, and where we may also experience a measure of healing if we are open to it.

I have come to the realization that I, like many others, have a history of leaving. This discussion is specifically about choosing to leave on your terms. What my experience does not speak directly to, but may have echoes of similarity with, are circumstances where people leave when something naturally concludes or comes to an end—the end of one's formal education, when a contract, trip, or other time-defined experience is over, when retirement comes to pass, or perhaps when a loved one dies. Endings like these are better explored in a discussion focused on adjusting to a natural conclusion of events. Instead, this contribution presents several critical considerations for when people choose to leave. The topic of leaving does not get much airtime in conversations, pop culture, social media, magazines, or books. When it does, the topic of leaving is generally viewed in a negative light and seen as a form of giving up, giving in, and even as a form of weakness or failure. I aim to provide a different lens from which to view leaving—to help you develop a new or different mental construct of how the process of leaving has impacted or may impact, your life.

I have a history of leaving and, perhaps you do too. I left my parents' home and childhood community, I have ended friendships, left partners, jobs, organizations, women's groups, my faith community, my family physician, and I left a twenty-year marriage. Leaving may portray failure, weakness, loss, and can feel incredibly burdensome even if it's for positive, life-affirming reasons. Leaving may convey cruelty and betrayal. There is something deeply foreboding about the loss experienced when one physically and emotionally leaves, even if it's a healthy decision, and even if it's the only option. There are common threads to my experiences of leaving. Upon reflecting on my personal history of leaving, I have come to appreciate the many lessons learned about scarcity, loss, conformity, loneliness, courage, self-reliance, acceptance, and ultimately, about love. While leaving may appear to be a single, definable act, a moment in time when things change forever, in reality, leaving is a series of decisions that lead up to, culminate in, and follow the moment of departure. Leaving is a process. Through sharing a few of my own personal accounts of leaving, I invite you to be open to what may be a new perspective for you on this shared human reality. I encourage you to begin to frame leaving in a new way and understand personal experiences of leaving, while also cultivating an understanding of those who may have left you. Leaving is not quitting; leaving is beginning anew.

Before delving further into the topic of leaving, I'd like you to pause here and consider a time when you have contemplated leaving—a job, organization, team, club, relationship—it can be anything that readily comes to mind. Close your eyes for a moment and revisit your thoughts on leaving this part of your life. Hold onto this idea and imagine it resting gently in the palms of your hands or perched upon your fingers like a bird on a branch. I'll ask you to hold onto this idea as we move through concepts connected with leaving. I'll ask you to come back to your idea from time to time and consider it in the context of the topics I will cover. The points I will present are not about helping you decide whether to leave or not to leave, but instead about acknowledging how the process of leaving may unfold if you enacted your own process of departure. You may have several scenarios of leaving you are considering. That's okay.

Choose one for this exercise. You may wish to jot it down or to sketch it perched within the palms of your hands or on the branch of your fingertips. Later on, I invite you to re-visit my chapter and consider other circumstances of leaving that may arise for you. Do you have your idea in the palms of your hands, or on the sturdy branch of your fingertips? If you are able, simply observe your thought—it's just an idea—it's neither good nor bad. This is a process of observation and of exploration of the topic of leaving. My hope for you is that you come to view leaving in a new way you may not have previously considered—in a positive way.

SCARCITY

Experiencing a period of scarcity during a time of leaving is inevitable and real. What is never apparent is that experiencing a period of scarcity will happen to you. Each time I left something or someone, I was unprepared for the period of scarcity I was entering. You may wonder why scarcity is the first point I mention in my discussion. It is because scarcity is very stark, apparent, and profound immediately upon the moment of departure. Once the choice to leave has been made and the steps carried out, scarcity becomes real. Scarcity means having less of something which you are accustomed to having a steady and plentiful supply of.

The learning curve I was on as a newly single mother of two teens after having been married for twenty years was steep. While I slowly learned how to navigate that tremendous learning curve, I had to do so in a way that considered living with scarcity in several areas of my life. There were many things that no longer existed: my "family home" and acreage life became a rental duplex in town, the household I was able to set up immediately upon my departure was exceptionally meager when compared with what my children and I had grown accustomed to, my double income household became single income, my personal reliance on two health care plans was reduced to one, and the list grew from there. The list was lengthy. I was prepared for and had even planned for most of these realities. However, it's one thing to understand something intellectually, and quite another to live through it. This is one side of scarcity I experienced.

The scarcity of these "tangibles" of daily living aside, there was a different type of scarcity I had not fully realized would happen when I contemplated leaving my marriage. The scarcity of human connection altered for me in a very profound way. When you leave a circumstance or a relationship, you also leave opportunities for connection with others. In the case of leaving my marriage, the connection to extended family and some friends altered; in some instances, it ended entirely. Invitations to holiday celebrations, birthdays, weddings, family reunions, special days such as graduation celebrations and other milestone events, became scarce and ended. Intellectually I knew this was going to be a result of my marriage ending. Emotionally, the lack of connection was profound for me for quite some time. I did eventually develop ways to maintain a connection through phone calls, visits, mailing letters, gifts, and cards, and to also connect digitally via email, texting, and social media. In some instances, people reached out to me, in others I reached out to them. Some connections lessened over time and some ended entirely. The ripple effect of leaving my marriage spread out into my wider circle of my friends and family; it was vast. There was no way for me to foresee that due to my marital breakdown, the lack of connection with others and the eventual end of some relationships would result in such profound scarcity. At the time this all came about in my life, I did not apply this term—scarcity—to what I was experiencing. After a period of adjustment, as well as with the work I've done to heal and move forward in my life, my connections and relationships have evolved to fill in the gaps that felt so deep and dark during that period of scarcity. This is not to say that I do not still think about and miss certain relationships and individuals who are no longer part of my daily life, I most certainly do. Eventually, the period of scarcity experienced immediately upon leaving becomes less intense; it decreases, and new relationships and connections emerge, and pre-existing ones deepen in some instances. The "new you" carries on and forges ahead.

What I wasn't prepared for was the loss of what was. In retrospect, I am uncertain if anything could have prepared me for the feeling and the reality of scarcity I experienced. Had someone framed things for me concerning how scarcity may play a role in my life during this time, or if I'd had a resource on this specific topic, I would have been more prepared. I knew there would be very profound differences in my life as a single mother and divorcee. However, it wasn't until very recently that I have identified scarcity as what I experienced then, and at other times where I left situations and relationships.

Along with scarcity—which may take many forms such as a lack of emotional and/or physical intimacy, friendship, financial resources, companionship, human contact, time, etc.—also comes a sense of loss. When you leave and experience a period of scarcity of any description, there is a period of grieving what was. Even when people intentionally delete things from their lives and replace them with what feels like new, exciting, and challenging opportunities, there is a period of scarcity and of loss that is also part of the newness.

I ask you to pause now and consider the circumstance of leaving you imagined for this exercise. What is it that you think you may lack if you chose to leave that part of your life? What may become scarce in your life, even for a short period of time, while you adjust and become familiar with your new situation? You may choose to mentally go through a list of possibilities, or you may wish to record them along with your initial thoughts if you are keeping notes. Scarcity is real. When you leave something or someone, there are elements that will no longer be part of your life. It's important to note here that not all areas where you may experience scarcity are even apparent until you are well on the way down your new life path. You will not be able to arrive at a complete list; however, the awareness that scarcity will accompany leaving is of value. Knowing that scarcity will be part of your journey will help you prepare mentally, emotionally, physically, and even spiritually for what's to come should you lift off and take flight in search of what's next.

CONFORMITY

Conformity becomes more comfortable as time passes, life carries on, and we stay in our lane, toe the line, and live up to expectations. Do any of these ring true for you? Have you thought about shedding one or more of the roles that define you? Eventually, everyone experiences a time when they choose to leave; we leave jobs, organizations, churches, teams, relationships, etc. The list goes on. When we get to the point that we must leave, and we engage the steps to finally depart, we enter into a period of scarcity and loss. At this same time, we also enter a time when we are no longer conforming to the norms we have established for our own life; we leave behind the defined duties and expectations of the role we once embodied. This is a metamorphosis of sorts—a shedding of our warm, winter down and trying on our new plumage for size. It's a time to see how we might navigate the world in our new, beautiful feathers. What becomes immediately apparent to the people in our lives is that we have changed; we cease conforming to the same rules, expectations, duties, roles, and predictable behaviors they are accustomed to. My father taught me that the only person I can control is myself. I was a heartbroken nineteen-year-old at the time my father and I shared a deep and thought-provoking discussion on human nature and relationships. It took me many years to fully understand and appreciate his precious advice. I spent decades trying to control my environment to make others happy, to soothe them, to make them proud of me, accept me, and to love me. I allowed myself to be controlled by the wishes, expectations, and desires of others, all the while forsaking myself. When we leave, we also cease our conformism. Our lack of conformity is an adjustment for everyone. Leaving conveys that we've had enough and are ready for something new, different, better, and something more; it's truly about ceasing to conform to what was and to move on, into what will be.

Stepping out of conformity and into the "new you" can bring with it swift and sometimes harsh judgment of others. You may experience shame, guilt, rejection, and betrayal. You may believe that you have become the topic of gossip and conjecture. During this sometimes-difficult period of adjustment when you are no longer conforming to your old way of life, it's wise to remember that the only person you can control is you. You have the right and the responsibility to speak your truth, to share as much or as little of your journey as you wish with whomever you wish, to do so fearlessly—even if you tremble when you find your voice—and to shed your layers of conformity as you move forward on your new pathway in life; the pathway you have chosen.

When I was in the process of deciding if I would leave my marriage, I was visiting with a friend on the phone one evening. She was concerned about me and wanted to know what she could do to help since she had observed that I appeared extremely sad, was increasingly more and more withdrawn, looked physically unwell, and wasn't behaving like the friend she knew. I responded by telling her that I just wasn't able to share anything at that time; that was my truth—my circumstance was too big, it was too deep, it was intensely private—it was terrifying for me to consider telling anyone. Her plea was that if I'd only share what was happening, then she would be able to help me through it. I didn't have the energy or even the words to share my circumstance with her. Further to that, I was paralyzed by fear. What would she think of my crumbling marriage? Of me? Of my immense failure? I listened to my gut; my intuition was saying to keep my circumstance, my decision-making process, and my next move to myself. At that time, I didn't even know for certain what may happen next; I truly didn't know if I could salvage my marriage or if it was broken beyond repair. I remember our phone call very vividly even though it was such a tumultuous time in my life; it was a pivotal moment when, for the first time in a very long time, perhaps for the first time ever, I took care of myself instead of taking care of someone else's curiosities, needs, and desires. I had no desire to feel like or to become someone's "project." I had no doubt my friend's beautiful heart was in the right place, and that the advice she may have imparted that evening would have been useful and soothing had I disclosed everything I was going through, but it was a time when I needed to be alone with my thoughts and move through my process on my terms; it was a time when I needed to remain firmly gripped to the branch of my tree even though it no longer felt sturdy or sure. I found a measure of courage I didn't know I possessed when I stopped conforming.

Pause now. Consider what roles you may cease conforming to if you left the relationship or circumstance you've been considering. Think about the variety of tasks you perform, duties you undertake, and functions you fulfill in the lives of those with whom you interact in this area of your life. Whether you experience rejection or acceptance of your decision to leave, there is value in recognizing that when you cease conforming the way the people in your life have become accustomed to, there is going to be a reaction. In fact, you will experience myriad reactions and you may find yourself called to answer questions, defend your decision, to celebrate your courage, and to address the curiosities and inquiries of those who know and love you. Conformity in some of the roles you perform in your life will cease when you leave. Consider this when you contemplate lifting off and flying toward the future that whispers to you.

LONELINESS

"I'm so lonely...I should be happy but I'm not. I've never felt more alone in my entire life." This is a phrase I know well and once embodied. It is also a phrase that people have confided in me about their own life circumstance—in their own words. When I entered my mid-forties, it became starkly apparent that many couples in my same general demographic were weathering mounting storms in personal relationships, and major changes in career paths seemed to be taking place. This is not to say that these issues are not present for younger or for older generations, however, I do believe that there is something undeniably true about the quintessential "mid-life crises" that has a kernel of truth embedded in it. This can be an extremely lonely time for many people. Being alone and being lonely are two different circumstances; they can co-exist or be mutually exclusive. Having left a twenty-year marriage, I know what to be alone in the world is like; I know it intimately like the lines forming around the corners of my eyes and lips as I age, the uproarious belly laughs of my children, and tight around-the-neck hugs from my grandchild. I chose to be single; I left. I have also experienced loneliness when I've been in a crowded room, and in a long-term relationship. Through my own experiences of leaving and in learning about the experiences of others (whether they were contemplating leaving or actually have), I believe that being alone and experiencing loneliness, either with others or in complete solitude, is the soul's way of yearning for healing. This is work best done alone.

For many years after my separation and eventual divorce, when I hugged my parents goodbye, my father would remark, "if you're lonely, call us." My tenderhearted mom would whisper to me while enveloping me in her warm, familiar embrace, "are you lonely? I don't like thinking about you going through life all alone." Her eyes would well up with tears and sometimes mine would too; sometimes I truly was lonely. At times I still am. What I remind and reassure my parents of is this: I chose this life path. It is challenging to find the words to explain to a couple married for over fifty-four years and counting—that when you choose to leave, there are consequences beyond just being alone that you must learn to navigate and contend with. I never could quite find the right phrase to describe my reality to them—the reality that being alone and being lonely are not the same, that while I'm generally alone, I am not always lonely. The choice to leave and the act of leaving are steps in a process of soul searching and a journey toward healing.

Can you think of a time when you have uttered aloud or silently prayed, "just leave me be," or had a teen rush from the room, slam the bedroom door in their wake and yell, "leave me alone!"? If you've ever lived with others or been part of a family (which most of us have), this is undoubtedly relatable. As humans navigating the world and searching out what will fill us up, feed our passion and settle our restless heart, when we inwardly, or perhaps even outwardly scream, "just leave me be," I believe this is when our soul is speaking most loudly. We can only ignore the pleas of our soul for so long. Leaving and entering the unknowns of scarcity, loss, conformity, being alone and experiencing loneliness, is the soul's outcry for solitude and the opportunity to heal. There is a commonly used phrase: "we cannot care for others unless we tend to our own needs first." The act of leaving, I believe, is the soul pushing to the forefront, calling out to be heard, and exclaiming that it's time for something profoundly different, even if it's terrifying and the outcome uncertain. It's time to tend to your own needs first. When it's time to leave a situation, the soul knows and speaks loudly enough that the mind and the body eventually hear, a plan is then generated, and the exit takes place. It's when we are alone, and experiencing periods of loneliness, that the soul calls out and takes flight much like a Great Grey owl does when silently in search of what is needed—to nurture herself.

Each of us has experienced periods of time when we were alone and times when we have endured loneliness. We are social beings wired for interaction, relationship and for love. Pause now and look at into the palms of your hands, or at the sturdy branch of your fingertips that you imagined and where your idea is resting. Gather your energy and lift off; fly up and into the future for just a moment. Contemplate what life may be like having left the circumstance you are considering. Can you foresee moments when you will be alone and moments where you will experience loneliness? Are your sensations frightening? Do they offer a sense of relief? Moments in solitude and isolation offer us time for soul searching. This requires being alone at times and it can also result in periods of loneliness. Acknowledging that leaving will result in both times when you feel all alone and are on your own, as well as the possibility of periods of deep loneliness and longing, is an extremely valuable exercise. If you struggled with this concept, you are in good company; you are not alone. Take comfort in this knowledge.

COURAGE

One of the things I still find so captivating about the experience I had with the owl on those three afternoons so long ago, is the owl's courage; she was brave. The courage to sit on that branch and hold her ground while I intruded on her space and inserted myself into her routine was very curious. Three times in succession she stayed the course, and on the third day, she took flight only to return immediately with her prey. It was fascinating and surreal; it was magical and dreamlike. Her courage to stand her ground despite what I know were real threats for her—human and machine—was bold. She displayed not only the courage to continue what she started but did so in what was an unapologetic, natural fashion;

she was getting the job done and doing so despite nearby obstacles and threats. Granted, she was a noble, wild creature—a bird, and a hungry one at that. I am well aware of my personification of her avian traits and the message I gleaned for myself from her natural instinct to hunt, however, our encounter served me and my desire to finally witness the sign I was praying for. Regardless of my perception of our shared experience and how I made sense of the events that week, I intuitively know that I received the sign that day. The sign was laced with courage. The message was to always listen intently to what my soul is telling me when I'm alone, in my times of loneliness and in my moments of solitude. My circle of friends, family, and colleagues noticed my shift—my shift from who I was to what I was becoming. Despite all their offers of help, ears to listen, and shoulders to share my burdens, it was a decision I came to on my own and the plan that was generated was mine. No one made me leave my marriage; I chose to leave of my own free will and volition. It takes a tremendous amount of courage not only to realize that you need to leave a circumstance or a relationship but to then also follow through; to leave is no small thing. Many in your circle may question your decision, they may not understand, and some may no longer even accept you. Possessing courage does not equate to happiness. Having courage does not mean that your journey will yield a process or an outcome that is easy. Finding and cultivating courage does, however, answer the call from your soul for attention and for healing.

You may not see this in yourself, but you do have courage to spare. You have the courage to face things you never thought possible and you can identify where this has already rung true for you in the past. Consider again the circumstance you are contemplating leaving. The palms of your hands or the fingers that form your sturdy branch are the current resources that support you in your present role. Can you envision lifting off and flying in a new direction? If you can, that is courage; the proverbial "wind beneath your wings" that will support you on the journey is your courage. If you cannot envision that, it's not for lack of courage but rather it's that this specific departure may not be the right pathway for you, or that you are quite simply not ready to lift off and trust the courage you already possess and that will see you through and support you on your flight. Just because you contemplate a change does not mean it will happen nor does it mean that it should. Taking the time to consider something new is evidence that you do have courage to spare.

SELF-RELIANCE

Cultivating courage, navigating solitude, scarcity, and enduring loneliness have all required me to become extremely self-reliant. The learning curve to survive and thrive on my own has been steep in the majority of my experiences. Self-reliance takes a lot of ingenuity and a measure of strength. I've had people say to me, "you're so strong. I couldn't have survived that." Trust me when I say that I have rarely felt strong in times of stress. When I look back at situations where I have made the choice to leave and followed through with my plan, my recollections are of extremely adrenaline-filled, anxiety-ridden, and in some instances, terrifying moments. What many people do not realize is that they too are strong and when the soul emerges and pleads for attention and healing, their strength rises too. The overriding emotion when the big day of departure arrives is rarely a feeling I would identify as strength. All of this said, people truly do not know how strong they are until they have no other choice but to be strong. Self-reliance takes on many forms depending upon your own individual circumstance, what you are seeking to delete from your life, and where you are headed. Self-reliance may be updating a resume to apply for a new position or filling out a rental application after having a joint mortgage for twenty years. It can come in the form of requesting your personal medical records be sent to a new doctor at a different clinic. Self-reliance can be cultivated when leaving a group or a team that you have been part of for years. All of these situations, and myriad others, required me to become self-reliant—to find my voice, to put words to the feelings I was experiencing, to make decisions and, like the courageous, confident owl, to stand my ground in spite of real or perceived obstacles and threats.

Self-reliance is rooted in resilience and like courage, you do have resilience to spare; you have the skills, knowledge, and tools to be self-reliant, and if you do not feel you possess them right now, or if you feel you lack a specific skill set, you will learn and develop what's needed. Self-reliance and courage are oftentimes cultivated simultaneously.

In looking again to the future for a moment and at what life may be like if you lift off and leave—if you soar toward your future—do you see yourself as a resourceful person with the necessary skills, knowledge, and tools to be successful? If you can envision that, and if you see yourself already as self-reliant, you are well on your way to creating the future you desire. What's important to note here is that it's not necessary to possess all the skills you may need before you set out on a journey. You will learn, adapt, grow, and change along the way; you will become more self-reliant over time and with experience. You will learn what works best for you.

ACCEPTANCE

Displays of outward strength and feelings of inner strength aside, once you find yourself in a literal new place, be that a new position at work, a new community, a new home, relationship, friendship or other life circumstance, you will also be required to adjust to your new reality. This is where acceptance enters the equation. Regardless of whether the people in your circle accept the "new you," you must come to accept yourself and your situation. Either that or you will continue to shift and make changes until things are right for you. The key in this last phrase is, "right for you." When something is right for you, it's absolute and undeniable; it's a knowing so profound that you don't have the words to share your experience and truly, words may not matter, what you know matters.

When the day came for me to leave my marital home, I was quite amazed at my measure of inner calm. Moving is stressful at the very best of times when life is going well, and plans are falling into place. Moving is fraught with the stress of logistics, packing, dust, and dirt, hunger, headache, exhaustion, disorganization, and flaring tempers. On the day I moved out of that house, my two kids in tow, I had come to a place of both knowing and accepting that I had made the best decision I could at the time; I was doing the right thing. I had heard the calling out of my soul and finally, after many years, I listened. I had received the sign revealed to me by the experience with the great grey owl only weeks earlier.

For those in my life who didn't have a clue what was transpiring and who were learning about my circumstance through the grapevine, and even for many friends and family members who were aware of my separation and the fact that I was leaving my marriage, their worry and shock were undeniable. I knew that while some understood my path and were working on accepting my new reality, there were others who were truly aghast and confused, and some simply could not accept or condone my decision to leave. What I found myself reciting quite often was, "... and that's ok." For instance, I recall this repeated thought, "my mom is worried and fearful for me and my children, and that's ok. We're ok. I'm ok." The comments and conjectures of others can be constructive, useful, and help inform decision making, or they can merely be heard by you and simply let go; what you choose to do with the information from others that comes your way is truly your choice. The impact that the ideas, theories, advice, and opinions of others have on you and your life is really up to you.

My process for deciding what will serve me and what will not, involves a quick filtration of information and acceptance of another's point of view. My acceptance of another's point of view does not mean I agree with that person; it simply means I accept and respect their stance. The acknowledgment of where another person stands is a double acceptance of sorts: you accept their stance and you also accept yourself and where you stand. Reciting, "...and that's ok," is a simple and effective method to move past any judgment you may feel from others, and any self-judgment as well. The only person you can control is you! I believe it is human nature to expend a great deal of time and energy worrying about and ruminating on what others think or what you imagine they might think. Unless we ask people, and unless they share and are honest, we truly don't know what they believe; it's a guessing game. Does it matter? It does. There are people whom we seek out for their advice, counsel and to help us in our times of need and with our decision-making. These people are invaluable and are often our most trusted and beloved. However, what if it doesn't matter what certain people think? Accepting where you are at right now, today, and being at peace with your process and your decision is an active, conscious act. When we accept our own reality in the present moment, we accept ourselves and I believe we are better able to make the tough decisions around things like whether to stay and endure, or whether to leave and begin anew. Acceptance is not only a positive result of a situation where you have left and are beginning anew, but it is also the starting point for what's next. Acceptance is what truly makes the world go 'round; perhaps that's what love is exactly; acceptance.

Self-acceptance can be very difficult to practice and to nurture. I have yet to meet anyone who isn't truly a work in progress in this regard. When visualizing yourself in the future, at your "new place" in life, do you experience a feeling of acceptance of that "new you"; can you view yourself favorably and with a desire to commend that person, to commend yourself, for the work you have done since lifting off and flying away to get to where you are? Considering the struggles, you may have endured along the way, and despite any mistakes you may have made, can you view yourself in a kind and gentle light and in a way that is self-accepting? If you can, that's a true blessing. If you are struggling with this notion and casting disparaging doubts on yourself for having left; if you feel you may have regrets, misgivings, and negative judgments about the person you may become or the circumstance you may find yourself in, this is not only normal and natural, it's also common for anyone contemplating making a huge life shift. Self-acceptance waxes and wanes for everyone. We are all works in progress. Acknowledging that continual work on self-acceptance will be part of the process of leaving will help ensure that you practice compassion for yourself in all the seasons of your life. Accepting where you are right now, and accepting who you are today, is a healthy way to make time and space for contemplating the idea of leaving and then imagining where you may be in the future and who you may become.

LOVE

Leaving—making your way through periods of scarcity, loss, conformity, loneliness, and cultivating courage, self-reliance, and acceptance—is all wrapped beautifully in a warm, feather-soft cloak of love. Leaving is truly about love. This is one lesson that has taken me the longest to learn. The people you leave behind in your wake—the confused, the hurt, the betrayed, the sad and the angry (even the relieved)—may not describe your leaving as a loving act, and that's ok. Leaving is never about them; as selfish as this may sound, it's about you. At a time in history when people are criticized for being overly self-absorbed, it may not be popular or well-accepted to say that leaving is about you and it is about love. We live in a time in history where people tend to praise values of selflessness, self-sacrifice, and benevolence toward our fellow beings—where caring for others is lauded and applauded. So, to suggest that leaving is about love, including loving oneself, may challenge the status quo on issues involving giving to others and supporting others. I will harken back to my earlier quote: "we cannot care for others unless we tend to our own needs first." I know this is true from experience. I believe many people will agree with this sentiment; we cannot give what we don't have, be it patience, time, money, resources, knowledge, etc. And so, we have this paradox to make sense of within our own communities and families, and also within each of us that states: on the one hand, we are obligated to care for others and give, give, give, and on the other hand that we must care for ourselves first or we won't be able to care for our loved ones. The later eventually rings true for most people when it becomes absolutely necessary to care for oneself when we can no longer physically, mentally, and emotionally care for anyone else. Leaving a situation may be the best choice to allow for self-care to take place; for some people, it may be the only choice.

Leaving is about not forsaking yourself. When you choose to leave a situation or circumstance where you could have otherwise remained, it brings with it a uniqueness; it's different than other types of leaving where things conclude and naturally end. When you could stay and "make a go of things" and you choose to leave to pursue other adventures and experiences, you will generally move through a similar process as described here. Will your process be the same? No. Will it be similar? Likely, yes. When the proverbial "dust settles" after leaving a situation or relationship, new routines become established, new relationships are forged, and what was once a brand-new rhythm to your daily life becomes a familiar and comfortable one. Upon reflection, you may be able to see a "bigger picture" and identify with the idea that leaving is a form of self-love: it's completely and undeniably, one hundred percent about you. Leaving and loving yourself is not something to ever apologize for, and it's also not something you owe anyone an explanation for. If you wish to explain your process of leaving to someone, that's up to you; it's never something that should be seen as "owed" to another.

I'll ask you to pause one last time. Ask yourself this question: can you project six months, a year, or even five years ahead into your life after having left the circumstance or relationship you have resting in your palms or upon the branch of your fingertips? Can you envision that new place—a different tree with a strong branch to settle upon and a warm, gentle breeze blowing with clear skies above? It's a beautiful day. You are healthy. You made good decisions. Your choice has yielded better than expected results. If you cannot envision this outcome for the change you have been contemplating, that's ok. It's perhaps not the right time. It's perhaps not right for you. Love is present in both visions, in both outcomes; love is right here. Trust this truth.

A universal human desire is to seek meaning in life—in our existence. When the soul is neglected, restless, unsatisfied, and lonely, it speaks. We look for signs or for clues to help us decide when the time is right to make a change. Just because you have considered leaving doesn't mean it's the right time and it certainly doesn't mean that you will leave. When those thoughts come to the forefront and wave a flag you can no longer ignore, when ideas of newness, change, and glimpses of a different future become more and more frequent, it's time to tend to that yearning. Leaving may be a consideration for you. Trust me when I say that when it's time to leave, you will know, no one will need to tell you. You will simply know. Remember that departing, the day you leave, is one small step in a process; it's not an isolated event, it is a part of your journey and does not signal the beginning nor does it signal the end. The topics I have highlighted are not meant to outline a series of steps to take or a checklist to follow, but rather are meant to be key considerations for things you may encounter on any journey where you are departing from the "now" and flying toward what is "next" on your journey. Having a resource to access and revisit when your soul is longing for attention and needs tending to, and when a shift or change is imminent due to either positive or negative life circumstances, may prove to be a valuable tool to have in your decision making tool-kit as you move through your process. We leave when our soul yearns for more, better, different, and new. There is no need to apologize for your natural, human inclination to depart—to move through your own process in search of what's next. Trust this process, your process.

Leaving is a journey through love and with love.
Leaving is a process of flying onward toward your future.
Leaving is not quitting; leaving is beginning anew.

Jennifer Albrecht
Teacher, Certified Coach Practitioner, Author

Hailing from rural Alberta, Jenn resides in a geographically diverse region renowned for its plentiful natural resources and situated in the foothills of the majestic Rocky Mountains. She has a deep and abiding appreciation for the many blessings found in nature, as well as for the people who choose to make this part of the world their home. Jenn values the beautiful ebb and flow of the lifestyle found in the small community where she lives and works. Jenn is an educator at heart and in practice, with over two decades in public education. Her love for mentoring others and learning alongside them extends far beyond her classroom walls and out into the global community where she is a volunteer, certified coach practitioner, and author. Jenn enjoys spending time with family and friends, reading, writing, traveling, gardening, cooking, and teaching.

Connect with Jennifer:
authorjalbrecht@gmail.com
www.facebook.com/JennAlbrechtAuthor

Creating Abundance

by Derrick Sweet

I began to understand the concept of "abundance" when I was sixteen years old. At the time, I was a high school dropout, and, to say the least, I needed some direction. My mother gave me my first book on the topic. It was Dr. Wayne Dyer's book, The Sky's the Limit. Never in my wildest dreams did I believe, as I was reading Dr. Dyer's book, that some twenty-five years later I would not only have the pleasure of knowing and working with him, I would also have him endorse my second book, Get The Most Out Of Life. On the front cover of the book are his words, "Pay Attention and Grow."

It's with this sense of possibility that I share my thoughts with you in the book on the process of creating abundance.

The principles I will share with you have helped me create the kind of life that some would call "a dream life." I agree. I do live a dream life with more abundance than I ever thought possible. I live on a one-hundred-acre ranch with a view of the surrounding countryside that is as close to heaven as you can imagine. My wife Marsha and I have a house high on a cliff some two hundred feet above the ocean in Nicaragua at one of the best resorts in the world (www.RanchoSantana), and I have many of the material possessions that a life of abundance often includes.

The attitude, philosophy, and habits of abundance have helped me attract the best business partners and friends that are a joy to know and work with. Most importantly, it has helped me find the love of my life… my wife Marsha, who is not only my life partner, but she also runs the day-to-day operations of the Healthy Wealthy and Wise® Corporation.

My hope is that after reading my contribution to this book you will not only have a better appreciation of the importance of creating a life of abundance, but you will also have the confidence to begin to take the steps necessary to create your ideal life; a life that includes everything on your wish list that can easily help you live a deeper, richer and more connected life.

I've broken down my thoughts on this topic into five sections; Understand, Decide, Commit, Act, and Succeed. And because the first step, to understand, is so important, it will take up most of our discussion.

Let's begin!

UNDERSTAND |DECIDE | COMMIT | ACT |SUCCEED

In Robert Emmons' book "Thanks: How the New Science of Gratitude Can Make You Happier," the gratitude journal scores big points on helping people live happier lives. According to a study published in Applied Psychology writing in a gratitude journal causes a noticeable improvement in sleep & mood quality.

Gratitude reduces stress! In a study published in Behavior Research and Therapy, war veterans who practiced gratitude experienced lower rates of Post-Traumatic Stress Disorder. According to a study conducted by Dr. Robert Emmons gratitude not only increases happiness, but it also reduces negative feelings like envy and resentment. So, if reducing stress and feeling better about life is as simple as writing in a journal, why isn't everyone doing it?

The habit of reducing stress and creating abundance isn't a switch, it's a process that takes time. It can be and usually is, an arduous process.

This chapter will take you no less than thirty days to complete because the purpose of this chapter is to help you develop a deeper, richer, and consistent experience of abundance. So, to understand the process, we need to know what abundance is and how to create it. Abundance is not merely having enough, or simply being grateful for what you already have, but in knowing that you can create whatever your intentions are. Intentions are more than physical or material goals. Intentions are more related to the kind of life we would like to consistently experience, while we're alive. Abundance, in this sense of the word, is closely linked to gratitude. Without gratitude, a life of real abundance is virtually impossible.

Let's begin with a better understanding of why so many people around the world have such a difficult time creating abundance. We all desire to live a life of abundance. In its most basic form, abundance is having a roof over our heads, food to eat, people who love us, and income to pay our bills.

Most people in the world do not live an abundant life. In fact, almost half the world's population – 3.4 billion people - live on less than $5.50 a day, according to recent numbers from the World Bank. A few weeks ago, I was in Nicaragua with my wife Marsha for a few days. Nicaragua is a beautiful country in Central America with a population of approximately six million people, of which nearly half live on just $2.00 a day. Nicaragua is the second poorest country in the region. Only Haiti has more poverty.

Driving from the capital city of Managua to our house on the Pacific Coast was a two-and-a-half-hour drive. Traveling along the roads in Nicaragua, we came across many wagons being pulled by cows, horses, or even oxen. It was like being in another world that has missed out on what we in the west would consider "a civilized society." For hours we drove past one poor community after another. Many of the people we saw were so poor that their small tin houses didn't even have doors…yet Nicaragua is known around the world as having some of the happiest people on the planet.

The two primary forces that predict our ability to create abundance are internal circumstances and external circumstances.

EXTERNAL CIRCUMSTANCES

External circumstances include circumstances that you have no control over like war, drought, high unemployment, government corruption, oppression, unfair trade practices, and natural disasters. Countries that have the most poverty often have the most greed and corruption. That doesn't mean there isn't greed and corruption in wealthier countries like the United States, England, Canada, Ireland, and Australia. Greed and corruption are everywhere; however, most developed countries have laws that offer their citizens some protection from greed and corruption.

Organizations like the World Bank and the United Nations have the collective goal of ending poverty, creating abundance, and maintaining peace around the world. These organizations are failing miserably because too many of the leaders running these organizations are greedy and corrupt, which is why, for generations, poor countries rich in resources, have remained poor. Quite frankly, the world is not fair, and it has not been possible for everyone in the world to create abundance.

Despite the greed and corruption in the world, despite the exploitation and oppression that continues to happen all over the world, abundance is possible when you create the right internal circumstances, even when the external circumstances are not in your favor.

INTERNAL CIRCUMSTANCES

Internal circumstances are the circumstances that you have created for yourself, consciously or unconsciously, that either create abundance or create internal roadblocks that prevent you from creating abundance.

I want to share with you four simple tools you have, or could have, right now, that can help you create as much abundance as you can imagine. The key word here is IMAGINE!

The four tools that can help you create as much abundance as you can imagine, include your thoughts, your feelings, your beliefs, and your expectations. These four tools create your internal circumstances.

THOUGHTS

Your thoughts are like a currency. Every thought buys a feeling that matches the energy of that thought. If you think a negative thought, it, being a currency, will buy a negative feeling. For example, if you're worried about your finances, you may notice yourself thinking a thought like, "I'll never get out of debt," or, "I will never be able to afford to retire."

FEELINGS

Like your thoughts, your feelings are also a currency. Your feelings work with your thoughts to buy certain beliefs that match the energy and the quality of these thoughts and feelings. All this happens automatically and quite often without our awareness. For example, if you have a feeling of stress after thinking you'll never get out of debt, you may unconsciously and automatically develop negative beliefs around money. And as the same negative thoughts and feelings around money are repeated, the belief becomes stronger and stronger.

BELIEFS

When you repeat the same belief over and over again, that particular belief that you have been repeating will buy expectations that will match the energy of that belief. For example, if you believe money is difficult to make, you'll always expect money to be difficult to make. If you decide to work on commission or start your own business, you will be guaranteed to fail unless you change this limiting belief.

EXPECTATIONS

Like your beliefs, your expectations are also a currency. When you repeat certain expectations over and over again, that particular expectation that you have been repeating will buy actions that match the energy of each specific expectation. For example, if you expect money is challenging to make, inaction may occur, and you will not do what you need to do to make money. Our expectations can keep us in a perpetual process of procrastinating. Is this what Benjamin Franklin meant when he said, "Most people die at twenty-five and don't get buried until they're seventy-five?"

If you haven't been creating the kind of abundance that you desire, then figure out what type of currency you have been taking to the market of life. The market of life is a metaphor for life. Life is always willing to sell you what you ask for. The problem is most people have been showing up to the market of life with the wrong currency; buying the opposite of what their true intentions are. The market of life is magical…or can be once you understand how it works. What it offers will depend on what kind of currency you show up with each day.

When I started the Healthy Wealthy and Wise® Corporation in 1999, I had no idea where it would take me or how much of an impact it would have in the world. Like any big idea, it was a struggle to get off the ground in the early years, but through the struggle, we grew. In 2006 we started the Certified Coaches Federation. Today we have certified over fourteen-thousand life coaches around the world, and it has become known as one of the best life coach certification programs in the world. It would be eight years later when we started the Healthy Wealthy and Wise® Coaching Program. Like a lot of good ideas, the Healthy Wealthy and Wise® Coaching Program was inspired out of frustration.

It was in 2014, and we had about ten-thousand certified coaches around the world. The problem with the coaching business is challenging for most coaches to earn enough money to create real abundance if they use the standard approach to build a coaching business. Virtually every coaching certification program in the world failed to offer a solution that could create real abundance. We knew something had to change!

My thought (currency) was "the coaching profession needs an innovative solution that can provide the kind of value and experience that can help coaches earn a lucrative income." This currency (thought) bought a feeling of joy and excitement. The more I thought about what we could offer coaches (solutions), the more positive feelings I created. This was intentional because I knew that all I had to do was repeat specific thought patterns enough and they would buy enough feelings (another valuable currency) which could help create other valuable currencies like beliefs and expectations. Simple!

Another thought I had when we were just starting the Healthy Wealthy and Wise® Coaching Program was, "We need to offer a program that is impossible to be duplicated or stolen." It needed to be unique…not found anywhere else in the world. That particular currency bought what is now known as our proprietary investment algorithm! This algorithm has been helping our members earn millions of dollars in the stock market since 2014.

In addition to our stock market research, we also created content that couldn't be found anywhere else. We offered programming like Spiritual Wealth TV, Emotional Wealth TV, Physical Wealth TV, Relationship Wealth TV, live weekly webinars to support our coaches and a business opportunity that would pay members of our personal development business and coaching platform enough compensation, not only to create wealth, but to create recurring quarterly and annual income! It worked! Four years later, in 2018, our membership grew by over five hundred percent!

CREATING COMPLETE ABUNDANCE

There are eight primary kinds of abundance. They include Physical Abundance, Spiritual Abundance, Relationship Abundance, Community Abundance, Professional Abundance, Emotional Abundance, Creative Abundance, and Financial Abundance.

Physical Abundance: This is the most immediate and necessary kind of abundance. Being physically fit, feeling alive and healthy …having enough food to eat and enough energy to go after your dreams…this is step one in the process of creating abundance.

Spiritual Abundance: This kind of abundance creates connections to others, to nature, and to an internal source of power and inspiration that leads to a life of abundance.

Relationship Abundance: There is no true abundance without love, meaningful relationships, and friendships with kindred spirits.

Community Abundance: We are social animals. No life has true abundance without close relationships with others. Being part of a community with like-minded people who share your values and will encourage and support you is what is missing in the lives of most people today. The right community can provide the platform to create a meaningful life and a fulfilled life.

Professional Abundance: We earn a living by working at a job or in a profession, but we create abundance when that job or career allows us to contribute and have a lasting impact. It gives our life meaning.

Emotional Abundance: Emotional abundance is the process of associating positive feelings with relationships, challenges, goals, and even inconveniences.

Creative Abundance: Creative abundance is by far the most important kind of abundance because, without fully developed creativity, it is virtually impossible to successfully navigate all the wrong turns, roadblocks, and setbacks that we will repeatedly encounter on our journey.

Financial Abundance: I could have started with financial abundance because this is what most people think of when they hear the words "creating abundance." It will follow the other sources of abundance if you lay down the right foundation, and that's what the rest of this chapter is about.

The Healthy Wealthy and Wise® Coaching Program helps our members develop all of these essential pieces of the puzzle. Learn more about the Healthy Wealthy and Wise® Coaching Program at www. wealthitforward.com. Mention this book and automatically qualify to join our community of big thinkers and game changers with a $100.00 discount on the first year of your membership!

UNDERSTAND | DECIDE | COMMIT | ACT | SUCCEED

The next section of the chapter will focus on how to DECIDE to commit to living a life of abundance. The process begins with gratitude!

The following is a very simple exercise that may potentially teach you how to create abundance. For the next thirty days, keep a notebook or laptop nearby and commit to just once a day to ask the same simple question, "What am I grateful for?"

Pick the most convenient time, like shortly after you wake up, just after lunch, or just before bed. Record your answers. Don't forget to reflect each day on your answers from the day before and any key lessons or perspectives you may have noticed. Without the habit of reflection, we seldom recognize what we are doing to sabotage our intention of living a life of abundance.

There is a difference between being distracted and practicing reflection. Reflection requires both awareness and an ongoing conscious effort to think about events before they happen, as they are happening, and after they've happened.

Then, after thirty days answer the following questions:

What's different about my life?

How is my life better?

What am I doing more of that inspires me?

What am I overcoming?

What is different about how I'm feeling about life?

What are some of the new habits I am now developing?

What are some of the old habits I am now retiring?

Am I more grateful today than before I completed this thirty-day exercise? How?

If you're not satisfied with your answers, my advice is to repeat the same exercise. Once you're confident that you have developed more gratitude, it's time to develop some new habits.

UNDERSTAND | DECIDE | COMMIT | ACT | SUCCEED

The next section of the chapter will focus on how to COMMIT to taking the action steps that can create a life of abundance. The process begins with developing with right habits!

GRATITUDE HABITS:

It's good for your health to be grateful! In a study published in Personality and Individual Differences, it was reported that grateful people have significantly fewer aches and pains, exercise more, and are more likely to live longer.

The daily practice of gratitude reduces toxic neurotransmitter, which reduces inflammation and other stress reactions linked to heart disease, dementia, cancer, and weight gain!

The following habits will be easy to develop if you've completed the previous exercise. There is some overlap between the next exercise and the previous exercise to help you develop your gratitude muscle. Like last time, you will need a journal or computer for this exercise.

1) Begin each day with gratitude shortly after waking up, and before you begin to think about the day ahead. You could begin with the thought, "Today I'm grateful for," and just notice what comes to mind. Doing this for just one minute will make a difference! Write down your answer.

2) Write at least one thank you letter, email, or text to someone you're grateful for each day before noon. Again, it's the habit of cultivating abundance that we're creating.

3) Because generosity is a type of gratitude in action do something nice for someone at least once a day. You have all day to do this. Here are some examples:

   • Open the door for a stranger

- Smile at a stranger (No, it's not creepy!)
- Pay for the coffee for the person behind you at the coffee shop or at the local drive through
- Always pay a sincere compliment to a minimum of one person each day
- Be kind to at least one stranger while out running errands

At the end of the day, record what you did to exercise generosity. Answer the question, "How was I generous today?"

4) Before you go to sleep each day look in the mirror and silently hold eye-contact with yourself for five to thirty seconds. Don't say anything...just allow yourself to slow down and get grounded. Notice your breathing. Slow it down. Breathe in through your nose...hold for a few seconds, then slowly exhale through your mouth as you continue to hold eye contact silently.

Before you finish, end the routine by telling yourself out loud what you're grateful for...pause and wait for the answer. Then, before you record your response, thank yourself for something. It can be for anything. Note: This exercise is similar to the first exercise you may begin your day with each day. Beginning and ending your day with thoughts around gratitude will create a mindset that reflects this process. It creates an attitude that attracts the right people into your life. And, most importantly, it creates a flow in your life that is very difficult to put into words.

You may have noticed how similar both exercises are. This was intentional. The purpose of performing these two exercises is to learn how to develop a deeper level of gratitude, and that's what can happen if you commit to doing both exercises!

UNDERSTAND | DECIDE | COMMIT | ACT | SUCCEED

The next section of the chapter will focus on what to do and how to ACT to commit to living a life of abundance. This process begins with understanding that you have no time to waste. I believe we are here on a metaphorical "three-day pass," meaning we have a short time and we should make the most of it.

IMPERMANENCE & NON-SELF

Once a student offered a length of cloth to his teacher and requested him for teachings but was put off. He painstakingly insisted again and again, so his teacher finally took the man's hands in his and said, "I will die, you will die" (three times).

And then added, "That's all that my teacher taught me, and that's all that I practice. Just meditate on that. I promise there is nothing greater than that."

When we forget that we have a very limited time on this planet, it becomes all too easy to waste time. We risk falling into the mental trap of doing something Seneca referred to as, "Loathing of the present & dreaming of the future," which is, in fact, wasting this precious moment.

When we remember that "we are going to die soon," we will naturally begin to accept our limitations and imperfections. We will stop taking ourselves so seriously, and begin to seek out the people, situations, and opportunities that can give our life more meaning, significance, and purpose. When we remember that we will die soon, we can become more aware of all the abundance we have in this moment, like the ability to breathe, enjoy the view of a sunrise, or simply enjoy a cup of organic coffee. Yes, organic, because you deserve it.

Poem From the book I wrote, You Don't Have to Die to Go to Heaven

"I will die soon, but today I have breath. Today I have life.

I am grateful for this life. Today I have a purpose, and I have opportunities and things to do, people to help, and causes to serve.

Because tomorrow is not guaranteed I choose to live this day, in its entirety, to the absolute fullest.

And because the end is near, I remain in full awareness how lucky I have been again today to have lived."

WHY MOST PEOPLE ARE NOT HEALTHY WEALTHY AND WISE®

Most people are not Healthy Wealthy and Wise®, not because they don't know what to do, but because they don't know how to think about the process of becoming Healthy Wealthy and Wise®. It's our thinking that either moves us forward or keeps us stuck. Everyone on this planet either wants to change a behavior or change how they feel. Most people go about creating abundance in the wrong way. Most people, when thinking of their goals, spend too much time thinking about the completion of the goal and not enough time looking forward to the process of achieving the goal.

The problem with this kind of thinking is that it is supported by the weak notion of perfection. You see, in the future, when you're imagining your goal being achieved, everything is perfect. In reality, the process of achieving any goal includes many setbacks, frustrations, disappointments, scary moments, tons of self-doubt, and anxiety. Too many people look at the process of achieving any goal as a "necessary evil."

PERFECTION (RESULT) VS. PROCESS (GROWING/BECOMING)

The steps we can take (process) to achieve any goal are seldom going to be perfect. And we are not going to be perfect as we take the steps in the process of achieving our many goals. Focusing on the process as the reward, rather than the completion of the goal as the reward, allows us to embrace the present moment. We can find joy in the growth that can happen when we lose ourselves in each part of the process of achieving the goal. It is real abundance to be engaged in the process, which provides an opening to experience a feeling of complete calm and timelessness.

Focusing on the result at the expense of the process blocks spontaneity and creativity, which are the very building blocks and any accomplishment.

Focusing on any task related to the completion of a goal as a means to an end often creates negative internal feedback loops. One of the feedback loops that is created is the negativity and stress combination that may be triggered each time we think about the steps needed to achieve our goal. Because there has been no "payoff" in the process when we think this way, we may avoid acting, and we're much more likely to say:

"This is too hard."

"I'm terrible at public speaking."

"I should have thirty clients by now."

"I don't like social media."

"I don't see why I have to make two videos a week to build credibility."

Because seeing each moment as a means to an end can be so exhausting, it doesn't take long to develop habits of procrastination to provide a brief escape. This may manifest as wasting time on the internet, watching too many Netflix movies and less time doing the things that really matter.

HOW TO PRACTICE NON-SELF LIVING?

Ralph Waldo Emerson believed that we are wiser than we know! What this really means is, we can make better choices than we do, eat healthier foods than we do, exercise more than we do, and be more productive than we are. If we start to question some of our outdated values, traditions, and beliefs and look at life with an open mind, we can eventually see how God dwells in everyone and in everything.

Emerson said, "the maker of all things stands in us and through us."

Because I realize not everyone is comfortable with the word "God," you can just replace it with a word that inspires you about our collective potential for good, like the words, "higher-self," or "spirit." Emerson believed that understanding God and your relationship with God and the universe, not to mention understanding your own soul, can be accelerated when we develop a connection with nature. He said we should seek to reinforce ourselves (self-actualization) by seeking God's presence in nature and to seek the truth, your truth, and to honor the truth!

No one woke up today intending to be worried or doubtful, critical, anxious, or mean spirited, but it happens every day to the majority of the people living on this planet. Crazy, isn't it?

Living in intention, on the other hand, can eventually liberate us from obsessive thoughts! Living with intention can get us out of the way of our old stories that have been holding us back all these years.

Emerson believed that God was not remote and unknowable, but a part of the very fabric of each of us. To become someone who enlightens others and helps them break free of fear, we can start by seeing the light in others, even when it's not obvious. This is easier said than done but when we remember to see the world this way, what we see in the world changes, how we treat other people changes and how we feel about the world changes. It's not easy, but it's worth the effort!

Emerson advocated for the abolition of slavery at a time when it was perilous to do the right thing. It reminds me today of the people speaking out on GMOs, Climate Change, or Geo-Engineering. It would have been "safer" than, like today, to do nothing, which is what most people did then and still do today. Emerson continued to speak out against slavery, and lecture across the country, throughout the 1860s, despite the criticism, the insults, and the threats against his life.

Emerson said, "To be yourself in a world that is constantly trying to make you something else is the greatest accomplishment."

This has not changed in 150 years. People today know conformity and complacency all too well. People today, most people today, live in the shadow of their potential because that's what complacency and conformity create. It provides a perfect environment for fear and self-doubt to fester, and that's what happens. Is this what Benjamin Franklin was referring to when he said, "Most people die at twenty-five and don't get buried until they're seventy-five?" Maybe!

The virtue valued most by society is conformity. The awakened soul knows that conformity is not a virtue but a virus that robs us of our potential to be Gods!

Emerson said, "Everywhere I am hindered of meeting God in my brother, because he has shut his own temple doors and recites fables merely of his brother's, or his brother's brother's God." In other words, the conformed have been conditioned to value name and tradition over experience and connection.

Everything looks permanent until its secret is known! Every solid (roadblock) in the universe is ready to become fluid when we live in intention because living in intention is living in fluidity! Seneca said, "Life is long enough if you know how to live." He also said, "We suffer more in imagination than in reality."

Seneca was astonished how easily people wasted time, how they gave up time without much thought, perhaps because time is intangible and invisible. If each of us could see the exact number of days of life we have left, and how many of these days would be wasted on worry, anger, self-doubt, wasteful vices, and procrastination, what would we do to avoid this outcome?

What vices would we give up? Smoking? Worrying? Doubting?

What habits would we start? Writing? Meditation? Exercise?

What rituals would be a part of each of our remaining days?

How would we deal with setbacks or frustration?

What would we do every day that honored our values?

What would we do each day to grow, learn, earn, and contribute?

"In reality, your life, even if you live 1,000 years and more, will be compressed into the merest span of time; those vices of yours will swallow up any number of lifetimes." Seneca

UNDERSTAND | DECIDE | COMMIT | ACT | SUCCEED

The final section of the chapter will focus on the true meaning of Success...Living a Life of Flow, Meaning, Contribution, and Connection.

You already know what flow is. It's that feeling of being fully engaged in the moment to a point where you almost lose yourself in the experience of whatever you are doing. It is a timeless experience.

Flow is an experience that is associated with total immersion, a loss of oneself, and a timeless sense of joy. There are several kinds of flow. Living an abundant live includes flow in each of these areas:

Stationary Flow: An experience that is associated with total immersion, a loss of oneself, and a timeless sense of joy while either watching an event or sitting still and just being quiet.

Activity-Oriented Flow: An experience that is associated with total immersion, a loss of oneself, and a timeless sense of joy while participating in a particular activity like playing the guitar, riding your bike, or just having a good talk with a close friend or family member.

Career Flow: An experience that is associated with total immersion, a loss of oneself, and a timeless sense of joy while performing the duties associated with earning a living.

Flow and intention are very similar. It is hard to remain in flow unless we are living in intention.

WHAT IS YOUR INTENTION?

You may say that your intention is to be kind, loving, happy, joyful, creative, generous, grateful, patient, compassionate, courageous, alive, aware, engaged, and offer the world your very best in this moment!

Notice, I didn't write, your best, I wrote YOUR VERY BEST! The difference in the sentence is just a word, but the difference in a life is immeasurable! So, don't cheat yourself from becoming the person you're capable of becoming. Don't offer the world your best...offer the world your very best!

TRAVEL LIGHT

Remember, you're only here on a three-day pass. Be happy. Make a difference. Become the person you expected to become when you were seven years old. I'd love to know how it all works out!

Derrick Sweet
Founder Certified Coaches Federation, Healthy Wealthy and Wise®

Derrick Sweet is best known as a popular corporate keynote speaker and author of three highly celebrated books: *Healthy Wealthy and Wise, Get The Most Out Of Life*, and *You Don't Have To Die To Go To Heaven*. Derrick Sweet is also the Chairman and Founder of the Healthy Wealthy and Wise® Corporation, the parent company of the Certified Coaches Federation™. The Healthy Wealthy and Wise® Corporation is an international training and development company known worldwide for our professional development courses and customized in-house programs.

Prior to starting the Healthy Wealthy and Wise® Corporation, Derrick was a Senior Investment Advisor and Vice-President of one of the largest bank-owned investment firms in Canada. Derrick developed Cognitive Reflex Conditioning®, which is a four-step behavior modification process that empowers people to reframe how they approach and achieve their goals. This life-changing coaching model, which has been endorsed by psychologists around the world, is only available through the Certified Coaches Federation® Life Coach Certification Training programs.

Connect with Derrick:
www.wealthitforward.com
info@healthywealthyandwise.com
www.facebook.com/healthywealthyandwisecoachingprogram/

A Warrior Woman's Road to Freedom

by Ronda Lauer

PRELUDE

It was an early Wednesday evening; the sun was obscured by the heavy cloud cover which briskly wisped through the dimming evening sky. She was exhausted after having worked most of the day, teaching others how to ride motorcycles with confidence and always, *safely*. The day, as usual consisted of both being on the heat on the asphalt, riding, instructing, coaching, and chasing down run-away motorcycles, as well as teaching in the calm, quiet classroom. She packed up her motorcycle, started up that Harley of hers, and headed on the long trek home, after ensuring her boots were laced and double knotted, motorcycle gear worn properly, including her riding pants, her conspicuous jacket, full-fingered gloves and well-fitting helmet. As always, the sound of that motor infused and lit up her soul and revved up her heartbeat every time she turned the key. It had a sweet sound that resonated with her and at the same time had a thunderous, commanding sort of sound, making the motorcycle vibrate with ferocity. That motorcycle holds more than its perceived monetary value. It represented her grit and unrecognized strength, it was magic beyond the normal coincidence, and delivered her the freedom she has always yearned for.

It was typically a two-hour ride for her, door to door. Appreciating her level of fatigue, she recognized that it would be best to have a bite to eat in a small town that she passed through along her journey, after she had cleared from the heavy city traffic. It took so much more stamina and concentration when on a two-wheeled vehicle, alongside motorists ignorant of how to safely share the road with those of us who are so much more vulnerable. She was ever-so-thankful that she moved out of that hectic lifestyle, to a calm rural community, albeit a bit of a drive for a contract position. The most excitement that she encountered in her small-town of one-thousand people was seeing a horse and buggy go through the newly opened Tim Horton's drive through, and the larger-than-life beavers who chomped down the poplar trees beside her weary century home in the late fall. Her mind worked in resourceful ways as she often pondered how she could do home renovations with the lumber that the beavers so helpfully felled, so very near her home.

She ate her nourishing veggie pita with great relief of having removed herself from the gloomy weather, sighing that there was yet another hour and a half of riding to go. A brief meditation occupied her mind, as she internally chanted, "I am resilient, I can do this." She mounted the motorcycle that she had bought just a few weeks prior, after redressing herself in all the protective gear she was wearing prior to stopping. The wind had picked up while she had her dinner, with a gusting force to be reckoned with, and the rain pelted on and off as the preparation for the ride began. A break of sun low in the sky to the west, gave her hope, as she headed out of the timid, Mennonite community, in the direction of that clearing sky creating the horizon. There was hope that there would be a break from the storm.

INTERLUDE: HER YOUNGER
YEARS

The young country gal had begun riding motorcycles after several traumas had impacted her life. Riding horses once gave her the enjoyment and freedom of self-expression, and love, as she would ride the strong and muscular, yet graceful and majestic beasts. The connection between her and her horse was magnificent. The horse, named "Betty," *saw* her. Her stepfather's horse represented a connection that she had with no human other than her mother. The horse was an ever-present strength, a strength that was so very admired, so beautiful and full of grace, but most of all, humbling.

After Betty had her offspring (she named this beautiful foal "Babedi" after the admired Princess Diana, for reasons obvious to her), and raising it for a mere eighteen months, she found that the financial strain of owning the foal was too much to handle on her own. There was no financial support, never had been, as at this time she was only eighteen, and paid for everything herself from the age of fourteen onward. After her parents had divorced, money was scarce indeed, and she put it upon herself to be self-supportive not to burden her broken, yet amazing mother. Money was scarce throughout her childhood, creating a money blueprint that burdened her long after. Full of angst, she sold her Babedi for a mere pittance, and planned the rest of her life, full of already broken dreams and annihilated promises of a better life.

As a young, innocent girl, her dreams of owning her own horse and having children of her own one day were the only dreams she envisioned. She had received a Barbie doll with a pink RV one year for Christmas, and a pinto horse with fencing and tack another year. That horse represented so much to her in those formative years. It was that time of her life when it happened; an assault in a sexual form, as a young girl playing joyously on the cold, hard basement floor. She didn't understand it, too young after all, but something changed in her. There were repeat occurrences, and she seemed to have become fallen prey to various predators growing up, and even into her adult years. Alcohol had also become a way of escaping, but only a problem when in the company of the most important adult role model in a little girl's life. He obviously had issues with alcohol; she became his worthy drinking companion from the age of fourteen on up. How murky the waters.

What was it that she missed so dearly after selling Babedi? It took some time of reflection and pondering. She sought time alone yet was a great and trusted friend to everyone. She had felt such loss in the universe yet was joyful. Her stepfather would say to her on countless occasions, "I wish you loved yourself." With no further information on what was taken as a sarcastic statement, she developed resentment for his words, yet loved. That girl grew up to be a sentimental and intelligent woman, and married her first husband, a true narcissist, yet she gave and loved unconditionally. The conundrum of her oxymoron lifestyle was hitting home hard as it continued without fail into her mid-adult years.

In high school, she was the first gal to achieve the status of multiple awards throughout her schooling as a French academic. Top of the class, top grades in the school for her efforts in French, she marveled at how she got lost in the beautiful and artistic language of love. She found a flow, and a form of brilliant connection. One would think she had all the confidence in the world, but that sadly was not the case. One may have assumed that she would one day be a French teacher, or in the least pursue her passion for the language as encouraged; neither occurred.

NEEDING THE MOTORCYCLE

She missed her experiences at the barn gravely, the grooming and leading of Babedi mostly. She missed riding through the bush, the crackling of the sticks below the hooves of the one she trusted, yet everyone knows you can't fully trust a horse. They too have a mind of their own. They will run in the opposite direction of your intention if spooked in any form or fashion. She missed the wind in her hair and the sunshine gleaming down on her entire being, warming her to the core. She missed the heightened aromas of the country air, the smells of the strawberry fields of late spring and the sweet cuttings of fresh hay.

Something enormous was missing in her life, and she couldn't quite put her finger on it, until one day. One day, it hit her with grand enthusiasm. It was recognized by her creative force, acknowledging that she loved her riding days, even her adventures of riding her burgundy-colored ten-speed bicycle with the downward curling handles down the lush paved country roads, on the treks of longer, faster, harder, that she knew so well. It was the freedom she so greatly missed, along with that feeling of being connected. It was as if the spirit from within hammered the gavel on her chest and spoke. "A motorcycle, that's what I need! I need to get myself a motorcycle! I will unveil my freedom and rediscover the connection, even if it is with a brainless iron horse!"

Her first motorcycle was a 1984 Honda Rebel, 250cc. It was particularly funny to her, as she was not rebellious as a young woman, that people knew of anyway. She had this tenderness that replicated the princess that she so admired yet raging inside of her was a female warrior. A woman who, if challenged, would rise to any occasion to make a situation better, as much as she was capable. She taught herself on the dirt roads of her small residential community, her stepdad cheering on from the sidelines (she couldn't hear a word he hollered) to "pull in the clutch, faster, slow down, *stop*!" Those were the days, the days of naivety combined with an unmatched determination to excel, no matter what happens. Independence as far as she knew, was a breath of fresh air once more. She rode her motorcycle to her high school for her last year, empowered.

THE RIDE HOME

As she bundled up for her tiresome journey, she felt content that soon she would be home to her eagerly awaiting family. She had turned right at the highway eighty-six, a busy road considering it is in the country. A curve up and ahead was traveled often by her, and the strength of the gusts of wind made for a challenge as it blew from the opposite direction of the curve. Thankfully, she teaches about riding safely on motorcycles and has practiced many great skills over her riding career. As she entered the lengthy curve, clear, double solid yellow lines gave warning that no one should pass another vehicle while in the contour. But she saw something odd. Her fingers tightened around the grips, and then she took a gasping breath, as she recognized that there were headlights approaching at lightning speed, in her lane, directly for her and her motorcycle. It was passing a long transport truck, an SUV, and another car, in the very lane in the curve that she was riding. She immediately gulped and yelled "Jesus!" She did what she had taught for her ten years of teaching experience. She kept her eyes peeled up and ahead, gained perspective of everything around her, checking her mirrors in haste. She push-steered to the right, managing to keep the Harley on the fringe of pavement that remained. It was truly a miracle that had occurred, but in slow motion. The oncoming, hurtling vehicle brushed by her with such proximity that had she extended her arm, it would have been severed. She pulled in her clutch and roared her loud engine, believing that the individual driver had no idea she was even sharing the road with the passers-by. She hoped and prayed that the noise of her engine would somehow alarm everyone. It did not. As a matter of fact, no one even stopped to see if she was okay. She felt completely alone in this moment, abandoned, and frightened to near death, quite literally. Her life passed through her mind in an instant over the fact that she nearly perished. Truthfully, had she been driving her SUV, she would have either had a head on collision, or gone onto the shoulder of the road and down a forty-five degree angled ditch and rolled it; either way, she was sure she would not have survived. That which people often utter "motorcycles are dangerous," is truthfully in complete opposition to what saved her life that day.

As no one that day paused for her, she decided to carry on home. What else was there to do? It was proof that few really care about your story and carry on with their own trek in life. Who knows if anyone truly saw her beast of a motorcycle, let alone her? Tears filled her eyes for nearly an hour and a half. She knew in her right mind that stopping would be best from a mental standpoint, yet the drive to get home safely was all she cared about. She dug in, with her mental grit, and stuck to her plan. She reasoned in her own mind that riding home to her husband and fur babies was better than sitting on the side of the road lost in emotional angst over the near-death experience. It was already in the past; move the hell on, get to your home and family, your anchor. The quandary has run its course, move on.

Her ride was truly a gnarly blur, and certainly she had gone through an adrenaline rush of post-traumatic stress. Again, although pulling over to stop would have been best, she found her way home, timelessly, tiresomely, but safe. Her husband met her in the driveway, and she could barely get her story out when he shared that a good pastor friend had just passed away. She nearly collapsed and worked awfully hard at not vomiting. It had all become too much, and she ran into the house and hid under a blanket wailing with tears. The night was long and dark. The conflicting feelings of life, and that of death; profound gratitude, as well as the grief that accompanies such great loss of another loved one, wrestled in her soul.

The following morning, she decided to investigate the paperwork from the motorcycle's history of ownership. She marveled at how a motorcycle in and of itself is considered dangerous by some, yet for her, a life saver. They told her at the Harley dealership just a few weeks prior, that upon purchase, this motorcycle had fourteen prior owners, and there were no liens against it. She flicked through meticulously, page by page of all prior owners, dealership to owner, dealership to owner unable to fathom the numbers. She nearly collapsed when she read on the last page, the final lines of black on the white crisp page, that the original owner of that very motorcycle some thirteen years prior, was that of her husband. He had not recognized it when she test-drove it five hours away from their rural home. There were a few modifications, but it was without argument, his original bike. She trembled in awe over the news. He had sold it ninety days to the day before her mom had passed away. At that point in their lives, they hadn't even met yet. She had bought the motorcycle the day that their pastor friend Terry had passed away. Far too many circumstances to be believed as just that by the general population. Angels keeping her safe on her journey, a great friend and mother deceased a few weeks short of eleven years prior, and her earth angel, her husband, who gave up riding a few years prior due to his poor health; she truly counts on for his soulful insight and support.

Divinity at work? Have you ever experienced a rush of coincidence that may have seen you at one end of the life spectrum, or the other? Have you ever been through such travesty and turmoil? Has adversity ever shaken you to the core? Life has been chalked full of such occurrences, and she continues to bounce back to a vibrant way of living. "How," you may ponder and query. For her, the term God-incidence seemed awesomely appropriate.

Knowing that imminent death may have been staring me in the face was frightening to say the least. It was not the first time, and I am sure it will not be the last that the proverbial flash of my life will traverse before my eyes. I decided in great haste, that this was not "my time to go." I had more time that I needed to share with my family and friends; more cherished moments and beautiful memories to create. I needed time to seek out more harmony, more beautiful people, and to realize the ripple effect of positive change that I sought, not only for myself, but for the lives of those around me, who were ready. An epic period of time was in the making, and it was magnificent. The remedy to my dire situation was answered in a mere split second or two. Interestingly, the force of nature was against me. It often seems to me that there is an opposing force to that of my mindset. The gale of wind rushed from the left, the long tight curve of road veered to the right, and creating the push on the right handle bar of the motorcycle had to be maneuvered precisely, in order to successfully land on the paved fringe of the road, without hitting the dirt, yet over far enough that I did not collide any part of my motorcycle or body with the lethal approach. Yes, it truly was a miracle, and one which I will be forever grateful.

In analyzing my feelings of being in the moment, I recognize that the force of adrenaline acted as a lifesaving mechanism. I did not fear the situation as there was simply no time. I reacted upon command, with exactitude that I marvel at. Practicing perfect, with every moment of my riding journey over the decades, is what helped to save me, along with my unyielding faith. For every error made, I have performed the remedy many, many times over, replaced with an improved and enhanced skill. Practice does not make perfect, although I have found that practicing perfect, over, and over in my mind, and consistently while riding has changed my capability and performance on the road. I have found life to be like this also. It is such as to the conscious vs the subconscious mind. If I were to have stayed "in my head," in the conscious mind, I believe that my time here would have be cut off tragically. Because I have replaced my thoughts from that of fear to that of practicing perfect at any challenge, and in this case, motorcycle related, that I reacted with commanding majesty. It is so hard to convey in words, the power of the trained subconscious mind; my seasoned subconscious mind, my motorcycle and God saved my life that eventful day. I discovered incredibly early on that if I keep repeating the same error over and over again, I simply continue to get better at getting worse. By not replacing old destructive habits or thought patterns, decisions and reactions can truly be fatal, or at least self-defeating. A shift of gears is vital, to lead onward to a more abundant and fulfilled life.

WHAT WORKED FOR ME, MAY WORK FOR YOU

Faith was indeed at the top of the list about having a successful outcome during this traumatic experience. I commanded my faith and hope in the situation with immediacy. Putting all the dooming, coinciding factors together that were against me, really says that I shouldn't be here any longer. Having said that, I admittedly was one with the situation. In that very moment, I had aligned myself with that which threatened my life. I was congruent with the challenges posed and am feeling very blessed to be breathing.

Trust was indeed and has been an ongoing threat to my existence. I certainly did not trust the driver of that vehicle, and I felt a loss of such for those that carried on driving down the highway without stopping to see if a fellow human being, me, was okay. Alone again, not seen, not heard, an energy occupying invisible space. I have had people of varying walks of life manipulate, lie, and deceive me; they have cheated against me those who said they "loved" me. I have recognized that I had even stopped believing in myself, and thus had no trust for the decisions that

I had been making. A great deal of mistakes and failures have followed my every attempt. It has been through the successive trips and falls, the near misses, the death-defying moments that I have realized that if I didn't start trusting me, I had nothing. It is like a relationship without the foundation of trust; it does not exist, nor does it thrive to survive. I have developed a new sense of being through the actions of others, to realize that it is not about me. Their behavior is owned by them, their own responsibility. My life may not matter to anyone else, but it sure does matter...to me, and the perception of others towards me no longer holds me captive to limited beliefs. This has taken a very long time for me to realize. Do you matter to you? Are you recognizing any traits that may be bringing you down, and tearing you away from your true potential? I decided to trust my instincts, and against all odds, I am still here. Learn to trust YOU, it may just save your life one day! It may bring you to your knees trying, you may ride on the last bit of pavement on your journey to who knows where; trust, you've got this!

There have been many times where I have questioned myself, broken-spirited and lost. Those who one would think would be along my side, were not. I was abandoned, criticized, and judged, alone and longing. Since the passing of my mom, my greatest fan, my idol of humanity, I have learned a very slow lesson. It has had me bleed from the inside out and the outside in. Self-worth and self-love were traits that had escaped my many years of development. A true conundrum was acknowledged, and at what point I am really unsure. It was some time after my mother had gone to her heavenly home. I was in a relationship that again left me feeling desperate and isolated. My children had grown up and were at the beginning stages of developing their own lives. I would put on a great show of confidence, whilst my heart was heavy and impoverished. Time, patience, and self-care have contributed to my improvement in these areas, the opulence leaving me bursting with newfound joy and bliss, a celebration for life! Your celebration of life is now, not when you are dead. Life, a certainty of the moment, and the moment I chose life during that summer evening ride, my story was one to be shared. How on earth could I have survived otherwise, without self-worth and self-love? How on earth could I truly *ever* care for and love others, if I didn't recognize the lack of such traits in myself first? These were other profound shifts.

STRONG AS A DAFFODIL

I am sure you have seen, in the very early spring, the daffodils pop up from the prior frozen ground, joined by the splendor of color of the crocuses and eventually the tulips. I have been awestruck every year, going through the tough times, that these precious gifts of hope for warmer days ahead, as delicately beautiful as they are, are resilient. Just because they have developed their rooted system for another season of growth, and just because they have managed to crack open their bulb of hope to generate a green stem and a most spectacular brilliant colored flower, does not mean that they are fragile, as one may assume. These little miracles are like our life story. They are so resilient that even upon an ice storm, another freeze, or a fresh dumping of snow, they maintain their level of integrity. Despite the ice, the snow, and the freeze, the flower continues to stand strong. If you are open to change, you too can maintain or grow in integrity, resilient to the angst of daily situations. The ride I had on the 1200cc Harley Sportster Custom, that blustery summer's eve, truly could have resulted in the end of my riding days. It would have been easy to hang up the keys, to sell the bike, to quit the job of teaching that I am so passionate about, because of a near miss. I am resilient, I have chosen to use this near-death experience yet again another lesson in my life story. I could be dead, quite literally. I could have chosen to be stuck in the thought of it all, remaining in the story of adversity. I have so much ahead of me, I choose to live my life. I saw the miracle; I saw the divine intervention; I saw the hope. I chose to continue my journey with grit, determined that if I was still alive, I deserved to do whatever it takes to make the greatest story for me, for others, to learn and grow from. How resilient have you chosen to be? It is really a decision, so decide.

Albert Einstein said, "No problem can be solved from the same level of consciousness that created it." If you choose to remain in the same headspace as that which you have found troubles, there will never be a lesson, there will never be a solid solution. Once you can elevate your mindset, any problem that comes up will have resolve, and a wonderful opportunity to share and elevate someone else's life path. I am feeling so blessed to share part of my story with you. I hope that this resonates with you on a level that you recognize as a potential to change. If we are not learning and growing, we are stuck, and that is simply not living life abundantly.

In fact, if we are stuck, often we shrink. Not only do some chose to be immobilized by fear, injustice, and opinions of others, but what occurs is that their soul starts to lack love for themselves. I have been here too, where I have felt my soul shrivel up, with a mere spark of inspiration remaining. It has taken work, don't be fooled, the grit necessary to choose growth is not for the faint of heart. You may be feeling this negative tape going around and around in your head, reconfirming that you aren't worth the effort, and the negation of an awesome future occurs. My heart feels so heavy when I ponder this aspect of my life, and that of yours. Pull your bootstraps up, get your head out of your ass and release the negativity once and for all. Learn to replace all the negative thought patterns with hope for the now and fill it with love. Allow faith to be your driving force. When I yelled out "Jesus," it was not simply a reactionary term. I had the faith, the belief that I was worth the fight. Growth can most certainly be painful, and uncomfortable, but the pain of being stuck or worse yet, shriveled up like a prune, is more challenging by far. Choose to *grow* and learn from all the lessons. Some of those lessons come in very tiny packages, and some of them could wipe you off the face of the earth, if it is your time. That day was not my time, it was my *day*, my day to *live* and to *shine*. Choose to grow through your adversity, it is easier on the other side of growth.

STAND TALL

I suppose what I have learned along the decades of my life path is that I have made conscientious decisions to stand tall; to be a survivor despite the odds. As tender hearted as I am, I am a true warrior. I have chosen to be courageous as such. I may crumble, stumble, and even fall on occasion, but you can rest assured I will get up out of the ashes and continue to fuel my flame. I will ride on, despite the near misses. I will pray to be a conduit for your growth, meaning that adversity will strike me again, and again, and I will carry the lessons like a torch to light your flame. It is in me to give, and I hope that one day, you feel strong enough to do the same for others. We are here but for a short time. In my time remaining, I hope to inspire.

Every tear she ever shed, was now recognized as the magical potential, the God-given gifts and talents that had been suppressed for so many years. The many tears that rolled down her tender cheeks, the prisms that they were, mini masterpieces of her future aspirations, visions, and dreams. Every pain had planted a seed for future growth. She has finally recognized that she is enough. I am enough. You are enough. The end, it is just the beginning.

Ronda Lauer
Certified Coach Practitioner, Certified Master Coach Practitioner

Ronda Lauer grew up in a small-town setting with the love of nature as a huge part of her soul. The essence of her free spirit shines through as she takes you on a journey of pure grit and determination, of the growth of her warrior self, to become all that she can be. A brush with death will give you chills, as she warms your heart with the many personal lessons, she shares along one of her tumultuous journeys. She is certified as a coach with the Certified Coaches Federation and will help to inspire you to become unstuck and discover your amazing life purpose. The end is just a beginning. She is now Healthy Wealthy and Wise and is ready to help you show your shine.

This chapter is dedicated to her earth angels and her guardian angels of the heavens.

Connect with Ronda:
www.rideofyourlife.today
www.facebook.com/profile.php?id=100008708594234
www.linkedin.com/in/ronda-lauer-2bb1b62

A Cowboy's Perspective

by Roy Gunderson

So, what is "adversity"? Oxford's dictionary of current English describes it as misfortune or distress.

I think experiencing something painful, that leaves you with limiting beliefs about yourself is very unfortunate and highly distressful. Especially, (for most people) the endless "beating up of one's self" by reliving some event or seeing and interpreting it in a manner that leaves you defeated and to blame. In a perfect world, we would all realize how very powerful we are, filled with infinite possibilities and love, but I feel that limiting beliefs have a way of keeping us in our place and living beneath our potential or in other words, "small."

So, how do you "handle" or deal with adversity? Maybe, just get on with it, or talk with somebody? How about, rather than intellectualize or try to "figure" this out, we just be willing to calm down and relax, then allow ourselves to be "vulnerable" if only for a brief time. You may be surprised how incredibly empowered and free you can become from this!

The longest conversation we will ever have in our lives will be with ourselves. Ideally that conversation will be a kind, empowering one. There is a saying or common belief that "always just work hard and keep busy in your life, and everything will be just fine." If only it would be that easy! Dedicated hard work is essential to any worthwhile endeavor's success, but it seems our western culture's primary focus is to ignore the source of these scars we acquire, but to ignore our own individual gifts. "Just get to work, and don't cause any trouble" is a common philosophy most people internalize while growing up. It would be great if that was all there was to it, but I fervently believe it's common for the little things in our personality or psyche which may not serve us well and literally hold us back, to be present in many of our "closets" where it's dark and buried and we seldom like to go.

To be just by ourselves, or if we were all just single solitary individuals, who never once interacted with anybody or anything else, then we could all just "exist" within our own little worlds, never feeling or be troubled by those scars. Conversely, you would never feel the heartbreak or the joy, or the stress and elation of engaging in "life" and all that it has to offer. To truly live life, within the "arena" of the human experience, complete in relationship with a spouse and raising a family, is an ideal not for the faint of heart. I feel we must learn to live consciously and on-purpose or it seems a certainty that these little triggers you would prefer buried, will find their way to the surface, too often in the most inopportune times. They provide us the opportunity to deal with them repeatedly (hopefully in a constructive manner) or react and attempt to bury them a bit deeper until they give rise to be revealed again.

I'm pretty sure none of us are perfect and depending on where you are in your life, I think we could all benefit from just admitting we are human (complete with the "warts" or the "beauty marks") and entertain the thought that our best selves are well within our reach and worth searching for. From the business entrepreneur to the diesel mechanic, or scientist to the horseman, in all walks of life, the better we can "connect" with ourselves through strength, courage, truth, and vulnerability, the better we can understand and relate to others which makes us all happier, more fulfilled and more valuable to humanity in whatever capacity we choose.

James Allen wrote in the classic "As a Man Thinketh," "The strong, calm man is always loved and revered. He is like a shade-giving tree in a thirsty land or a sheltering rock in a storm." In my life of working with horses and people, some people who may be a bit unsure of themselves, or like a horse who may be skittish a bit or quite a bunch, I think James Allen's quote is both true and extremely helpful.

You may be asking yourself, "so, what does this have to do with adversity?" Well, there was a time in my life that, whether it may be from limiting beliefs or perceived sense of worth, that I felt unworthy and thereby susceptible to guilt and projections of others. My life was a roller coaster of trying to please everyone which inevitably lead to a place when life did not hold much of a future for myself with pain as my prevailing state. I'm not sure if it's a blessing or a curse, but I have the ability to feel things very deeply, both good and bad. Believe me, I was on the road to personal disaster unless I learned a way of gaining an empowering mindset and turning this curse into my blessing.

Let me tell you my story and explain my perspective on the parallels I have seen and how the perception of adversity or limiting beliefs can reside in the body and rob you of your happiness, health, or life's potential. Hopefully, you may recognize some insights and use these tools to work through unhealthy patterns and free your inner giant!

My childhood was like many others; I grew up in Canada, which by itself made me one of the most fortunate people on earth. It was everything it could be, plenty to eat and drink, a safe place to live and the security of belonging to a loving family. Then again, there were some parts I wish would have been different, better said, I wish my interpretations and then ultimately the lessons I adopted, contributed to my empowerment rather than contributing to thoughts and feelings to keep me in my place. As a result, for many years, I carried around with me limiting beliefs and interpretations which did not serve me well. My thoughts of unworthiness and of not being important to anybody seemed to pre-dispose or be at the forefront of who I was and somehow shaped the quality of my life. I believe the quality of our lives can be summarized down to the pictures we "see" in our minds, and the "language" we use to describe what those pictures "mean." The pictures we see in our minds of a life event for instance, are "colored" by or "interpreted" in a certain manner depending on our most predominating attitude and beliefs (whether that belief is acquired through personal experience or social conditioning). For example, two people can witness the exact same event, but when asked to recount what that event consisted of, it can be two totally different stories. We see or "imagine" things in our own certain way, whether it be happy or sad, good, or bad. Since the dawn of the human species, we have survived by our innate tendency to scan our surroundings in a negative way, to cause us to exercise caution, shrink back, stay with the familiar and what we know as true. All this is nature's way of not only keeping us safe but ensuring our survival. Thus, the power of our imaginations, to "see" something in a certain way. First and foremost, the number one function of our primitively programmed brain and nervous system is to process the billions of bits of information coming at it "negatively" and discern through our colored glasses what is dangerous, then fundamentally, "keep us safe". Of course, now we can intellectualize and use logic to determine reality, right? Just imagine for a moment that there is a four-inch-thick piece of plexiglass laying on the ground, no problem, you can walk on it back and forth so what's the problem? Now just imagine that you are up on top of the Calgary Tower or CN Tower in Toronto and step out onto the section with the same glass floor! We know "logically" that it has been engineered to support any amount of weight that we might exert on it, but those butterflies in our stomach will keep most people from trusting it! Imagination trumps logic every time! To see things in your imagination "positively, empowering," now that is the process we will entertain later in this chapter.

I grew up the thirteenth child of hard-working parents. I had seven brothers and five sisters, and I was the youngest. Most of my siblings were much older than I, with lives and interests of their own, it seemed (whether real or perceived) that me being around, or my existence was something of a bother and a source of stress. My parents were the salt of the earth actually, whom I love and appreciate very much. When I think of my folks, I think about how hard they worked for their family, even in their senior years, they toiled day in and day out. I know that's who they were and what they had always done, but I did feel an incredible amount of guilt on being a burden and another mouth to feed. Being the last kid and quite a bit younger than most of my siblings, I somehow gained the label of being "spoiled." I realize my bias now, and I certainly was no angel, but considering today's standards, I honestly do not know why it was that way. Other than my mom did her best to smooth or shield me from the occasional barb or remark from my siblings, derived from family dynamics of "favorites" and "sibling rivalries." Be it right or wrong, that was my reality growing up. My parents, father especially was quite elderly in his life and passed on in 1976 from cancer at the age of seventy years, I was sixteen years old then. All my siblings had moved away with their own lives by then and our mom was taking the loss of father with difficulty. Although mom did love to travel, she never went far from home in those days and as I was still in school and living at home, I did what I could to get mom out into the world of the living. Quite often she would come with me to the rodeos to watch and loved to "mother" my young cowboy friends as well! At seventeen years I graduated from High School and wanted some adventure, so I went to live my dream by hiring on and riding for "Falcon Farm," a Thoroughbred race-horse training facility near Crossfield, AB. So started my dream career of making my living riding horses.

As a kid we always had horses and naturally I wanted to emulate my brother's (who I thought were the world's greatest cowboy's!) From my father, I observed his quiet appreciation and connection of respect for all the horses but especially for his saddle horse "Birdy," a Thoroughbred mare (who could run like the wind!) which I remember very, very well! One time as a lad back home in the rolling hills west of Water Valley, Alberta, I was out with a couple of my brother's riding to check some cattle and they thought it a big joke to let Birdy run off with me on our way home (which was a huge no-no! Not so much the running off with me but letting any horse run on the way home!), as well, as a youngster I had to ride bareback as that was the way all the kids had learned to ride. I'm sure that was dad's way of keeping us safe riding as kids. From his cowboy days I'm sure he witnessed enough wreck's, that he did not want his kids to inadvertently run a foot through a stirrup or arm through a coil of rope and get dragged, injured or more than likely, killed. (My uncle was killed in a horse wreck when dad was a youngster.) Dad rode in the Calgary Stampede as a young man in the 1920s, and I'm told rode for Pat Burns, one of the original "Big Four" who had financed the first Calgary Stampede in 1912. So, my dad was the real deal and yet a mystery to me as he and I never really talked or "connected" in the way I yearned for. It seemed he was always away working and when he did finally come home to stay, it was short-lived as his health deteriorated and he passed away.

After high school, I could not wait to be off on my own, and making a living riding Thoroughbreds, well, that was a dream come true! I had many adventures with horses as a youngster but from my experience riding Thoroughbred racehorses galloping on a track, I found out just how fast a horse could run! If I had owned a set of goggles at that time, I would have worn them but I did not, so I used to keep my head kind of tilted down behind the horses neck somewhat so I could see and my eyes did not fill with tears from the wind! To see and feel the horse change leads from the straightaways into the corners and back was like (what I imagined) "Mario Andretti" would feel like changing gears in his favorite race car! Those horses were spectacular and after a mile or so flat out on the rail and then another half mile or so at a lope, they would be ready to move to the outside rail and pull up into a trot and eventually a walk and cool down. It was incredible!

Like most things, in those days I was looking for variety and when a chance came up from a family friend, I left the Thoroughbred farm to ride at Nashlyn PFRA pasture, (Prairie Farm Rehabilitation Administration) at a fifty-seven thousand six-hundred acres (two point five townships) grazing reserve south of the Cypress Hills in southern Saskatchewan. Once I got my directional bearings, sometimes riding alone checking cattle on what was a vast, never-ending prairie, was without a doubt, a life-changing experience for me. It was there that I gained my deep appreciation and wonder for the capabilities and depth of a horse's stamina and heart. It may sound like a load of BS now but on a few occasions, we would ride upwards of fifty miles a day just doing our job. I had brought one of my brother's mares with me from Alberta but the other horses I rode were from the short grass country, so they were well prepared for the long miles. Depending on whether we rode out from the yard, or on how far we could trailer, or rather "if" we could trailer. In the odd time it rained, the soil or "prairie gumbo," is one of the absolute worst types of mud you could imagine. More slippery than ice and stickier than a handful of molasses. It balls up around the wheel wells on truck and trailer and makes for a very unpleasant experience. This inevitably would result in some extra miles a-horseback. As well, the pasture I was on is dry-land native range meaning it has never been touched by a plow (except for the fire-guards which dissected the prairie) and is the same "shortgrass" or same types of native grasses, as in the days of the buffalo. Shortgrass, which is typically made up of distinct species of grasses, is predominately made up of "prairie wool," (just one of the varieties of hard grass native to the prairies). In a nutshell, because it is so nutrient-rich it is pure "hi-octane" to a horse, and the power it gives a saddle-horse along with their typical daily grain ration in the barn, seemed to rival or surpass the nutrition received by the racehorses I rode for stamina, staying power and longevity. Mile after mile at a long trot, it was nothing short of truly jaw-dropping for me to experience the heart and power those short grass horses had. One morning in late September we helped a neighboring PFRA pasture (Battle Creek) with the gather going on there that day (to prepare a herd of cattle to ship back to their respective patrons). We left our bunkhouse at 3:00 a.m. to trailer over to Battle Creek. Being only seventeen, amongst much older riders, it was an exciting time for me to learn from their experience. At that hour, we could not see anything that was not directly in front the lights of the truck and after we drove for a while, in my slumber, I marked the miles traveled by the abrupt vibration of crossing over the cattle guards (Texas gates that mark the separation of fields). I was dropped off with my horse and instructed to "ride that-a-way and gather stock, and we will meet back up with the herd closer to the corrals." This proved to be quite an experience for me coming from the rolling hills and foothill country of Alberta to the vast expanse of prairie in southern

Saskatchewan especially at this hour of the morning! (I remember the metaphor, "it's the darkest before the dawn" and yes, I found that to be true!) As I rode along, I encountered the occasional dark shapes of cattle which I got started to move along in the direction I was instructed to go. In my seventeen years up until then and in all the years that have past, I have not seen anything as beautiful or brilliant as what happened next! As dawn began to break in the east, the glow of early morning started to emerge over the distant ridge exposing the vast valley before me carved out of the earth during glacial times. The typical golden and green of the prairie was intensified by such a glorious spectrum of color that it is hard to explain the magnitude! Red, blue, orange, purple, yellow and green the prairie came alive with a vibrant surreal glow. It was truly magnificent! I would never have dreamed anything could be so beautiful! It was brilliant! The creak of my saddle, the footfalls of my horse and the odd "moo" of a mother cow calling her calf were like music to my ears, the air was so crisp and clear that every once in a while, I could hear the conversation of the other riders, who were now mere specks on a distant ridge, like they were riding right beside me! It was amazing! The peace, harmony, beauty, and immensity of the prairie, the livestock along with me & my horse is something that has stuck with me to this day and always will as a feeling to "ground" me in nature and life. We covered a lot of ground on that circle and I marveled at the impact the horse has had on civilization and how he changed the course of history forever! When I hear the Ian Tyson song, "La Primera," I'm always transported back to that morning, alone with my horse on the magnificent prairie.

Over the course of the next few years on multiple occasions, I had the opportunity to work with my brother Wally during busy times of the year at the Calgary Stampede Ranch south of Hanna, AB. The ranch is twenty-two thousand acres of native range short grass as well. The horses, (mares & foals, stud horses and broncs) were as sound and hard as rock (in great shape) from distances traveled and again, the hard grass! When gathering a field, once the herd was out along the road the majority of riders would need to ride ahead of the herd, waving their ropes and doing everything they could while riding flat out to keep the herd back behind and keep from overtaking the lead riders so we could not miss bending the herd down the lane to the corrals. The heart and power those broncs showed on their home range carried through to what outstanding athletes they are in the rodeo area as well.

Over the years I have witnessed this "heart" and drive that I'd seen in those horses, shine through in some people as well. I think most of us can admit, we all aspire to this magnificence, but somehow, something has a way of sabotaging our true brilliance. This "saboteur" that steals our freedom is, unfortunately ourselves complete with the limiting beliefs, that we claim, fiercely defend, and drag with us through life. I have found that only through self-reflection, and a willingness to grow we can affect miracles within ourselves through strength, courage, truth, and vulnerability.

My love and affinity with horses was a major factor in my career choice for the next twenty-five years, both working for Alberta Public Lands Division, Grazing Reserves as well as my own company, Excalibur Equine starting colts for any discipline and working with horses from pleasure to cutting horses.

This background of mine is not just idle ramblings, but to illustrate my experiences that support the parallels I see between working with horses and working with people. We can intellectualize and talk ourselves into or out of anything, but how we feel "deep" inside, is something that is difficult to mask successfully. We can try, but as we all know, if there is too much incongruence in how we really feel and act under stress, we can experience all kinds of issues from social anxieties to health concerns that may very well stem back to, those beliefs we harbor deep inside our nervous system. The metaphor I want to use here is the illustration of the fear or need for self-preservation that is so prevalent in horses, especially a "green" one. Their being is all about self-preservation as exhibited by instinctual head high, eyes wide, and snorting (clearing their nose/lungs of air thereby allowing an immediate, olfactory intake which may warn of any impending threat.) Not unlike somebody who is always defensive or threatened, under stress by the thought of standing up confidently and asking for what they want, possibly from fear of being ridiculed, mocked, or rejected. Of course, any number of social idiosyncrasies could be played out here.

This essay is by no means meant to be a "how-to" in working with horses, or a "blanket" approach to heal the human psyche, but a visual illustration that hopefully is both helpful and easily relatable to you, the reader.

There is such a thing as "it's not what you do, but it's in how you do it." Such as helping a troubled horse who struggles with being anywhere around you in a "learning" (so to speak) environment. If you are genuine about wanting to help the horse learn rather than jam your presence down his throat, you might not only allow, but encourage movement of his feet. In human terms, this is synonymous with allowing someone in a stressful or awkward situation to "save face." In some cultures, this could mean everything, the absolute gravity of saving face is paramount in building trust and building an environment of safety. A horse's feet are everything to him and to "move" is allowing a chance to assimilate and learn while still honoring his need for safety and self-preservation. In an extreme case whereby the horse struggles excessively with containing his own nervous compulsion to react (either buck you off and run away or come at you with teeth, strike or kick), at times it can be beneficial to help the horse to lie down, not for a rest as some readers might think, but to, in other words, experience vulnerability, NOT domination. A word of caution, this should ONLY be entertained by an expert horseman as the exercise may prove detrimental, if not downright dangerous and counter-productive if not carried out with utmost feel, timing, and balance. This is much like being present with someone in a delicate or uncomfortable conversation with emotionally charged or extremely sensitive subject matter, the outcome could go either way depending on your skill as a friend, therapist, or communicator.

As mentioned above, "it's not what you do but rather, how you do it." Teaching a horse to trust you and helping him when needed is a series of progressive steps. This is NOT something a person can ram through the motions and use this in an attempt to intimidate, such as in elementary school days, maybe when some bully delights in dominating a smaller student by pinning them down, and then spitting in their face! Only someone with acute horsemanship should entertain this cathartic experience. As shared earlier, a horse's feet are everything to him and the act of him laying down and thereby losing the use (temporarily) of their feet, is to the horse, the epitome of vulnerability. In his instinctual nervous system and in every cell of his body, to lose mobility in his feet is coming close to experiencing his own death. Remember, the instinctual needs ruling his innate ability to be safe, are the same instincts which ensured survival of the species for fifty million years! This need for self-preservation is still alive and well in every living thing and fundamentally is still working in us as human beings. Thank goodness or else Lord knows if we would even still be here! In basic function, our brain is the same as our primitive ancestors who occupied this earth roughly six million years ago. Its primary job is ensuring our "survival." As mentioned earlier in this chapter, according to research, our conscious mind (what we are aware of) can process about forty bits of information per second, while totally out of our awareness, our subconscious mind can handle approximately forty million bits of information per second! That is amazing! Our RAS (Reticular Activating System) is that part of the brain which filters or evaluates all this data down to, what is important and what it perceives to be DANGER! In today's modern society, the need for "fight or flight" is not as prevalent in our daily living as it once was those millions, or thousands, or hundreds of years ago, but those same reflexes and instincts lie just under the surface ready to strike out or react in a milliseconds notice. An example is when we get startled or perceive a threat. This self-preservation is hardwired right into our very nature but of course, shows up in each of us depending on our paradigm of trust or desensitization. One example is how comfortable we all are as human beings piling into a busy elevator or bumping around in a crowded lineup at a sporting event. On the other end of the spectrum, could be the extreme of a wild horse who will not be cornered, contained, or restrained in any way and would rather kill himself than be touched by a human hand. He will not risk being vulnerable.

Can you remember when you were the most vulnerable (helpless and naked)? Depending on, "where" you were or "who" you were with, it was either the most horrific or most pleasurable experience you have ever had. You can be terrified to the point of your nervous system temporary shutting down and you get lightheaded or faint, or you could feel showered with waves of excitement and ecstasy while in the arms of your lover. Fundamentally the same thing, vulnerability, but obviously so vastly different. There may be those of you who maintain that you have always been in "control" and never feel vulnerability, it is "weakness" to feel vulnerable. Well, how is that working out for you? If good, then I applaud you. I applaud your spirit, your effort, and your tenacity, but oh does it ever become a heavy load to bear. I know from experience. In life, I believe we can do anything for a while but, not forever. You get tired, you get worn out and you become burned out. I invite you to be "willing" to become vulnerable; to become "real" and experience truth. Going there, to that dark place, but with the willingness to feel it constructively, and the willingness to feel whatever is there fully until you do not have to anymore, (you will know.) As well, the willingness to come through the other side free of the grip of whatever the fear was that had been paralyzing that area of your life and forcing you to be "in control." That is where the miracle lies.

Once the horse "let's down" and lies down, they can go through a cathartic experience groaning and releasing much the same kind of tension and stress, as you or me in an emotional or traumatic release.

As a human being, it can be quite scary to go through this experience, or let me rephrase that, "damn terrifying" to tell the truth! I can fully identify what a horse may be feeling at a time like that as I have been through it myself.

That saying, "the thing that you run from, will in turn, run you" is so true, and get stronger, if left to persist!

To experience this change for yourself, I invite you to make the agreement not to hurt yourself or anyone else, make yourself comfortable, either lie down or sit either by yourself or with someone you trust, then just calm down and breathe deeply in your abdomen. Then just decide to "let down" and allow to be present with whatever comes up in a constructive way. Breathe slowly, breathe deeply, or breathe whatever way feels right for you at that moment. You may yell, you may scream, you may cry, you may shake, you may get angry, you may shudder like never before just like in your worst thunderstorm complete with multiple cracks of lightning! This is where most people have learned to, "I've got to stop this., just get over it., grow up!" This is where I invite you to stop that thinking, (it's sabotaging your freedom!) and allow yourself to feel everything that comes up, and then, dare to feel it even more! (Bring it on! Give me everything you got!) Exaggerate whatever movement or sound (constructively) that brings up feelings even stronger, be fully present and do not try to "put a lid on it," or "suppress" your feelings on and on, until you do not have to feel it anymore. I'll bet you will be astonished at just how easy that was and may even find yourself laughing and thinking, "is that it? Wow, that was easy!" If felt completely, I guarantee just like that thunderstorm, the negative feelings will just dissipate, the rain will stop, the clouds will part, and the sun will shine even brighter than before (you know how awesome it feels after a storm has ended!)

What you will find out is; those "thoughts," those things that made us "feel" a certain way, used to rule, or govern our "actions" and thereby we would experience whatever "result" we had become accustomed to. So goes the perpetual loop supporting our "old" beliefs, "I can't do this…" or, "I can't do that…," "I'm not pretty enough." or "I'm not good enough." Well now you know, you ARE enough, and we are not our thoughts, we have thoughts, or thoughts are not us!

When you do not like the result you are getting or limiting beliefs are keeping you down, and living up to your potential seems an impossibility, then "change" your thoughts, change what you are putting into your mind deliberately into life-giving, empowering thoughts which over time and repetition will compel you to "feel" energized, empowered, and ready to achieve whatever plan you set out for yourself, and next most importantly, take the required "action" as outlined in your plan to accomplish this goal, the result is, how did it make you "feel" to accomplish this goal? So becomes the "new" perpetual empowering loop supporting the paradigm of your own design of the new unstoppable you!

Be advised, our minds or paradigms are so incredibly powerful that when you least expect it or especially in a moment of weakness, your old limiting beliefs will sneak up and try to take you back, down to the old and familiar way of feeling bad about yourself or disempowered about something. This is normal and just like re-writing over an old hard drive or cassette tape (for those of us who remember them) little fragments of data are still there in our minds vying for position in our thoughts. Lasting transformation requires repetition and reinforcement of your new, empowering beliefs in the form of an incantation or mantra which I suggest you repeat over and over again, ideally ten times in the morning upon waking and ten times at night prior to going to sleep. You must replace the old familiar disempowering thoughts with new exciting empowering thoughts, just like you can dilute a glass of murky water by pouring in clean new water until the glass is effectively left full of crystal clear, clean water. For increased results, link, or charge that mantra with emotion. Then, when you really "get" or understand that our thoughts are NOT us, then boom, in an instant you can decide "no more...." and replace that old disempowering thought that does not serve you, with a new empowering. One that is now in line with the new definition or self-image of who we are and how high we set the standards in our lives.

We may learn healthy strategies to "cope" through exercise, working too hard, deep breathing or "swearing like a sailor," or any of the unhealthy choices we have at our disposal may be drugs, alcohol, smoking, abusive personality etc. the list can be exhaustive. Typically, we (society) just chalk these vices up as "something we do," you know, it doesn't really mean anything, and we could "quit" or change if we really wanted to. Sure.

It seems everyone has their "thing" that very skillfully, and "naturally" we file it away in our psyche and when life is good, it exists in the dark and it's like nothing's there at all! But, under the stress of modern life, be it a close call in traffic, public speaking, making that pitch for the perfect job, listening to an opposing political view (list is endless) but, the best one, the one that can make these little touchy spots feel like they are raw wounds is under the bright light of an intimate relationship. I think among the many obvious reasons a healthy loving relationship is good for us (we statistically live longer!), it is our opportunity to address and heal these little "things" in ourselves that can keep us from living a full life; unbridled from the little insecurities that hold us back from the limitless potential we all are capable of. I'm speaking from experience; everything we need to deal with the undesirable things in life, we already have within us, waiting to be unleashed. There is nothing to gain from using vices to beat our demons, in fact it will only get stronger and hungrier than ever. I'm saying when you indulge or use as a means of making an unwanted feeling go away, you are on a slippery slope and statistically, it does not get any better. Either dramatically, or subtly, a belief can manifest itself in unwanted behavior which can live on through the generations. "We learn what we live, and live what we learn," that is a profound statement explaining cause and effect.

The way we can help ourselves as well as the generations to follow, is to grow and discover who we really are, without the baggage of misconceptions and inhibitions. Rather than suppress and numb out, thereby resign to live another day feeling this way, is to take a stand and do the inner work on yourself and agree to "feel" and be with whatever comes up in a constructive way. You may say, "come on now, that's just ridiculous," but imagine, how much better our world would be if we all learned just how we are all connected. That to live to our potential and be the best version of ourselves for our families and society, can only help us all evolve to a better understanding and way of being. At this point in time, our world needs "new" inspired ideas and solutions to bring us into the future rich with hope and possibilities. It's been said, "everything that ever was and always will be, is already here in front of us, we need just the eyes to "see" it."

Therefore, I invite you to be like that wild horse running high up on a ridge with the wind in his mane and power exploding from every muscle, running not, from whatever is chasing him, but running to his unbounded destiny!

Now, I really applaud you from the bottom of my heart for your courage, leadership, and conviction to doing your part to this evolution and making our world a better place for today and generations to come.

Roy Gunderson, Certified Coach Practitioner, Certified Master Coach Practitioner

Roy Gunderson grew up in southern Alberta and spent most of his life working with horses. Through experience as well as connecting with some of the industry's great teachers in both horsemanship and personal development, Roy has gained many useful insights and sees parallels between working with horses and working with people. He is a passionate optimist on human potential as well as a certified master coach practitioner, author, and speaker. Roy is a husband, father, and grandfather, real estate investor and life-long learner.

Connect with Roy:
www.linkedin.com/in/roygunderson/

Claim Your Power and Heal from Narcissistic Abuse

by Gina Papanou

O ne day it struck her like a ton of bricks. She had awoken like so many times before with that nauseated feeling in the pit of her stomach, her mind racing, knowing her life wasn't what she had imagined it was, and that it was far from what she'd hoped it could be. This particular morning, however, she had the realization she'd been living a fantasy for a very long time. For years, she had been choosing to believe the illusion because she didn't want to face the reality that things weren't right. Then she'd have to do something about it, which was even more frightening. The extent of the dysfunction she had been living was too agonizing to admit to anyone, let alone to herself.

It seemed easier going through the motions, pretending she didn't see the truth of her disheartening situation, so she could stay complacent in the story she had been telling herself. For a long time, she had turned a blind eye to the cause of her deep personal pain. Instead, she had been suppressing her feelings to endure. She had not been living a life that was true to herself. Rather, she had learned to betray herself because she didn't know anything about personal boundaries, let alone have any in place to protect herself from those who were inclined to take advantage of her.

Like many young women, she had imagined a beautiful vision of what her life would look like when one day she would fall in love and get married. She believed she would grow old with her husband and together, they would raise a family making special memories that would last a lifetime. Like most people, she wasn't fully conscious at the stage in her life when she made that momentous decision about who she was going to build her future with. Having lived a sheltered life growing up, she had little wisdom and she was far from independent. She hadn't learned many valuable life lessons yet, and to boot, she got married at the tender age of nineteen. The truth is she decided to get married because she thought it would offer her the freedom she desperately longed for. She knew marriage was the only peaceful option she had to move out of her father's house.

She grew up in a dysfunctional home. Her father was a narcissist and he ran the household with fear and an iron fist. Growing up her dad was so strict she wasn't allowed to go to friends' houses, parties or sleepovers. Her dad was very oppressive, and he was paranoid about "stranger danger." He was regularly suspicious of her whereabouts and she often had to lie to him just to be able to go out and do things that normal kids took for granted.

The times he caught her deceiving him there was hell to pay. As a consequence, she spent much of her childhood at home, often in her room engrossed in books and listening to music to escape, and to avoid being targeted during those terrifying moments where he would fly into a rage. A couple of times she planned to run away and once, at the age of fifteen, she even had her bag packed but she didn't go through with it because she had nowhere to go. There was always a sense of helplessness present in her that she can only describe as a feeling that she was in a prison with invisible bars.

With the understanding she has all these years later, it was no surprise her father behaved this way. It was a natural consequence to his childhood experience, which had been a traumatic one. As a young girl, she didn't have the capacity to understand why her dad acted the way he did or that he suffered from complex post-traumatic stress disorder. All she knew was the confusion, anger and resentment she felt towards him. She grew to learn that he was a good person with bad behaviours. After years of therapy and reflection, she developed a compassion for what her father went through. He was a deeply wounded person who endured a horrific childhood. Her dad suffered greatly during the Second World War. He was orphaned, losing his mother at the age of seven and he had grown up in post-war poverty.

The stories her father rarely told were unimaginable and disturbing. One example was the time communist guerillas were invading his family's village. Her grandfather, frantically ordered her father, who was age nine at the time, to run off as fast as he could and hide in the mountains, for fear that he would be captured and taken by the soldiers, who were rumoured to kidnap young boys to train as child fighters for their cause. Her dad escaped into the mountains in terror, where he survived alone for three days and three nights before returning to the village. As a result of this kind of anguish, he wasn't capable of being an emotionally healthy husband or father. He was just too wounded. A narcissist can't love themselves, let alone anyone else. Like Narcissus in the Greek myth, a narcissist is more preoccupied with his reflection, false-self or "image" of what others think of him, than he is with knowing and developing his authentic, real Self.

She grew up living in a state of continual fear of verbal, physical and emotional abuse - like her dad had in his childhood. The circumstances were different of course, but the family pattern was the same. She developed codependency, like her mother, in order to cope. Getting married right out of school was a way of escape to her then young and naïve mind. What she didn't realize at the time, was that she had attracted someone into her life who mirrored aspects of her father. That is what human beings unconsciously do. We "fall in love" with someone who subconsciously feels familiar, usually a person exhibiting similar traits to one or both of our parents. This happens so our childhood wounds can come to the surface to be healed.

It's important to understand that narcissism occurs on a spectrum and not everyone who exhibits occasional narcissistic traits has a personality disorder. The exact cause of narcissistic personality disorder is unknown, but psychologists agree it's probably a combination of early childhood experiences, genetics and psychological factors which include excessive criticism, over-praising, excessive pampering, trauma, abuse, insensitive parenting, and unpredictable or negligent care. Although narcissists can leave a path of destruction behind them, it's important to understand this behaviour is unconscious and to have compassion for what they've suffered. At the same time, it's also vital to remove anyone exhibiting toxic behaviour from our life so that we can heal because whether we realize it or not, our health is negatively impacted in these relationships.

Codependents play an equal role in the dysfunctional family dynamic and are also responsible for their own healing. Condemning narcissists or feeling sorry for codependents doesn't serve anyone. We're all adults running the unconscious programs we learned witnessing others from birth to age seven and even though it wasn't our fault that we were "programmed" in that way, as adults, we are responsible for healing and developing ourselves. Education is vital to gain understanding, so those still in the dark can move to the light and see the reality of their situations. Only through awareness and acceptance can a person take right action towards real recovery and thrive.

Codependence is caused when a child grows up in a dysfunctional family and comes to believe they don't matter and may conclude they're even the cause of the family's problems. This happens when well-intentioned parents don't have the capacity to provide a stable, supportive and nurturing home environment and at times, as in her case, the child becomes the caretaker. Codependents suffer from Self-Love Deficit Disorder, a term created by Dr. Ross Rosenberg of the Self-Love Recovery Institute in Chicago.

Growing up, she learned that people who say they love you, might hurt you and due to many experiences in her family system, she became a people pleaser. She often felt guilty, unworthy and fearful and she had difficulty trusting people. As a result, she regularly felt alone, wouldn't ask for help and became controlling in order to feel safe. She learned to react to everyone else's problems and to respond to their needs. She would give a lot more care, respect and love to others than she would ask for or expect to receive. She often found herself being overly responsible for the emotions and actions of others, and she would even help other people at her own expense. She wasn't in touch with her needs or what she was truly feeling. She suffered from low self-esteem and she gave up her power because she had never experienced what it was like to have any. Then at times, she would feel angry and taken advantage of.

Codependents repeat relationship dynamics and unresolved issues even though they are deeply unfulfilling, confusing and scary. They repeat them because they're familiar, they feel "right" and because they don't know what a healthy relationship looks like.

A lack of boundaries manifested itself in harmful ways in her life; she had an ongoing identity crisis because she didn't really know who she was or what she stood for, not having the opportunity to live on her own and individuate as a young adult; she was approval-seeking so she had difficulty saying "no" or setting limits; she had a hard time when it came to asking for what she needed; she also had difficulty making decisions; and she didn't feel comfortable receiving from others.

The gaslighting was the worst. It was the pervasive wearing down of her self-esteem that eventually caused a downward spiral into hopelessness and depression. It led her to doubt herself and to second-guess her perceptions and memories of events that had taken place. She regularly experienced a "twilight zone-like" sensation accompanied by anxiety. She had become convinced there was something wrong with her and she was unlovable. It was a horrible feeling when deep down, she knew she was a good person, but she lacked comprehension of the situation, and she was blind to the unconscious patterns that were running her.

Narcissistic abuse is the gradual, intentional erosion of a person's sense of self-worth aimed at undermining the person's identity for the purpose of gaining control over them, for the narcissist's personal gain. Narcissistic abuse causes psychological damage. Narcissists insist their version of reality is the truth because they have a powerful need to be right. They are experts at everything, making up fiction they themselves may believe and arguing it as fact. They will lie to your face with such insistence that you can't help but start to believe them, even questioning everything you know because they can be so incredibly persuasive. Narcissists are quite arrogant and self-absorbed. They'll exaggerate their accomplishments and take credit for yours if they can because they feel threatened by another person's achievements, as if they are a direct reflection of their own inadequacy.

Narcissists usually have a small circle of supporters who on the surface, they treat very well, as long as they remain loyal to the narcissist's agenda. A narcissist can be especially kind when you go along with their perception of life on their terms. Studies show most narcissists are men, although women can also have the disorder. Narcissists exploit and manipulate people for personal gain such as to receive attention and admiration from them - this is their narcissistic supply. They will even turn family members against each other, inciting competition, to gain control over them. Narcissists are unable to sincerely apologize for anything and they will deflect blame as they are extremely vulnerable to criticism. If you confront them with their behaviour for example, they will act like they are the victim and immediately divert attention away from themselves by pointing the finger elsewhere. They refuse to see or admit there is a problem, except when it comes to you.

With a narcissist, arguments are left unresolved and hanging in the balance. They will reject your feelings, thoughts, needs or perceptions because they believe they know better what you are feeling and thinking. Guilt-tripping is another way they gain power and control over others to satisfy their needs while effectively appearing kind, generous and selfless. Some make themselves indispensable by gifting things, helping out materially and never asking for anything back, in order to appear altruistic, yet there are always strings attached.

The narcissist's need for attention and admiration is at the expense of anyone who is willing, gullible or dependent enough to give it to them. You can bring up a topic in conversation for example, and they will find meaning in it for themselves, jump in and hijack that conversation. They have a need for all eyes to be on them. They take control of the conversation and don't give you a chance to speak, all the while not even being conscious of what they're doing, and they can go on for hours talking to a captive audience. Their relationships are generally void of mutuality and reciprocity and they don't truly know how to care for or anticipate the needs of another person. This is because one of the key traits exhibited by a person with narcissistic personality disorder is a lack of empathy. Recent studies have shown this is tied to a reduction in the volume of gray matter in an area of the brain that correlates to emotional regulation and compassion.

Not all narcissists are overt, loud or gregarious. The covert narcissists are the hardest to recognize because they can be quiet, insecure, and passive. They will also give insincere apologies to placate and manipulate another person if it suits their purpose.

Having boundaries is essential for any loving relationship. Healthy boundaries keep harmful elements like negativity, manipulation, harassment and abuse out of your life. As a codependent with a lack of boundaries she unconsciously attracted a familiar, toxic relationship where she could continue; to accept and justify unacceptable behaviour; to blame herself when things went wrong; to continually apologize; to allow others to demean her by staying silent; to avoid confrontation at all cost; and to feel invisible.

She didn't feel whole and loved because she didn't love herself. That was the crux of it all. She suppressed her personality to avoid conflicts and allowed problems to be repeatedly swept under the rug, never to be solved. She was stuck doing the same thing over and over again expecting a different result, praying for some external miracle to happen that would change everything. Albert Einstein calls this the definition of insanity and she would have to agree. Her experience as a codependent in relationships with narcissists was indeed "crazy-making."

Depression is caused when your thoughts and beliefs are not aligned with your feelings. Living an illusion, she wanted to believe, while feeling more and more emotionally, physically and spiritually depleted, led to hitting rock-bottom where she also became physically ill and developed suicidal ideations. She reached a point where she could no longer function and struggled just to survive each day.

Going through a challenging divorce where her needs were completely dismissed as were all the years of devotion and building a life together was brutal. Healthy people remember the good times - not just the bad. You might be getting divorced, but it doesn't mean that your life together didn't have some happy, valuable memories. For a narcissist, it's like it never happened. You're no longer useful to them so they discard you, casting you aside and they go further to create a smear campaign so they can sabotage you with your friends, extended family and even alienate you from your children if they can. They will do this all the while playing the part of the victim, looking like they care and are genuine.

Her father passed away a few years after her divorce. On his deathbed, he apologized to her, deeply regretting that he had limited her choices as a young woman. He was very sad that her marriage hadn't been fulfilling for her and she assured him she was well on her way to a brighter future. Her father's remorse and the gift of her forgiveness was cathartic for the both of them.

Reasonable people who have empathy, respect another person's boundaries if they are cut off. They also self-reflect and feel regret about their behaviour. They don't try to have others "talk sense" into that person or talk badly about them behind their back. There is a certain level of respect for the dignity and wishes of another person by people who have a healthy sense of empathy.

Ending a relationship with a narcissist doesn't follow the normal recovery time for a breakup. When you're a survivor of a toxic relationship like this, it takes much longer to heal and feel whole again, especially if you're still in contact with the narcissist who confuses obsession with care, and control with security. Control is power and self-preservation for the narcissist. Remaining in any kind of contact gives them further opportunity to gaslight you, to use triangulation, etc., which hinders your ability to recover.

To truly restore your mental and physical health, you need a peaceful space to rebuild your self-worth, and discover the inner strength and sense of confidence you've been lacking. This requires faith, patience and time. Breaking all contact with the narcissist gives you the best opportunity to heal because you can't recover when you are still experiencing pain. In a safe space you can effectively express your truth and safely cleanse your emotions.

Dysfunction is passed down through the generations. Most people's core beliefs are rooted in fear because we live in a fear-based society and because most of our parents' core beliefs were rooted in fear. Perfect parents don't exist. Our parents did the best they could but unknowingly programmed us with the same angst and prejudices they learned from their parents. The good news is we have the power to reprogram ourselves as if we had perfect parents raising us, if we're willing to do the work. Some people had emotionally available parents and the blessing of a well-adjusted, contented childhood. This doesn't appear to be the norm.

Dysfunction is revealed in behaviours that are passed down from generation to generation because people do what they know. If you're a member of a dysfunctional family, you are most likely completely unaware of it. You might suspect there's something wrong because you're unhappy and missing a sense of wellbeing, but you can't put your finger on it and you won't find out unless you are brave enough to take a critical look at your situation and start asking yourself the hard questions. First, you need to accept there's a problem and in order to do that, it helps to be aware of and understand healthy boundaries.

When a person goes through trauma, their focus is on surviving, not thriving. Personal boundaries can only come into a person's awareness once they are secure in their survival and only then can they strive to reach their full potential. In Maslow's Hierarchy of Needs for example, the first level a human being requires for survival, is basic physiological needs like food, water, and sleep. Level two is safety and security and level three is love and belonging. In other words, until you have these three foundational areas in place, you can't reach level four which is self-esteem, confidence, achievement and respect of and by others, where you can actually develop into your highest and best version.

In our busy, often distracted daily lives, we seldom take the time to become quiet and still, to go within and listen to our feelings and what's really going on inside our bodies. Our bodies don't lie to us. That gut feeling you have is actually your subconscious mind talking to you. Science has discovered the brain-gut connection and your subconscious mind communicates with you through emotions sensed by your gut as well as through pain and illness, which acts like an alarm to alert you to problems you need to address.

Most of us ignore our body's signals until eventually, they come back to bite us with a huge message like a serious health issue of some kind, which is designed to rudely awaken us so that we have no other choice but to take notice. Louise Hay, in her best-selling book, <u>Heal Your Body</u>, discusses the mental causes for physical illness. It's an excellent resource to get insight into the thought patterns going on in your subconscious mind that may be manifesting as dis-ease.

As a result of childhood trauma and societal judgment around the expression of negative emotions, many people stoically push their feelings down without realizing this suppression leads them to become numb to their feelings. We're taught expressing our sad or angry feelings is a sign of weakness. Actually, it's the opposite - vulnerability and authenticity are in fact characteristics of strength. Only a strong person has the courage to express how they really feel and allow themselves the space and self-compassion to sit in non-judgment with their feelings. A person with low self-esteem, is afraid of being authentic because they're more concerned about maintaining their image, in order to protect against anticipated criticism and judgment from others. They're afraid to feel their feelings because they have bought into the "rational lies" that if they're not always happy, there's something wrong with them.

She used to be one of those people who felt embarrassed to show her feelings and especially, to cry in front of people. This is because she had been so often ridiculed and humiliated when she did. The challenge for her was that she felt teary a lot of the time because she had been living a life so untrue to herself. It was like the chicken and the egg story - she wasn't sure which came first, depression or living with a narcissist? Studies show narcissistic abuse causes anxiety, depression and complex post-traumatic stress disorder.

It is said that our souls choose our parents based on lessons we want to learn here on "earth school". We all have the same life but each one of us has a different exam and there are no enemies, only lessons. Her lessons in life have been like those of many others; to learn self-love, self-worth, and healthy personal boundaries. It wasn't until she started recovering from burnout that she realized her breakdown was actually a breakthrough. No one wants to experience that kind of anguish but it's only through heartache and adversity that we can learn, grow and evolve. Although it can be deeply painful, this creates an opportunity for you to have a major breakthrough that can lead to a beautiful new life if you're willing to trust your journey, do the inner work and persevere.

Healthy boundaries start with you. If you often find yourself feeling sad and frustrated, holding in negative feelings to the point of angry outbursts, constantly complaining, feeling unwell, perhaps feeling taken advantage of or even powerless, then you're playing something called the "Blame Shame Victim Game" which isn't serving you. This approach will keep you stuck forever with no opportunity for recovery.

True healing starts with taking responsibility for yourself and for your own life. When you're able to respond instead of reacting to what's going on around you, such as people trying to hook you into an argument for example, you're able to develop that sense of inner peace and wellbeing because you are aware you have free will choice and you have stepped into your power.

This is why it's important for women to speak our truth and share our stories. So, we can help those who are struggling along their own journey of personal turmoil or breakdown. It's essential to know there is hope no matter how bleak things may look right now. You will come out the other side, into the light victorious, transformed like a phoenix from the ashes, as long as you don't give up on yourself. We often hear it said, "Your life falls apart so it can fall back together in the best possible way for you and for the highest and best good of those you love and serve."

She made a huge commitment to her recovery because she knew she was the only one that could. She was open to new ideas and personal growth, and she also knew that it would take warrior strength and courageous action to make the necessary changes. She knew she would have to take a leap of faith into the unknown and it was terrifying, but she did it anyway. The alternative was to give up and say goodbye to this life and there was no way she was going to do that to her children. Her love for them is what kept her going through the darkest nights. She often wonders, how this has affected them. She is determined to heal and break the cycle for future generations.

Therapy was where she started her healing journey and it was extremely helpful, but she needed more. There were times she would be up all night, alone with anxiety or panic attacks and waiting for next week's therapy appointment just wasn't going to cut it. She created a support system around her of people she could trust and depend on, who truly cared about her wellbeing. She tried several life coaches and chose the one she resonated with the most and she invested the time and resources it took to benefit from the coaching.

As she grew stronger, she participated in a variety of personal development courses and experiential healing programs. Her exploration was limitless. It was a long, arduous journey yet she persevered, one step at a time. Fortunately, she is healthier now than ever and she feels strong, joyful, grateful and more self-loving than she has in her life. She truly feels blessed. Our healing journeys are ongoing.

As a life coach, I have met far too many women like this, who are suffering from narcissistic abuse and codependency and whose children are caught in the no-man's land of the battles they are fighting. If you are in this position, it's essential to remember there is always hope.

Learning and implementing boundaries is a vital part of your healing journey. I cannot stress this enough. If you're experiencing anger, complaining, feeling defensive, or feeling victimized then you have some major clues about the boundaries you need to set. Setting and implementing boundaries takes determination. Many people don't set boundaries because they're afraid of what other people will think, or that they'll be upset with them. Sometimes they just don't want the hassle and prefer to go with the flow or they're afraid of being seen as "selfish". Sometimes they just don't know where to start.

You can't simultaneously set a boundary with someone and also take care of their feelings. They may feel hurt, angry, or disappointed and that is not your problem. At first setting boundaries might make you feel uncomfortable and afraid and this is normal. It's like exercising a muscle, the first few times it's going to hurt and then the muscle is going to grow stronger and you'll feel stronger too. Your life is your business, and no one has the right to tell you what to think, feel, or do. You have a right to your own thoughts, beliefs, feelings and values and you don't have to be nice to people who are not treating you well.

A person with healthy boundaries feels the need and has the right to love, respect, and stand up for themselves. You have the right to live your life on your own terms regardless of whether other people like it or not. And you don't have to feel guilty for not behaving the way others want you to. Choose you over the expectations of others. You can still be kind and have boundaries. To say no to others means that you also need to be okay with others saying no to you.

When you have healthy boundaries; you don't tolerate abuse or disrespect; you're in touch with your own wants, needs and feelings and you're able to communicate them clearly; you're committed to your healing and take responsibility for nurturing your full potential; you realize that you're responsible for your own happiness and fulfillment and at the same time you allow others to be responsible for theirs; you don't absorb other people's feelings; and you're able to ask for help when you need it. Most importantly, you don't compromise your values or integrity to avoid conflict or being rejected. You listen to your inner voice and you know that what other people think of you is none of your business.

People want to believe in their illusions. It's easier to stay in the comfort zone of what you know and continue on the path you're on - even if you're unhappy. To truly embark on your recovery, you must be willing to face the truth of any misconceptions in your life. Learn to depend on yourself and take responsibility for yourself by boldly taking action in response to new learning and information. Self-love is being okay with the work in progress that you are and being self-approved and comparing yourself only to who you were in the past and not to other people.

We can never truly heal if we stay engaged in the struggle. Trying to keep the narcissist accountable keeps us hooked, so we must let it go and focus on the only person we can control - ourselves. Forgiveness is not for anyone else, except "for giving" yourself another chance. Learn to trust yourself, feel your feelings and be compassionate with yourself.

You must be the change you wish to see in your life. Embrace new experiences and new people in your life in order to learn, grow and raise your awareness. Spend time in nature, meditate or listen to music that moves and inspires you. This is very restorative and will help you get in touch with your inner self and the present moment. Over time, you will learn to think and act spontaneously rather than from distrust based on past experiences. You will lose the tendency to worry, you will lose interest in conflict or interpreting the actions of others. And you'll lose concern in judging anyone, including yourself.

Stay away from people who make you feel you're hard to love. Let go of those who walk out of your life - they're not meant to be there. Boundaries will help you remain honest, healthy and living a life that is true to you. You will become the role model your loved ones need. As your energy changes, you will manifest like-minded people into your life.

If someone crosses your boundary then you must enforce it with consequences or else, it isn't a real boundary. We teach people how to treat us by the conduct we're willing to accept. Your personal boundaries protect the essence of your identity. You don't need to justify, apologize for, or rationalize the healthy boundaries you're setting. Just be calm, clear, firm and respectful. Validate your own feelings and know setting boundaries is a form of self-care. When you fill your own cup first, you can give freely of the overflow to others. What's best for you is best for the people in your life as well. They will benefit from a healthier, happier you and as you valiantly shatter illusions that don't serve you, others will be uplifted to do the same.

You can break out of the scary story of illusion into a beautiful, new experience of personal exploration and positive change. Healthy boundaries will lead you to the happy life you deserve. Having a life-coach or mentor to guide you will keep you on track and accelerate your progress as long as you believe in and stay committed to yourself. You are here for a reason and you have great things to contribute to this world.

Finally, know along the way you will experience fear but if you keep the faith, you will persevere. FEAR can mean "Forget Everything And Run" or "Face Everything And Rise" - the choice is yours. Heal from narcissistic abuse and thrive because you are worth it. Break the cycle because future generations depend on it. The Divine Feminine is the warrior and the healer. You can meet your inner warrior and rise to the occasion of your life. She is sacred. She is you.

"Every woman who heals herself, heals her children's children."
Liezel Graham

The events are portrayed to the best of the woman's memory. While the story is true it may not be entirely factual. Some identifying details have been changed to protect the privacy of the people involved.

Gina Papanou, Certified Coach Practitioner, Certified Master Coach Practitioner

Self-Love/Narcissistic Abuse Recovery Expert

Gina Papanou is a Teacher, Author, Speaker and Women's Empowerment Coach who is passionate about helping others step into their power through self-love recovery, and heal from narcissistic abuse. As a survivor herself, Gina understands the pain and life challenges experienced by victims. Gina helps you connect with your inner warrior so you can get in touch with your authentic power, overcome your fears and live life from a place of joy and inner peace again. Narcissistic abuse is not well understood in our society and this lack of knowledge has led to a lack of power. Be brave enough to listen to your heart, bold enough to stand for yourself, and strong enough to take the first steps towards loving your life again.

Connect with Gina:
www.facebook.com/TheConsciousThriver/

Crushed Under the Roof: Overcoming Life's Challenges

by Gabrielle Manski

Have you ever had a day where you felt like the roof of your home came crashing down on you? Imagine you are pinned down by the crushing weight of the walls, the beams, and ultimately the roof. You wouldn't be able to move forward, backward, right, or left. You would be unable to shift your body away from beneath the oppressive weight of the roof and you'd be unable to breathe, amidst air thick with dust and debris. Darkness and fear engulf you as you look desperately around for a ray of hope and light, a breath of fresh air, to show you a way out. This was what it felt like on the day I was shocked to read a full-page article in a national newspaper that my father was being cared for in a hospice. I was mesmerized by his hopeful eyes looking back at me from the half-page picture included in the article. Sitting on the edge of his bed, he was accompanied by my mother and a hospice worker. Unbeknownst to me, he was dying of prostate cancer. Emotion overwhelmed me as though my world was caving in on me, plunging me further down into the depths of despair. It was a life-altering moment, but only one of many I was to experience.

In my early forties then, it may have superficially appeared that I had it all. Married to a successful professional, two beautiful children in private school, a cottage on the lake for weekends, a housekeeper, and a gardener to boot. Busy days as an entrepreneur interspersed with volunteering and commuting were the daily routine. But below the surface, there was a choppy sea of emotional stress that had just become a tidal wave. My father was dying, and I hadn't known about it.

My parents immigrated from Germany to Canada and settled west of Toronto to Hamilton, Ontario in the late fifties. Both of my parents were injured in WWII, my mother most severely having been shot in the head and losing the sight in the right eye. Postwar Europe was desolate with little to eat and few opportunities to work and make a living. Boundless futures in Canada were attainable to those who worked hard. Family and friends wished them bon voyage one gray November day and off they sailed on a freighter to Halifax, Nova Scotia and then began their three-day journey by train to Hamilton.

My father had an entrepreneurial spirit in his blood. We moved often, each time when a better bigger business was purchased. My mother took whatever employment she could, even though she had a university degree. With no family and no daycare in those days, she needed flexible hours so she could look after me.

The next decade and a half were a time of striving, building, and supporting a secure future for our little family of three. Life moved upwards to better, bigger homes in Burlington, a bedroom community for those working in Hamilton. We moved a total of nine times which meant eight different elementary schools for me. It was a lonely childhood with no lasting friendships because of the many moves. A sense of stability eluded me.

Perfectionism, independence, self-sufficiency, and goal orientation were instilled in me from the time I was a toddler. My grades were excellent, and I was always one of the top students. But it was sadly never "good enough" for my mother. I spent much of my childhood and

95

even adulthood trying to please her and secure her love. From about age eight, I spent Saturdays cleaning the house and doing the laundry. Several years later I added cutting the lawn to please my father. Sadly, it was never enough for my mother. It chipped a fissure into my self-confidence. The harder I tried to climb up the slippery slope of my mother's love, the quicker I fell into the depths of despair for not being enough.

As a teenager, the situation at home escalated. Emotional, verbal, and physical abuse became more frequent. Life was on a roller coaster. Which kind of day was it going to be? Loving-kindness or yelling tirades with handy household items being thrown at me? Life was like standing at the center of a teeter-totter. Again, I continued to feel the lack of stability deep in the core of my being.

My father was even tempered but also a bit of a coward taking a passive role during this time. He turned the other way and retreated, hoping to not get caught in the crossfire. No support there for me. Eventually, he too became "not enough" in the eyes of my mother. My dad had the option to escape to work and come home late.

As a child, I intuitively always felt there was something not right, something wrong, or amiss. It made me feel that I had to behave better, be more compliant. The corporal punishment that I received was not justifiable. As a teenager, I still didn't understand the complexity of my home situation and felt powerless to make a change. In those days there was not much out there about mental illness or abuse.

The only respite was school, which I loved, my part-time job, and time out with friends and boyfriends. As my social circle expanded, I received positive reinforcement and was well-liked by others outside my family. I felt more relaxed, happier, and confident. But whenever I was home with my mother, the black cloud of negativity, stress, and abuse descended over me. I felt at times that I was two different people. Out in the community I was accomplished and likable, but at home, I was often considered to fall short of my mother's expectations. Deep down I knew I had to remove myself from the family home. How could I accomplish this? I needed to formulate a plan for the transformation my life was about to undergo. As Benjamin Franklin said, "If you fail to plan, you are planning to fail."

I kept my awareness open to any opportunities but for a long time, nothing presented itself. Until the day I walked by the guidance department message board at my high school and saw the first step to my solution to be happy and independent away from a troubling home. I become aware of early-admission opportunities offered at two different Ontario universities. Skip a year of high school and go straight to university. To qualify for this fantastic opportunity to escape home, you needed to have exceptional grades and recommendation letters from two teachers to secure one of a limited number of spots for a six-week university-level program on campus. If you passed the university exams you qualified for fall admission without finishing high school.

YES! this was the answer to my decision to get away from home as soon as possible. I studied even more diligently and completed some extra advanced level high school courses to give me an edge over my fellow competitors. And I made it!

My plan also involved a financial aspect. I saved most of the money from my part-time job during the school season and summer was occupied with full-time employment. But it still fell short of what I needed to live on in another city and go to school. Student loans made up the shortfall.

Living away from home lowered my stress levels. I made friends with fellow students, did well in my studies and maintained my own finances. There was never a free ride at my house. But weekend visits home became a nightmare. You had to be prepared to go into the "war zone" of emotions, battle it out with mother and attempt to mitigate the damage before returning campus Sunday night.

One weekend it was different. I drove my old blue Ford the sixty kilometers home to peace and quiet. What was going on? My father sat me down on the living room sofa and gently explained that my mother was locked up in the psych ward of the local hospital. He asked if I wanted to see her. To say I was scared was an understatement. What was wrong with her? What had happened to cause this? How was she going to act now?

The drive to the hospital was completed in heavy silence. I walked nervously with my dad down the sterile hallway not knowing what to expect. We gained access to the locked door of the psych ward and passed through to be greeted by my mother. She was dressed and smiling obviously aware of our arrival. After some small talk, it was obvious she was trying to make light of it and was embarrassed that it had come to this.

It was the first of several other occasions when her doctor had her committed for depression. On one occasion she was even in a catatonic state at home and my father had to bring her in himself. I only heard about it after the fact, but it got me thinking. What was wrong with her? Why had it affected our relationship? Why were the problems escalating? Hindsight together with numerous psychology courses led me to believe that it was most likely manic depressive or bipolar disorder as we know it today. Extreme highs and lows of emotion. I was never aware of any drug therapy or counseling being undertaken to improve her condition as I got the "glossed over" version of the problem. Today it is also well-documented that people who sustain any type of head injury during any period of their life, such as being shot in the head as my mother was, are likely to develop and exhibit symptoms of brain damage or disease later in life.

In two years, I successfully completed an undergraduate degree while working full time during years three and four, got married and finished my master's degree also while holding a full-time job. Two children were to follow to make life complete. I was now forty-two years old. I had created a sense of stability, support and sharing in my own home.

My mother's unhappiness with life, with my dad, and with me, worsened over the years. She compared my life to hers and developed feelings of resentment and jealousy. The criticisms flowed each time we got together. Eventually, my husband became a target of her verbal abuse. He then slowly realized what I had been going through for most of my life. Her role as grandmother was of no interest to her. In the end, I came to a fork in the road of life. It was an exceedingly difficult decision to make. It took some time for me to build up the courage to have this conversation with her.

This next step had haunted me for years. Things had to change, or we would have to part ways. My health was suffering from the emotional turmoil and I had a family to take care of and a business to run.

She chose her path without me and my family. The estrangement continued over a period of years even though I made several attempts to approach her and see if she felt any differently. Not everything was still my fault. The estrangement lasted about five long years.

While sitting at my work desk one summer day in August, I saw the story about my dad in the newspaper. I was devastated and overwhelmed with emotion. My dad was dying of cancer. I at once phoned home but the number was disconnected. They had moved yet again. I had no idea where they lived and couldn't secure a phone number for them. I decided to contact the newspaper and connect with the person who authored the article. Several days later the writer contacted me and told me more bad news, the story was written four months ago, and she was not sure if my dad was still alive. She was however immensely helpful in giving a location for the hospice. A hospice worker reluctantly let me know that my father had died in only the month prior but would not give me the whereabouts of my mother. After several more conversations with the hospice, they decided to have my mother contact me.

Nothing had changed with the ensuing conversation. I had hoped that my mother might come around now that she was alone and make an effort to reconnect, but it was not to be. It took many years to forgive her for not letting me say goodbye to my father, to reassure him that I still loved him despite everything. She had taken that great opportunity away from me.

During the next several years, more attempts to reconnect were initiated by me, but to no avail. I had to get on with my life. She had written me off. My mother has since died, but I remember her, the young loving mother, in my heart.

"No matter where you are on the pathway of your life, please don't let the pain of an imperfect past hinder the glory of your fabulous future." -Robin Sharma

Along the journey of life, there will be many challenges. Challenges growing up or growing old, relationship challenges with family members, friends, coworker or spouses, physical challenges, professional, educational challenges, anxiety, depression and more. Life's challenges afford an opportunity for transformation and growth. How you approach your life's challenges will determine if they will make you or break you. Just like the pruning of that beautiful rose; the stress of pruning will either stimulate the flower to become more vibrant and lusher, resulting in a beautiful transformation, or if pruned incorrectly, it will cause the rose to die.

The challenge you face may become an opportunity for learning and personal growth or it may stop you in its tracks and result in you becoming a victim of circumstances. Therefore, you have two choices to make about your approach. You can choose to be proactive; get past the emotions, develop awareness with regard to your challenge, be open and attuned to the choices the universe provides, take control of the situation, set a goal, and form a plan of action. Alternatively the second choice is to continue to be reactive to circumstances, allowing negative and perhaps overwhelming emotion rather than logic to guide you, identifying with the victim image with a belief that you have no control over the outcome, make excuses, project responsibility to others, lacking confidence with the belief that nothing can be done and life is over.

Shifting your perception from "I can't" to "I can" is critical. With heightened awareness, your level of confidence will soar and assist the shift in your perception. By making the shift to "I can" you are taking control of your life back, shifting the power of your being back into your own hands. Only you are the master of your life.

Each of us is unique physically, biochemically, genetically, and environmentally. There lies a potential for greatness deep within each of us like the bud of a flower with nurturing will gloriously bloom one day. When a life challenge such as abuse, an illness, divorce, death, job loss or whatever it is, comes to the forefront of our lives, it is prudent to follow a strategy to treat that as a temporary detour to overcome, a period of transformation in the journey of life. It is an opportunity to grow and flourish with increased dimension, strength, and confidence.

The development of a self-directed holistic strategy for successful transformation was a compilation of years of experiences, the creation and application of tools and best practices that may be applied to any challenge and can be undertaken by anyone. It is called the Manski Protocol.

The Manski Protocol inspires, explores, and provides a unique foundation and action plan which puts you in control to become the architect of your own life. Each solution is unique to you and your transformation. You select the pillar(s) that represent the dimensions of life that you wish to develop to assist your transformation. You choose the tools that will rebuild and fortify that pillar. The Manski Protocol is thus a multifactorial approach, whereby one or more pillars need to be addressed at the same time to reach your transformational goal.

Remember the roof? Rebuild and fortify the ten pillars of your life to lift the burden of your challenge off your shoulders. Each pillar represents a dimension of your life: physical, intellectual, emotional, character, social, quality of life, goal setting, financial and/or career, spirituality, and life purpose. The pillars support each other and are interrelated as well.

Ten simple pillars to rebuild the solid foundation that supports your being, ten load-bearing columns that support you during the five steps in your transformation.

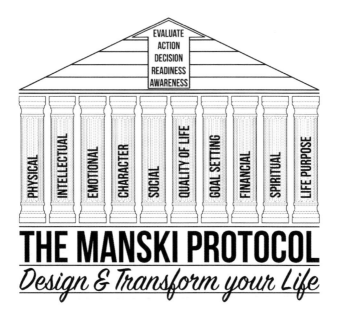

THE FIVE STEPS TO TRANSFORMATION

STEP ONE: AWARENESS
TOOLS: Mindshift, Journaling, Affirmation, Vision Board

The first step according to the Manski Protocol is awareness. Awareness involves gathering information, learning, and growth. Better awareness starts by listening to your body. The gut-brain also is known as the second brain of the body was the first place that signaled me that something wasn't right in my childhood. Listen to and understand how your body responds mentally, emotionally, physically, and spiritually to that stressor or challenge. Listening to your body is a part of the information gathering process that is necessary to build your awareness of what the problem is and how it affects you. Actively seek further facts to define your challenge by speaking with others in your community, seeking out professional advice, networking with other people who have effectively managed similar finding support in books and the internet. What you learn in the awareness stage of your transformation will provide keys to the solution in the latter part of your journey.

While you are in the awareness stage in the first part of your transformation, allow your mind to be open and flexible to what the Universe provides. Gather information, ideas, and opportunities for assessment without judgment, which creates the opportunity for a mind shift. If your mind is closed, you will be unable to see the resources and opportunities out there and will stay in the perception of "I can't."

During the awareness stage, it is an ideal time to begin journaling. The daily habit of journaling is recommended as a safe place to release suppressed emotions, to work through confusion, increase clarity, to support changes in your perception, to express gratitude, to make note of your progress and to take note of ideas and solutions. Write in your journal daily as many times as you desire. It is important to reaffirm self-love and confidence here as well.

Another effective tool to use at this stage is an affirmation. Repeating self-affirmations daily will aid in building your self-esteem, improving your level of confidence and increase feelings of self- worth and love. You can select any affirmation that is meaningful to you. An example is "I am worthy of love and joy" or "I approve of myself." Begin each day by repeating your chosen affirmation quietly five times in your mind, five more times by mouthing the words without sound and lastly, five additional times reaffirm your affirmation out loud. You can change your affirmation anytime you wish.

Another effective tool to help you focus is the creation of a "vision board." Start a vision board when you feel ready to sharpen the focus on your transformation. Close your eyes and visualize what life will be like when you have achieved the transformation in your life. What will it look like? How will you feel? What will you hear, smell, and see in your new life? Cut out pictures and words from magazines that exemplify what life would be like when you reach your goal of transformation. Consider all ten pillars of the Manski Protocol to aid you in your selections. Paste them onto a large piece of cardboard. Keep developing and adding onto your vision board as you progress through the five steps. You don't need to finish it in step one necessarily. Display your vision board somewhere in your home where you will be able to see it daily.

In summary, the awareness stage is the initial period in which you become aware of a problem, gain clarity about the challenge, gather information, and define the problem in your life. Your awareness becomes more focused with tools such as journaling and the vision board. Coping skills such as journaling your emotions and thoughts and making affirmations are explored. There is a significant mind shift to be proactive, to stay positive and to control your destiny with a plan in step one.

STEP TWO: READINESS
TOOLS: Stress Management, Meditation, Exercise Nutrition

At the end stage of awareness, it will become apparent when you are prepared to move onto step two "readiness" before committing to a decision for change and taking action. You will be ready for transformation when the advantages for change and a better life far outweigh the disadvantages of staying in your present situation. You will be ready to move towards happiness and to distance yourself from pain and suffering.

Information has been gathered, avenues of opportunities and obstacles are listed and considered, perception to "I can" is solidified, power and control have been taken back for your transformation. Your readiness phase involves making the best choices for your transformation, methods of implementation, and execution of the select courses of action. In the readiness step, the rays of hope will begin to shine and illuminate your path for transformation.

The readiness phase needs to be particularly supported because you have most likely been experiencing a high level of stress. Stress affects the physical, emotional, and mental pillars of life simultaneously. Short term stress and its effects can be overcome, and the body will return to homeostasis or balance. But chronic long-term stress affects the human body profoundly both in visible and subtle ways. Its effects are far-reaching emotionally, mentally, physically, and spiritually.

Stress puts your body into the fight or flight mode (the sympathetic nervous system). It activates your adrenal glands to secrete a host of hormones such as cortisol in preparation for the fight. Much of the other hormonal activity in your body is put on hold. Blood is directed to the extremities and your senses are elevated as are your heart and blood pressure. Chronic long-term stress leads to adrenal burnout and the thyroid, the master gland that controls metabolism, will also become compromised. Stress is the leading cause of disease and even death in our current Western society. Stress management is key to support your physical, mental, and emotional health.

A variety of tools can be accessed for stress management. Listening to your favorite music, reading a book, connecting with nature, getting a massage, a restorative yoga session, anything that works for you.

Support your readiness phase as well as the following phases of your transformation with one of the best tools; meditation. Meditation is wonderful for stress management because it shifts you from the sympathetic nervous system, the fight or flight mode, into the parasympathetic mode or the rest and digest mode. Meditation even changes and slows your brain waves. Begin with just five minutes in the morning before your day starts and/or five minutes at the end of the day. Select a quiet space inside your home or outside in nature and unplug your devices. Sit tall, close your eyes, and align your mind, body, and spirit. If sitting is uncomfortable, lie on a yoga mat. Focus on your breath. This is the best way to begin a simple meditation. Inhale and exhale in equal amounts keeping the breath steady. Imagine the energy coming into your body to restore and rejuvenate you with each inhalation. Release and let go of anything that no longer serves you with each exhale. Open your eyes again when you are finished your meditation. Keep your journal close by. At the end of your meditation, note down in your journal any emotions, ideas, and thoughts that came up during that time.

There are many ways to meditate. There is no set time. There is no right or wrong way, so do what works best for you. It takes, on average, sixty-six days to develop a habit. Start your meditation practice right away. In the morning I meditate in a special spot I have set up for meditation. I allow my mind to be open and relaxed. I reflect on how the day will flow and express gratitude. But I also meditate while running later in the day. Not only do I get my cardio exercise, but I also benefit from the relaxation that comes from meditation. Some of my most creative solutions to nagging problems have come to me via meditation. If I meditate at the end of the day, I reflect on how the day has gone and formulate thoughts of gratitude for each day is precious, each day is priceless never to return again.

Next, it is critical to support readiness and the steps beyond with the physical pillar which includes nutrition and fitness. In times of crisis, health and self-care are often neglected. This may result in weight gain or weight loss, low energy levels, digestive issues, anxiety, depression, reduced immunity, physical ailments, poor concentration, irritability as well as other symptoms.

Make your health a priority. Self-care is self-love. If you have been sedentary, begin by walking fifteen minutes just three times per week. Gradually increase your duration and frequency and vary your routes and terrain. Dress for the weather. No excuses. Consistency is key here. Work your way up to an hour a day seven days a week. You will feel amazing. Walking will increase your stamina, raise your energy levels, increase metabolism, assist weight loss, and make you feel more confident in yourself. It's also a great way to relax and connect with nature.

When this habit has been nailed down, add in resistance training one to three times a week. Bodyweight training, functional training, and Pilates do not require any equipment and can be done right at home. Resistance or weight training is the key to mental and physical health and longevity. Again, be open to different types of training. Hire a trainer or visit appropriate classes in your community if this is a financially viable option for you. Remember the best exercise is the one you will adhere to in the long term.

The third aspect of fitness is stretching and relaxation. Try a yoga class. The benefits of yoga are too numerous to list here. Many kinds and styles of yoga are offered, so again find an instructor and a style of yoga that resonates with you. Yoga helps you connect with your innermost true self and clarifies your life's path while performing asanas and finishes with breathwork and meditation. Perfect for supporting your transformation.

If you have a history of participation in the three areas of fitness (cardio, resistance, and stretching) but have neglected this area of your life, start gradually to get back into the routine. By rushing too quickly into any fitness regime, it will just become another stressor in your life. Take your time and listen to your body.

During my transformation, I realized the profound negative effects it was having on my health and my body. Weight gain, lack of energy, and a whole lot of small physical complaints that were getting bigger over time came to me at the awareness phase. Although I had been active in sports all my life and had enjoyed working out as an adult, much of this fell by the wayside during the late stages of my challenge. But I decided to institute a change by getting out there and walking. It was the only thing I could fit into my busy schedule and it didn't cost anything. After a few weeks, I started to realize the benefits and changes walking made to my life. After several months, the weather turned, and I bought my first treadmill. I was not going to miss one day of walking.

Later that following spring I added weight training to my fitness protocol. I joined a gym and hired a personal trainer. At about the same time, I resumed my yoga practice with a studio I really loved. I felt so much better, understood myself better and came away much more positive. All those physical complaints had disappeared too.

Sleep hygiene is an additional tool that is so important to your health and wellness. Sleep quality is also quickly disrupted by stress and lack of exercise. Good sleep habits are needed to support your transformation throughout the various phases. Sleep supports the physical, mental, and emotional pillars all at the same time.

Keep a regular sleep schedule of seven to eight hours of quality sleep retiring at the same time each night and waking at the same time each morning. Sleep in a dark cool quiet room. No blue light devices should be near you, nor are nightlights advisable. Precede your sleep time with a relaxing activity like reading, listening to soft music or your meditation. No television. A good night's sleep is good hygiene for the brain which is cleansed in sleep. It is also equally beneficial to the body. It is during sleep that the body restores itself. Between 1:00 a.m. and 4:00 a.m., the growth hormones are at work to repair and restore your body. If sleep is disrupted, it will affect your energy levels, your ability to focus and pay attention, your emotions and increase your appetite.

Nutrition is key to the pillar of physical health, especially during this time. During a period of stress and change, the body has an increased need for nutrients, that is vitamins, particularly Vitamin C and all the B vitamins and minerals too. Most often though a person will crave fats and sugars when under stress and eat more processed and refined foods devoid of those very nutrients most needed. Whole fresh and preferably organic foods should be a part of a healthy diet. Complex carbohydrates, healthy fats, and protein in proper proportions are best. The daily food intake should be largely alkaline rather than acidic in nature for optimal health. Eat the colors of the rainbow with what is in season - lots of vegetables and fruits. And lastly, hydrate your body with eight to twelve glasses of spring water every day, plus more water during exercise. Good nutritional practices support brain health, keep your body systems functioning optimally, mitigate the effects of stress, provide sustained energy, help with weight management, assist with emotional health, and keep you away from the clutches of chronic disease.

A solid foundation of physical, emotional, and mental health via nutrition, fitness, stress management, meditation and journaling protocols will make coping with the different phases of your transformation easier.

With increased awareness, mental clarity, and renewed confidence, you can make better choices in phase two and transition successfully to phase three of your transformation. Phase three is the decision-making phase.

"Many of our professional and personal desires really can come true — if we write the script." -Robin Sharma

STEP THREE: DECISION MAKING
TOOLS: S.M.A.R.T. GOAL SETTING, SCHEDULING, YOUR TRIBE

Step three of your transformation involves goal setting specific to the development of the plan of action for change. The first decision "to make a change" in Step Two is followed by a significant decision now in this step to identify and commit to the best alternative for change after weighing all the options. Your decision to initiate a change involves the development of a plan consisting of a specific action to be executed in a specific way with a timeline set. Applying the S.M.A.R.T. goal setting tool focuses your efforts to act most effectively. The S.M.A.R.T. goal setting acronym stands for Specific, Measurable, Achievable, Realistic, and Time-Based.

During high school, my specific goal was to become independent and leave home, my timeline was a year and a half to move and begin a university course of study. It was measurable by being accepted into the special entrance program. It was achievable by studying hard, undertaking extra courses, and applying my efforts even more on my education. It was a realistic goal considering my past academic performance and relevant to achieving independence.

Running parallel to the main goal of independence, I also had a financial goal that enabled me to leave home and be able to pay for university as well as all my living costs. I developed my financial goal to be able to support myself in the same way. Working part-time three times a week, full-time employment during the summer and government loans helped me secure an independent future.

Planning and goal setting are particularly important. They are key to your transformation and a life of greatness. They shift you into becoming proactive and help you design your sequence of steps to arrive at your desired goal. Both short term and long-term goal setting bring your plan for transformation into sharp focus. Your plan begins with a long-term goal(s). Your long-term goal is then broken down into smaller short-term goals that when completed will bring you step by step closer to achieving the long-term goal. For instance, my two long term goals were to leave home and to become financially independent in a year and a half. Another easily understood common example is weight loss. Specifically, the goal might be to lose twenty pounds in four months. This is the part where most people stop planning and wait for the magic to happen. But they never achieve their goal because they failed to support their big goal with short term goals. As a result, they became lost, overwhelmed, and unsuccessful in meeting their weight loss goal. It is important to realize the significance of the supportive role of short-term goals to the larger long-term goal.

Short term goals use the same S.M.A.R.T. goal setting strategy as long-term goals. But they are broken down into daily, weekly, and monthly timelines and actions. For our twenty-pound weight loss example, success would mean a weight deficit of five pounds per month or just over a pound a week. That's specific. Now that sounds doable.

How can you measure your progress? The nature of measurement will depend on your specific goal. For the weight loss example, measure it by how much better you feel, how much more energy you have, your vitality, your improved performance at work, how your clothes fit and so on. Journal your progress daily.

What actions will help you achieve your twenty-pound weight loss? Long term goals will include nutrition, exercise, and sleep. Short term goals will specify these same goals to manageable daily and weekly actions. Daily for improved nutrition, eat the rainbow of vegetables, consume at least .8 grams of protein per kilogram of weight, drink at least eight glasses of water and avoid sugar and refined foods. Daily, just move as much as you can for at least ten minutes at a time in addition to at least a half hour of formal exercise. Lastly, get eight hours of quality sleep to restore and rejuvenate your body.

Schedule your actions in a daily as well as a weekly timer. Print off blank daily and weekly schedules from your computer or do this on your phone app. Commit to your schedule and have it close by. Note down how and when each action is going to occur and be completed. In this way, you won't get caught short at the end of the day having had no movement at all and having skipped lunch.

Keep in mind that life is not all black or white. If you couldn't complete all your actions today, just keep to your action plan for the next day and don't quit. Don't throw away all your efforts because one day did not work out as planned. Everyone has challenges that come up at work or at home that may override the day as planned. Just stick to your plan and to your goals. You are developing and reinforcing important habits and it takes time. Think of a baby learning to stand. How many times does a baby fall and then try again? The baby never gives up and does learn to stand on its own.

During the steps of your transformation, it's also a prudent time to consider the social pillar of your life. Who are the people who support you, understand you and are on your same wavelength? Which people around you are enjoyable to be with, energize you, accept you the way you are and make you feel happy? These people are your tribe. They instill a deep sense of connection in you. Keep them close. They are your true friends.

On the opposite spectrum of the social pillar, who are the people who are negative, critical, and suck the life out of you after being with them just a short while? They are not on your same wavelength, do not support your beliefs and see little value in your character. Distance yourself from them. They are not part of your tribe. They are not part of your support system.

My mother was increasingly not part of my tribe nor my support system. I was often left on my own as a child. If I wanted to go to the ballet recital or join tennis camp, for instance, it was up to me to figure out how to get there and pay for it. I learned independence very quickly.

Social connection is particularly important on so many levels. Sometimes a person will isolate themselves during a period of transformation. They may be afraid of being judged or feel ashamed of the circumstances they find themselves in or criticized as to how they are handling their challenge or the validity of the choices they are making. Trust your tribe and share only what you feel comfortable with. As you experience that feeling of deeper connection and acceptance with them, you will be able to share more about your transformation.

My social connection was developed largely outside of the family. There were no other relatives to connect with. Friends from school, work, and sports communities were my tribe. These people, never knowing my situation, accepted me, and just made me feel good about myself.

Today you can also make social connections online and through social media. Look for experts who may give your insight and knowledge on your challenge and for groups of people whose goal is like yours.

Step three of your transformation plan requires the decision to commit to a course of action from all the viable alternatives. The development of long- and short-term goals with respect to the one or more of the pillars of the Manski Protocol bring specificity and substance to your plan for change. S.M.A.R.T. goals, both long and short term, illuminate the direction along the path for change and the improvement in the quality of your life.

STEP FOUR: ACTION
TOOLS: Persistence

Step four is the call to action. It's time to implement your S.M.A.R.T. goals daily, weekly, and monthly to achieve the overall goal of your transformation. Excitement fills the air. Feelings of anxiety and doubt may flutter in the background of your newfound confidence with respect to your goal and the action plan you are about to implement. Firmly shut the door on fear and any other negative thoughts. Open the next door to positivity, success, transformation, greatness, and bliss. Stay focused. Stick to your goal and be persistent in your effort to achieve that goal. Many people give up too quickly at this stage and lack the skill of persistence to see their goal to fruition. Review your S.M.A.R.T. goals daily, weekly, or monthly to mark your progress as well as to modify your plan. What is working and not working with your plan? What actions are effectively bringing you closer to your goals? Refine your plan whenever needed.

The vision board of your goal that you created in Step One should be in a place where you can see it daily to remind yourself of what life will be like when you reach your goal. Visualize your life when you've reached your transformation. Appreciate all the lessons you've learned on your journey and the new positive habits you've established in your life.

"Success in life comes when you simply refuse to give up, with goals so strong that obstacles, failure and loss only act as motivation." -Tony Horton

Persistence is key. Each day you undertake your short-term goals you arrive a step closer to your long-term goals. If you give up and stop your efforts, you will slide quickly back down into your old life. Small steps lead to big changes and big successes. In yogic philosophy, it is said that no decisions are bad ones. Each seemingly bad decision is just a detour that leads one back down their special path in life. Consider it an occasion for great learning, growth, and reflection. If your action plan is ineffective or too slow, it is time to re-evaluate which is Step Five.

STEP FIVE: EVALUATION
TOOLS: S.M.A.R.T.

Evaluation of your S.M.A.R.T. goals may lead to their modification to overcome weaknesses in your plan. Was your goal realistic and specific enough? Was the timeline too short or inappropriate? Were the actions congruent with the goal? Resetting and fine-tuning your S.M.A.R.T. goals whether they are short term or long term can be an ongoing process in order to achieve successful transformation. Check your progress and reevaluate each factor of the goal setting formula regularly. Avoid waiting until the timeline runs out of your long-term goal. Make changes in a timely fashion. Assume the perception that it was not a failure but an opportunity for reflection, learning, and tremendous personal growth.

"We lift ourselves by our thought, we climb upon our vision of ourselves."
-Orison Swett Marden

Life around you is constantly changing and you are always in a state of change to some small degree. Change is the only certainty in life. As you evolve into the person you want to be today, rest assured that you can meet the next challenge with confidence using the five steps for action, incorporating the ten pillars of the Manski Protocol with your goals and enhancing each step successfully with tools from the toolbox of the Manski Protocol. Apply this method to write the script of your life, to design your life with the facets that are meaningful to you. Think big. Big thoughts, big life. Discover the greatness within you. Whether the goal is personal or professional, the Manski Protocol is your guide to successful transformation.

Gabrielle Manski, B.A., M.A. Certified Coach Practitioner, Certified Master Coach Practitioner

Owner of Balanced Life Solutions® and creator of The Manski Protocol®

With over thirteen years of experience in the field of holistic wellness, Gabrielle is passionate about inspiring and guiding clients in their midlife who feel stuck to tap into their inner strengths and find greatness both professionally and personally. The Manski Protocol, a multi-disciplinary approach, offers a unique solution towards successfully achieving each client's ultimate goal.

Gabrielle is the owner of Balanced Life Solutions. She is a highly regarded speaker, author, and master life coach. She is an authority on fitness, nutrition, and holistic wellness. Gabrielle's professional background includes over twenty fitness certifications, holistic as well as clinical nutrition studies, Reiki 2 practitioner, certified Ontario teacher, master life and executive coach (CCF) and holds a master's degree in administration (finance).

With a lifelong passion for sports, Gabrielle has been an avid runner competing in half marathon, triathlon, and marathon.

She is married and is a mother of two children.

Connect with Gabrielle:

www.gabriellemanski.com

mp@gabriellemanski.com

www.facebook.com/mpgabriellemanski

www.facebook.com/blsgabriellemanski

www.instagram.com/gabriellemanski_coaching

www.linkedin.com/in/gabriellemanski/

Have You Felt Like You Are a Prisoner?

by Monica Arango

ARE YOU LIVING YOUR LIFE OR SOMEONE ELSE'S?

Our lives sometimes get controlled by a person, action, or habit. The worst part is that we are not aware that we give away that power. We may end up unable to decide where to go or what to do because we are being held prisoner, but we do not know how, why, or when it began.

MY YOUNGER YEARS

I grew up in Medellin, Colombia, a beautiful city with the most fantastic weather, twenty to twenty-five Celsius (sixty-eight to seventy-seven Fahrenheit) all year round. It's found in the Aburra Valley and its surrounded by the Andes Mountains range. My father was an IBM technician, and as such, our household provider. If you remember those big computers in the sixties, he installed and maintained them throughout South America. My mother was the home administrator and the kids' director. We were four kids; my sister who was two years older than me, my two brothers, were one and two years younger than me respectively, and the baby was four years younger.

In Colombia, we were eligible for free primary education, but that was considered of lower quality and for families with low income. For post-secondary studies, we had the option to go to a public or a private university or college, where they consider the economic capacity of those admitted when setting the tuition. The public universities in my day were not safe because they had so many strikes and were often the place where political and social violence broke out.

If we had the good fortune to attend a private high school, we were expected to go on to achieve at least a bachelor's degree, become a lawyer, doctor, engineer or another prestigious career. If you didn't follow that path, you could be seen as dishonoring your family and society.

After graduating from Santa Maria del Rosario high school in 1981, I went to EAFIT University, one of the most prestigious private universities in Medellin, to study production engineering. At that time, Medellin was transforming, and you could feel it in the air, see it on the streets, and you could see it on the news. From being a city with hardworking people, vigorous, entrepreneurs, and honest citizens, we declined into one of the most violent and unsafe cities in the world. With the arrival of drug traffickers, the mafia, and specifically Pablo Escobar, killings, crimes, and the most indescribable tortures were commonplace in the news.

1984

We dreaded going to bars, nightclubs, parks, the mall, or even going to school as our lives were always in danger because no one was safe. Anything could happen, from murder in front of you to a bomb in a shopping mall.

In 1984, after the assassination of Rodrigo Lara Bonilla, Minister of Justice, President Belisario Betancourt ratified and implemented an extradition treaty with the United States of America. The situation got increasingly tense, as the Medellin Cartel created "Los Extraditables" (The Extraditables). They had the motto "it is better to have a grave in Colombia than prison in the USA." Eventually, all the cartels joined forces, achieving so much power, arms, and people, that our city was officially a war zone.

At this point, not even at home, you were safe because a stray bullet could reach you from any location in any neighborhood.

MY TWENTIES

In 1986, my boyfriend went with some friends to a bar, having parked his car very close to another vehicle. Not long afterward, somebody entered and asked for the owner of the yellow car. My boyfriend got up, and without one more word, was shot. He was just twenty-seven years old, and he was the happiest person I had ever met and a dream boyfriend. He was a true gentleman and romantic, even serenading me regularly. All his friends loved him, he was a hard worker, and entrepreneur, with so much future in front of him. Always ready to help his family, his friends, and his employees. All lost because he parked his car too close to the wrong person.

Not far away, a friend was living in Laureles without knowing their next-door neighbor was one of Pablo Escobar's relatives. One day, unexpectedly, the army and police forcibly entered the neighbor's house to capture him. My friend hid under a bed in the back room without knowing what was happening; all they heard were shots and the neighbor's house being destroyed.

Throughout these and other tragedies and challenges, in June 1987, I got my degree as a production engineer, and immediately got an excellent job for one of the most critical fashion manufacturers in the city. It was the degree I was meant to have and the job I deserved to get.

One day, while out shopping for shoes, I met an amazing man. He had an impeccable presentation, he was well educated and seemed to be a good man in every way. He was from a good family, grew up in El Poblado, one of the best neighborhoods in the city, his father was a supreme court justice, had excellent financial stability, and he had recently returned from the USA, to live in Medellin.

The same day we met, he invited me to his sister's wedding. We soon started a relationship, he brought me to beautiful places, and we had amazing conversations. Drinking was "normal" in my culture, and at the end of the day, almost everyone did.

We got married in February of 1988 and I centered my entire life around our marriage. This meant that I left my full-time job, partnered with my cousin on new business to have more time at home. Despite all this, things became increasingly challenging.

While I didn't know it at the time, this was an example of how our minds can trick us by trying to avoid pain in a big way. Proof of that was thinking that having a child would help our family and the challenges we were having. We agreed, and I got pregnant. While becoming a mother was my dream since I was a little girl, it evolved into an overwhelming situation, and despite my high expectations, things became more challenging at home. I had the responsibilities of caring for our family, and my business that was not going as well as I expected. I was busy but unfocused amidst the chaos.

Things got worse over time with situations too difficult to convey here. I reached a breaking point for what I was willing to endure, and I got divorced in 1990. My husband understood and agreed, so our divorce was a peaceful process.

I got back on my feet and started to build my life up again; I moved to an apartment with my son while my mother helped me a lot.

Because the Medellin cartel was united in avoiding the government's extradition treaty, the death toll was rising. In response to the escalated violence, the government created "the Search Block," an elite special forces unit, to capture Escobar. In turn, the cartel began to recruit mercenaries of different nationalities to confront the Search Block, which led the country to a war that resulted in more than twenty thousand deaths.

In June 1991, Pablo Escobar turned himself in to the police, under the condition that he build, manage, and live in his own private prison, called "la Catedral" (the Cathedral). We hoped life would be different in Medellin, but we were wrong. I remember distinctly that even with Pablo Escobar in his "prison," Colombia was in the middle of a cartel war, so President Gaviria declared a state of emergency capping one of the worst years in the Colombian history.

It was 1992, and I was hoping it would be one of the best years of my life. I brought my brand-new home for my son and me, and after an exhausting interview process, I began working for one of the biggest textile companies in Colombia. It was an ideal position that included six months of training with a Canadian Institute. Our Canadian instructor, amongst the many technical things he taught, introduced me to the Canadian way of life, explaining real quality of life, including the freedom not to worry about safety and the access to quality education and health care.

At the same time, the Columbian government was in negotiation with groups such as the M-19, heavily armed guerrillas, who agreed to surrender their weapons. For this negotiation, one of the de-armament camps was set up on our farm. Unfortunately, the process with other groups, such as the ELN (Ejército de liberación Nacional) and FARC (Fuerzas armadas revolucionarias de Colombia) was not successful, and they joined forces with the cartels. The ELN and FARC provided security, maintained order, and defended the coca fields from the army and the police. In turn, they charged a percentage of the profits from the sale of drugs in foreign markets because they had power, and they were better trained and armed than the police.

Because of the unsuccessful government negotiation taking place on our farm, we were warned that the guerrillas around our farm were looking for us, to kidnap us for ransom. As a preventive measure, my father and my youngest brother rented an apartment in Santa Rosa de Osos, a small city forty minutes from the farm. They went to the farm in daylight and left before sunset. We were sure everything was safe with these measures in place.

January 13, it was a sunny day in Medellin, Colombia. My brother was in Santa Rosa, going to the farm first thing in the morning, My father, and the rest of the family in Medellin. I was at work around 10:00 a.m.; I received a call from my mom telling me that my youngest brother, was kidnapped, by the guerrillas. He arrived at the farm around 7:00 a.m., and about one hour later, the guerrillas took him.

When my mom told me, I felt like my world physically stopped, a feeling indescribable with words. I don't even remember how I arrived home. While my mom was crying, my father was busy with people all around, there was so much noise, but I could not hear anything. Nothing else seemed to matter, and even though we were not kidnapped, it felt like we were held with him, our thoughts, feelings, family, financials, emotions, and our spirituality were their prisoners.

My brother was twenty-four years old when kidnapped; his captors were even younger. Most of the guerillas were minors, from fourteen-to-eighteen years old. The guerilla's methods of recruitment are to enlist illiterate children from rural areas; giving no choice to their parents. These kids grew up with no other concept of life, and they believed that being a guerilla was the right thing to do. While captive, the only thing my brother was able to do was to write. Because his captors were not able to read, my brother started to teach them some writing and reading, and while they did not free him, that small kindness may have begun to change their minds.

My brother's captors dressed him in the same clothes they wore, and told him that if any confrontation happened, he would be taken or killed as one of them. My brother believed what he was told by his captors; that he would not be identified as a prisoner, but as a guerrilla. About thirty days after he was kidnapped, there was a confrontation between the army and his captors. During that confrontation, my brother had a slim opportunity to run to the army and be freed, but he didn't because he was afraid the army would kill him.

They took my brother deep into the jungle. We had no idea where my brother was, how he was, not even if he was alive. So many things went on in our minds, we tried to keep our lives going, we prayed, we looked for answers, saint, spiritism, fortune tellers and more, and still, there was no communication for two months.

Eventually, my father began negotiating with the guerillas, but they kept wanting more. They were not only looking at my father for money, but my uncles and their families as well because they owned businesses in Santa Rosa de Osos. Ultimately, my father paid the ransom and rescued my brother. When my brother came back, he was never the same, neither were we, and we were never able to go back to our farm.

In another situation, my father escaped from an attempted kidnapping by the guerrillas in Medellin. My uncle sadly didn't have the same luck that my father had. My uncle lived in a beautiful apartment close to our house, and one day, the guerrillas arrived at his building. Heavily armed, they arrested the guard, and they went to his apartment, entered, and murdered him in front of his fourteen-year-old son. My cousin committed suicide eight months later.

It may sound like a movie, but unfortunately for us, it was not. My parents moved to another neighborhood, and I left for another city.

1994-1995

Everything went back to be a little bit more stable and safer for us. My parents went back to their house, and I came back to mine.

That year, at my fifteenth-anniversary production engineers' class reunion, I was so excited to see my friends; one in particular. We were so close and shared so many things at the time we were in the university, and while we hadn't had contact the previous five years, we had so many things in common, we were from the same neighborhood, we spent so much time together, we were close friends, and we were from the same social circle.

After the class reunion, we went out and started seeing each other romantically, and he introduced me to a new relationship with God, and six months later, we got engaged. I was in love, and I wanted to allow myself to have that family I dreamt of when I was a little kid. What influenced me most was the fact he was Christian; it was the "wand" of my decision. We got married in December of 1995. My father was not that happy, because he saw things that I did not.

Things were not good at home, and yet there was pressure to have more children.

1996-1998

In January 1996, I got pregnant, but I was not feeling well. My older sister was a doctor, and she rushed several tests, discovering my baby was implanted in my right fallopian tube; a dangerous ectopic pregnancy. Thanks to my sister, it was detected early, but sadly, I lost my baby. The only blessing was my fallopian tube was not damaged. Although my gynecologist insisted that I wait at least six months before getting pregnant again, I became pregnant three months later. We had a beautiful girl in January 1997 and another girl in April 1998.

On the outside, we were the perfect family. Three kids in our custom-made, brand new one-thousand seven-hundred square foot house with no mortgage, on the outskirts of the city, on a lot of a quarter of an acre, with living room, dining room, music room, library, four bedrooms, employee area, a more than full kitchen, marble floors, stained glass windows, with views of the city and a nature reserve. The kids were in the best schools, but happiness was not there. I went to work with my father's company to have a more stable income and try to stabilize my marriage.

The kids were growing, and safety was not getting any better, and the economic boom in Colombia gave the next generation a different vision and new opportunities. We started talking about immigrating and began the process. We considered Canada and Australia, but the time difference with Australia meant we would have challenges communicating with our families, so we applied to Canada for landed immigrant visas.

In addition to the English test, some of the requirements included having professional degrees, being married, having kids, being able to pay the immigration fees, and having financial resources to sustain the family for six months without work.

We followed all the process and received the immigration documents in January 2000. We had to land first and only had ninety days to complete everything. My husband arrived in Mississauga, Ontario, in February of 2000, staying at the home of my father's friend. He was responsible for searching for a job, a place to live, and finding a car. I was responsible for packing our home in Medellin, renting the property, and storing or selling our furniture.

Saturday, March 18, 2000, I arrived at Toronto's Pearson International Airport with my three kids; Luisa eighteen months, Maria three years old and Sebastian, nine years old. The following Monday, March 20, 2000, my life in Canada started, and the first thing on my to-do list was to drive my husband from Mississauga to his work in Brampton, about a forty-minute drive, taking highways 401 and 403. The differences between driving in Medellin and Canada made this a big deal because the fastest highway in Medellin is 60 kph (in Canada, the main highways have a speed limit of 100-120 kph). In Medellin, everyone drives aggressively, with people regularly cutting you off, and stopping is more like reducing speed because, at night, stopping might mean getting robbed. In Medellin, the motorcycle is a cheap and easy way to get around, the weather is perfect with millions of them in the streets, rarely following the rules, so if I drove like that there, why not the same way in Canada?

With everything that needed to be done including school registrations, health insurance, social insurance, bank accounts, I knew I could drive with my Colombian driver's license for three months but had to start the process to get the Ontario license as soon as possible. In Ontario, they have three driver's license levels: G1, G2, and the full G ("g" stands for graduated). If you can demonstrate your driving experience, you can challenge the full G, but if you fail, you must go for the G2 and wait two years to get the full G license.

As a mature Colombian Driver, with more than fifteen years of driving experience, I assumed that some rules would be different, and I studied for the theory test G1 and passed at my first try. After this achievement, I was so confident I decided to take the risk to challenge the full G test. I failed badly, frustrating me. I went to my father's friend, and he helped as much as he could. I retook the test, now for the G2, and failed again. So, I went to driving school, where they taught me well, gave me the chance to practice, and finally, I passed.

For some, it was "just a driver's license;" however, having a license helped me to build up my life, but without it, I doubt I could have gotten my life insurance license in 2001, my designation as a mutual fund agent in 2003, my realtor designation, or my coaching certification.

Many Colombians arrived in Canada between 2000 to 2005, with the wrong idea. While one of the qualifications for residency was to be a professional, we thought that as soon as we arrived here with our university degrees and years of Colombian experience, we would get the same or better job position we had back home. The reality is different because, with the language barrier, no Canadian experience, and no Canadian recommendation, this process was neither easy nor natural.

My first step was to improve my language skill, I went to the school full time. After six months, I felt that I was not advancing, and my husband started to pressure me to contribute to the house expenses. While it was a significant change from being an engineer, I got a job packing cameras in a warehouse. It was a minimum wage, but I was so happy because my main objectives were to practice English, get Canadian experience, and generate some income. I knew that it was not what I want to do for the rest of my life, so I started to investigate different possibilities.

In February 2001, I started to study for my Life and Sickness Insurance license. In September I obtained the designation, and within the next two years, I worked hard, networking, doing promotional seminars, events, radio, writing articles, doing advertisements, all in addition to constant training to be a better agent and serve my clients accordingly. Progressively, my income started to increase, and in my second year, in 2002, I had an income of seventy-five thousand dollars. That same year I got the Silver Self-Management Order of Merit; second-best designation in the company. I was within the best ten to one-hundred fifty agents at my office in Richmond Hill, Ontario.

Life at home was not easy. The relationship was in decline, my income went down, and to make this situation more challenging, my mother in law came to live with us. Ultimately, we got divorced. This divorce was extremely challenging.

I was here in Canada with three kids, two divorces, no financial support, no family, no Canadian degree, and an expensive custody fight. I had hit bottom. I was tired of feeling that I was "the victim" of this world, all these lousy things happening to me, and the people around me. Then I realized that the common element of all these dreadful things was *me*, and my search started right there.

TURNING THINGS AROUND

I could have stayed in the complaining phase, but I realized that the only role-model my kids had was me, I wanted the best for them, and for me as well. I had two options; go back to Colombia, as my father at once offered to me, or stay in Canada with the plan to give my kids and me a better lifestyle. I must confess; what my father offered was a good solution in all areas, including financially, family, social position, not to mention going back to be an engineer. He was ready to rescue me as he rescued my brother when he was kidnapped, but I didn't want the option of escape.

I decided to help myself and start a new process with many ups and downs, not the more accessible and shorter path and tools to discover my real potential and try to help others. I decided to fight for my kids and me, and the discovery that I had the opportunity to overcome my failures by improving myself,

I started first with my physical aspect, going to the gym, then starting to know who I was, looking the purpose of my life, self-study, workshops, networking, seminars, therapist, coaching, praying, certifications, joining associations. I wanted to have answers.

I started volunteering to lead a group of families; I had the heart and skills to do it, and we grew so much and learned from each other. Part of the dynamic of the group was to have an individual appointment when someone had special needs. Women came to me for help, and I listened. In some cases, I helped them by searching for tools to be safe. But I always had that feeling that was something else still had to be done.

I led three more groups, I got closer to God and his word, and I was able to save families. Not all the marriages were saved, but these women live now with purpose, happiness, and strength, ready to be the support and example their kids, partners, and society needs.

Forty-three percent of divorces happen between forty-five-to-fifty-nine years old, and depression is forty-five percent more frequent in women than in men. I realized that the divorce process does not start at the point where we begin to express or externalize, "I can't do this anymore," some studies suggest that the frustration builds, and disconnection begins ten years before the decision happens. The detachment is a slow process as we begin to distance ourselves to avoid conflict and please everyone and somehow kept the peace in our families.

I started to see a pattern, to realize that whatever I do or do not do in my life is a result of my decisions and that when I do not evaluate those decisions, life itself makes the decisions for you, not always with a positive outcome. I am the one how must assume the consequences of those decisions.

THE THREE PHASES OF FREEING YOURSELF

What I have discovered is that women can find freedom by reuniting themselves with their true identity. We are going to go on a trip together to see your own route to reunify your soul, body, and spirit and discover your purpose in just three phases; "Where do you want to go," "Define yourself," and "Boost your Potential."

WHERE DO YOU WANT TO GO?

We all have the need to change or improve our body, mind, or spirit. We want to be a better professional, better mother or father, lose or gain weight, learn a new language or a new skill. Sometimes these changes affect just one, or more often, affect multiple areas of our lives. These changes help us evolve, improve, and grow, and this can happen in either our conscious or subconscious mind.

When we start a new year or new phase of our lives, we typically set goals, but we usually are not specific enough, and we end up with an unrealized dream, frustrated and may avoid setting new goals and just return to our previous comfort zone. The difference between a goal and a dream is that the goal should be measured and specific, a dream is not. For example, "I want to lose weight" is a dream while, "I want to lose five pounds in thirty days by eating more vegetables and fruit, less carbohydrate and exercising two times per week" is a goal.

Our beliefs play a significant role in our subconscious mind goals. Remember the situation wherein my brother was kidnapped. Of course, his goal was to be free, but his captors seeded his mind with doubts. In addition to being afraid to run because the army might think he was a guerilla, he was subject to the "Stockholm syndrome," whereby the prisoner begins to connect with his or her captors. He tried to avoid being harmed, so in his mind, he began to sympathize with his captors, and hoped they wouldn't mistreat him.

Our mind always looks for safety. When we do not achieve our goals or dreams, we tend towards not setting goals.

Some questions to consider:

1) If you want to change something, why you want to do it?
2) When do you want this to happen?
3) How can you measure this process?

The need to adapt to your circumstances, to be accepted, to feel safe, to be loved, to fulfill that emptiness that takes us to depression, anxiety, and stress. The sensation of failure is part of being human, a part of an internal battle within our identity.

DEFINE YOURSELF

We have two different versions of ourselves:

1) The person I am pretending to be to satisfy society, primarily what the people who do not know me can see
2) The person I attempt to be for my family, my friends and the people close to me
3) The person who I am, in the inside.

What people see on the outside is not how I am on the inside. How people see me on the outside is not the true me. How does that affect my life? Well, if we aren't true to ourselves, we eventually lose our passion for living our lives, because we end up living someone else's life.

We often choose to go for an automatic pilot, looking for a comfortable and safe zone. We start to lives adapting to what people want to see in us. We transform ourselves into something we were not created for, it is a slow but aggressive process that can affect any or all areas of our lives.

The tension between living someone else's life shows in different ways, we can go from the extreme of eating healthy and exercising to not eating or overeating and not being active. We can be a workaholic and, in a depression, and not been motivated at all, to being angry and looking for a fight with our kids, friends, or spouse, to be overprotective, to convert yourself into a true shopaholic, or to be a tightwad and a cheapskate. These consequences do not show as a one-day event but fracture our lives slowly and progressively.

While I was growing up, because it was socially acceptable to drink, I saw the drinking, including adults sending their minor children to the liquor store to buy their liquor and adults bringing their teenage kids to the bars. I saw all the consequences; however, because it was programmed in me as normal, I ignored that information, and the alcoholism around me defined that phase of my life. We cannot let a situation define us.

Most of us live with that discrepancy between how the people see us, what we pretend to be, and what we are or what we want to be. All this is happening inside of us, and that discrepancy defines us. At the time we start to be aware we can change what we are. We must decide to shift the focus of our lives to the definition of ourselves. Are our thoughts and our life perspective, creating who we choose to be?

Some questions to consider:

1) How you describe yourself?
2) How you qualify yourself? Why?
3) Is any person, past situation, or fear defining you?

BOOST YOUR POTENTIAL

I have good news and bad news; we are not perfect, and we are not going to be. Neither your husband, boss, kids, or the people around you are perfect. The world is not perfect. We are not bad or good; we are what we think we are.

Three years ago, I bought a brand-new computer. The software need for my work was installed by the technicians at the store. It had full functionality, speed, and the battery was full. For some time, it worked perfectly, but with time and new requirements, I had to install new programs from the internet. I started to notice it was getting slow, and the possibility it had been infected with a virus was high. Sometimes viruses cannot be detected, but you experience that the computer run slow, with different unwanted messages appearing without our control, the system not working as it should be. Only when I brought the laptop to the computer store to clean it up and install antivirus software, can the computer return to working the way it should be.

Our brains are like the computer, because some of the ways we make decisions or the ways we process information, were created from the time we were on our mother's womb. While we retain all the information collected by our senses, not all the input can be processed at all, or in part. Some of this information we are aware of (conscious), some we are not (subconscious).

Can you remember when you wanted to learn to play piano or any other instrument or learn how to drive, initially you have to use all your senses and pay close attention to each move, each decision you have to make to get the right result, after practice you do not need that attention because that program has been already installed.

That program can be installed correctly or incorrectly. When I arrived here to Canada, I had been driving for more than twenty years in Colombia, with Colombian rules, very different from the Canadian rules. It took me three times to get a Canadian driver license, not because I did not know how to drive but because I had a different program installed in me, and if I kept pushing with the Colombian rules in Canada, I never would be able to get the Canadian driver's license.

I have access to different tools to transform your minds after we are aware that is something we want to change or improve and get better results in our lives. I used the most powerful of all. You are going to discover that tool at the end of this chapter.

We must not carry our past on our backs. Learning from and releasing, our history will help determine our future. Forgiving, forgetting, and learning from failures and triumphs will take us to that next stage. This is sometimes more challenging than our skills allow, which is where a coach or counselor can help us discover those past lessons that can be used in our growth. If you want to stop being a prisoner to your past, you can embrace that it is you that put the bars up by repeating the same cycle of behavior over and over again.

We all have the right to fail and make mistakes, but we can also decide what to do with the information because failures don't define who we are. We can remain who we are or choose to be that better person with a real purpose in life that can embrace and make you happier.

Some questions to consider:

1) what is your success/ failing definition? Why?
2) Do you know what areas of your life can be boosted?
3) Can you do it by yourself?
4) Are you open to accept the change?
5) Do you know this is a process?
6) How can I help you?

There are times in our lives, where we must decide to lead our lives. We can choose to look forward or continue to guide our lives through the rear-view mirror. Continue living with the fear of failure, and in safe mode, without taking the risk of experiencing all the amazing things we can achieve and discover the purpose of our lives reinventing and rediscovering new paths.

After my second divorce, I decided to live my life fully. At that point, I was a believer for about ten years, but I never realized the great Love of God, and only then I internalized my life star to be transformed.

I got re-married some years ago. We are not perfect. We have some differences, and the way I see it, those differences, and knowing more about how and why I react the way I do, must happen with myself first. I know that I cannot change him, but I can change myself and my approach to the situation.

I acknowledge now that my marriage, my husband, and my life are a masterpiece work in progress. The messages I give to myself daily are going to increase the happiness of my life, my husband's, my kids', my friends', and furthermore society's.

Life is not to observe; it is to experience.

My final questions are these:

1) What is the legacy you want to leave?
2) Do you want to be that person who never found and fulfilled your purpose or a successful person with a fulfilling goal?

It is not going to be easy, but I am sure it is going to be exciting, so do not give up. Don't try and find the perfect person, the perfect job, the ideal life, but with the support you want and need, you can create your best life and truly connect with and achieve all your goals.

Monica Arango, Certified Coach Practitioner, Certified Master Coach Practitioner

Dream Strategist and Founder of Boost Your Potential®

Monica has dedicated her life to guide families and individuals to renovate their lives. After experiencing a total remake of her life in 1997, Monica vowed to passionately help others on their own journey of rebirth and set out on a mission to discover the secrets to what makes Dreams come true. Since then, Monica has not only studied and got degrees in these areas, because she is a Certified Master Life Coach Practitioner, NLP Master Practitioner, and Happiness life Coach.

As a highly entertaining and insightful speaker, Monica has featured the stage of prominent organizations such as GROW, CBWN, Speak Up, and many others. She is a sought-after Dream Strategist, who focuses on helping women to find their identity, purpose, and happiness.

Monica's premiere workshops, Insulated from Happiness, renovating your relationship, Love and be loved, and Purpose quest is receiving awe reviews from "women only" audiences.

Connect with Monica:
www.boostyourpotential.ca
info@boostyourpotential.ca
780-707-0737
www.facebook.com/boostyourpotential/
www.linkedin.com/company/18751375/admin/
www.linkedin.com/in/connectingneeds/

I Ran *from* My Children, not *to* Them: Surviving Postpartum Depression and Anxiety *by Melissa Anne*

"Sometimes when you're in a dark place you think you've been buried, but actually you've been planted." -Christine Caine

Buried. As I ran from my home leaving behind my baby girl and my two-year-old, the tears streamed down my face. I got into my car and drove into the night, not knowing where I was going. Anywhere, in the quiet car was enough. I knocked on a friend's door not knowing how I got there or why, and when I entered her home, I was acutely aware of her own children, the same age as mine, sleeping not far away. I apologized for intruding, and as I fell into a chair, buried was the only word that came to me. Not buried beneath piles of dirt but having fallen into that deep dark place. Unable to climb from the bottomless hole, alone, cold, and dark. As I cried sitting in her living room, not even her presence took away the feelings of despair and loneliness that I felt. I didn't know how to climb out of the hole. It would be another year before I discovered that "buried" was a gift, an opportunity to grow.

I was born the middle child of three girls, twenty-eight months apart. My parents separated at about the age of ten, and we all grew up fast. My older sister took care of us while my mother worked full time and finished her education. We had a weekly visit with my father, where we would visit with my grandparents as well. Although things were in turmoil, we always knew that we were loved no matter what our family situation was. My mother looked after every need or want, and my father unfailingly made it clear that his daughters were more important than anything in his life.

I was what you would call a geek in elementary and high school. I had good grades, but I worked hard for them. I was the typical overweight Italian kid with glasses and braces. I was shy, and my perception was that I had no real friends, but rather acquaintances. I was continually in trouble for staying out late doing homework, even though I stayed away from parties and bars until I was in university. I thinned out at the beginning of high school and got rid of the braces just in time to start university. Although I had changed physically, the mental scars of being overweight and being made fun of for years never left me. Years later, at thirty-five and one-hundred and thirteen sickly pounds, I still looked in the mirror and saw flaws that I wished were not there. Even today, I sometimes see that overweight, shy kid that nobody paid attention to. The difference is that now I recognize those thoughts as anxious ones that distort reality.

My high school boyfriend treated me like a princess, and his parents gave me refuge whenever there were issues at home. Those issues seemed to pop up a lot during my last few years of high school, as my mother graduated with an art degree and my sisters and I had grown some independence. I fought with my mother for that independence quite frequently, which invariably ended with my father negotiating my return home. I remember continually begging my father to take me away from there, and the words were always "you are strong, and you can get through this." I hated that he left me there and resented being called strong when I just wanted someone to be strong for me. Years later, I would truly understand those words. "Strong" was the highest compliment that he could have ever given me.

My faith played a large part in my life during my elementary and high school years. I regularly attended mass with my mother and was a member of the church choir as a youngster. I began working in the church rectory on Saturdays at the age of thirteen, was a member of the youth group and a lector at the Saturday evening Masses. Those Saturdays in the rectory with the priests and another student working there were like being with family. I had a purpose, I was accepted, and I was good at what I did. Father Wayne, now a Bishop, listened without judgment and was unfailingly there for me through all the turmoil at home. The church was my haven, and Father Wayne was my best friend. Years later, I would re-connect with that student after his ordination into the priesthood, and he would help guide me to myself again.

When the opportunity came, I moved away from home to attend University. Although I had longed to run from home, I was incredibly homesick and never found a place where I fit in. I lost touch with my faith and found my studies to be difficult. I poured myself into jobs and my academics, and I began to turn away people in favor of work. It was during this time that I was first introduced to the world of yoga, and it was one of the best things that had ever come into my life. The yoga studio in the woods was peaceful and calming, and yoga became a lifelong calling for me. I went on to attend other yoga classes and eventually met my longtime mentor, who has been guiding me for eighteen years now. Just as the church was once my family, Burt became a source of love and encouragement. Even after absences and crazy life experiences, my return to Burt always felt like I had never been gone.

Fast forward many years later, Burt had seen me through a second degree, two marriages, countless jobs, and a relocation to Ottawa and back to Niagara Falls. My son had been born while in Ottawa, and I was now expecting my daughter. To everyone on the outside looking in, life was great. We were about to have what people call a "million-dollar family"–a boy and a girl–and were living in a half-million-dollar home. I had been with Canada Customs for ten years working a job that I loved. I had met people along the way that enriched my life and shared terrific experiences. I had worked for managers that were the best people. Yet, I was stressed beyond belief. I had a toddler potty training, a huge house that I didn't have the energy to clean and I was getting ready for a new baby while running my toddler to all his activities. In the office, I was overworked and tired. New work was piling up while I was trying to wind down and it hit. A panic attack like no other.

Regardless of all my knowledge and experience in handling panic attacks, this one hit hard. I remember it like it was yesterday. I was in the bathroom, sitting, rocking back and forth, and breathing. Deep inhalations and slow, steady exhalations. My heart was pounding. I was in a cold sweat, and the room was closing in on me. I was scared because I didn't know how this would affect my baby in the womb. I called for my husband, and he stood by my side holding my hand until it passed. There would be other milder panic attacks and anxious moments throughout the rest of my pregnancy, as I became more stressed with my workload. The more the anxiety appeared, the more I begged my manager to lessen the load. But it never happened. I was told that I was the only one that could write what needed to be written and they didn't want to make others feel bad. It was the first time in my life that I wished I had a lower work ethic or that I dared to stand up and say no.

I didn't say no, and I paid the price. I suffered a panic attack in the middle of childbirth and was forced to take medication to get through the labor. My daughter was beautiful and perfect in every way. She was in an incubator for a day, but otherwise a healthy baby girl. The date was August 8, 2011. We took her home and began the journey of settling in with a newborn and a toddler. Only the panic didn't stop. It was there at every turn. First, I panicked about getting her to breastfeed. Then I panicked about the fact that she was breastfeeding, and I was never going to be alone or be able to go anywhere alone because she was tied to me. Then I cried over the guilt of having those feelings, and I kept crying day after day, week after week. At the time, this distorted thinking was so real in my thoughts and in my reality that I couldn't make it stop.

For the first time, I made a choice to medicate. While I understand now that it was what I needed to do to heal, it was devastating for me. It was my choice, but it felt as though there was no choice at all. I lost a small connection with my daughter, as that decision meant that I could no longer breastfeed, but at the same time, I was relieved. The fear of judgment gripped me, and it took many years before I could let go of the guilt of that relief.

The day of our six-week checkup, we found ourselves in the emergency room. My daughter had spent the day vomiting every bottle. This time I didn't take "no" for an answer. I pushed back. I told them I wasn't leaving and watching my daughter starve all night. I demanded to see a pediatrician. It's funny how we stand guard for our loved ones, but not always for ourselves, and looking back, it was such a pivotal day for us. We were admitted overnight, and my daughter's ultrasound found an enlarged kidney that we would not have otherwise discovered. That was also the day that I was taken with severe diarrhea and, since I had no idea what was wrong, I was kicked out of the hospital, which was on alert for C-difficile. Six weeks postpartum and my baby was in the hospital with her father while I was home on the bathroom floor feeling guilty and my mom was watching my soon-to-be three-year-old. At the time, I wished that some of the people around me could have been more supportive about my illness instead of being angry that I had to rely on them to care for my baby. It felt like the low point of my life, but I could never know what was to come.

Everyone around me passed it off as the baby blues, but I knew different. This was not the blues—It was deep, scary, and dark. There was no way out of the hole. Nine weeks after my daughter was born, my doctor diagnosed postpartum depression, and I was entering a new phase. I was medicated with Sertraline, an SSRI drug that is commonly used for depression. I took that first dose with such hope, and I lay in my bed with such extreme anxiety, awake for thirty-six hours straight. We were back in the emergency room for medication that would finally allow me to sleep. I spent the next week in bed while my mother cared for my children and my husband lay beside me. I was grateful that he was able to take the time away from work to be there with me. That was when my mom—the strongest woman I know—decided that I was going to make it through this, whether I knew it or not. She would spend the next two years making sure that happened. Phone calls were made, and the chain of support was put in motion.

It was October 20, 2011, when I began phone counseling through my Employee Assistance Program (EAP). I was pleasantly surprised with the counselor, as he was well versed in anxiety and introduced me to triangle breathing and "chillout" by Ze Frank:

"Right now, it feels like I forgot to turn the light on
And things that looked so good yesterday are now shades of gray
And it seems like the world is spinning while I'm standing still
Or maybe I am spinning...I can't tell
And then you say...
Hey...You're okay...You'll be fine.... Just breathe
And now the women sing:
Hey...You're okay...You'll be fine (you'll be fine) ...Just breathe
Now everybody sings:
Hey...You're okay...You'll be fine...Just breathe
Hey...You're okay...You'll be fine...Just breathe
Hey...You're okay...You'll be fine (you'll be fine) ...Just breathe"

The song was so impactful on my life and on my son, who played it over and over. The EAP program is not meant to be a long-term solution, but the counseling carried me through the beginning stages of illness while I couldn't leave the house. I didn't realize at the time the kind of baby steps that I was taking; instead, I was grateful for someone to talk to that understood. No one, including my husband, could ever really understand what I was feeling, and I wished every day that they would just talk to me about it. Severe diarrhea continued, and between the unknown cause of that and the depression, I stayed home and, for the most part, in bed. Any time my husband was at work, my mother was there raising my children–very literally, raising them. I could not be alone with my daughter. I could not feed her a bottle or change her diaper. I could not be in the same room when she cried, before the panic set in. I was lost. I was broken. I was becoming buried and the light of day was moving further and further from my grasp.

By November, my mom had found a local support group through Niagara Public Health that was called Moms Offering Moms Support (MOMS). While I struggled to get out of bed, she was planning both my first group meeting and my daughter's baptism. The MOMS group was led by a public health nurse and three community volunteers that had suffered and survived various levels of postpartum depression. Their mission statement was simple, yet so effective–"To provide non-judgmental support in a safe environment to facilitate the understanding that this is not your fault, you are not alone, and you will get better." It was an incredibly safe space where I spent every Thursday night for four months (and sporadically for three months after that). I spent most nights running to the restroom while I was there, but just talking about my feelings with others that could understand first-hand was comforting. I struggled immensely to be there and participate, but it was a big step in my recovery. They accepted me as I was and never made me feel embarrassed about my condition.

On November 20, 2011, Monsignor Wayne baptized my daughter. I had managed to shop online for favors and have input into the decorations in the church hall. I sat with my father and the caterer and ordered a full Italian meal that I would never be able to eat. I even managed to order the most beautiful cake covered in white chocolate curls over the phone, while my mom handmade and iced cross cookies for the reception. The whole family pitched in and made sure that my daughter's special day was perfect. It should have been the happiest occasion, but all I could think about was how I was going to survive the ceremony without soiling myself. I had spent months staying close to a restroom and soiling myself just getting to the next room. It was more embarrassing to me than medicating my anxiety, and it took several discussions with my mom before she convinced me that it was ok to wear adult diapers. When the day came, we celebrated my beautiful baby girl surrounded by the love and grace of all our family and friends. The caterer provided the most incredible luncheon and, with my sports drink in hand, I made it through to the end. We thanked everyone for coming, said our goodbyes, cleaned up the hall and closed the doors–just as I needed to run to the restroom. No words can describe the embarrassment I felt, and nothing will erase the memory of cleaning up the hall and standing outside the newly locked doors soiling myself. The day of pretending to be okay had exhausted me, and I was thankful for adult diapers. Until answers were found, they would become a staple in my wardrobe. Some people used humor to deal with it, not knowing how deeply embarrassed I really was and how much their humor hurt me.

It was at the MOMS group that I learned to advocate for myself. I learned that there are so many places to get help if you fight for it. I learned that you never give up and there is always someone else out there that is experiencing the same or worse than you. The brave survivors that shared their stories gave me the strength to fight and the knowledge in which to do so. With their support and guidance, I began the journey to find a psychologist and to be accepted into the Women's Health Concerns Clinic at St. Joseph's Hospital. It was an OHIP-covered (Ontario Healthy Insurance Plan) clinic that took self-referrals, with an exceptionally long wait list. I spent the next month making phone calls, leaving voice messages, and speaking to whomever I could, to get on the list. And when that didn't work, I decided not to take "no" for an answer. I summoned up the strength that I had found for my daughter that night in the hospital, and I refused to hang up until I spoke with a live person. And when I got her, I refused to hang up until I got the right person. I told each person whom I was transferred to that, if I were going to kill myself, I would have done it by now, and they would have missed the chance to help me. I spoke from my soul to every person—I advocated—until the right one answered. On December 5, 2011, I sat in the office of a social worker and a psychiatrist with the Women's Health Concerns Clinic. It was the day before my thirty-sixth birthday.

Postpartum depression and both generalized anxiety and health anxiety were confirmed. I was started on a new medication that was not an SSRI, and a referral was made to the Anxiety Treatment & Research

Centre, which was also located at St. Joseph's Hospital. I remained in their care for the next year and traveled to Hamilton for monthly visits to check in. While I was getting settled into the new medication, my mother was busy setting up social supports as well. I was already attending the MOMS group, but I was so sick that I had not seen any friends since the birth of my daughter. I distinctly recall making a trip to the mall with my husband and my children to buy a pair of jeans, as I had lost a tremendous amount of weight. I was nervous about being there and full of anxiety about making it to the restroom. I remember flying out of a change room and running past my family, pointing in the direction of the bathrooms. They knew where I was headed, but nobody else would understand my urgency. On my way, I ran into a friend and apologized, but I just couldn't stop to chat. In the end, I didn't make it in time. I walked the mall back to my family, soiled, to get my change of clothes from the diaper bag and I alienated a friend. It was that same friend whom I visited that fateful night in tears and that same friend who, years later, I discovered wasn't on my path. It was in severing that friendship that I truly understood that everyone enters and exits your life for a reason.

The importance of the MOMS group to my recovery was never more evident, as these women truly understood what was happening. I would have given anything at that time to have my husband speak up on my behalf and explain what was happening to my friends–to rally them around me–and have their support. It was during this time that my mother called my childhood friend, Monsignor Wayne (now Bishop). He visited my bedside and didn't leave until we had discussed every option that he was aware of to help in my recovery. Although it would be some time before I forgave God for what I perceived as a punishment, Bishop Wayne has remained one of my oldest and dearest friends. He forgave what could have been a mortal sin, should my suicidal thoughts have turned to action.

By the end of December 2011, I had passed my four-month check-up and lost more than fifty pounds. The weight loss was bordering on dangerous, and the reality was that recovery was a full-time job. Hard work every day to wake up, face everything anew and make the conscious decision to survive what the day had in store. The new year began, and so came the trial of a higher dose of the medication I was taking. Two weeks into the trial, as we walked the grocery store parking lot, I told my mother that I wasn't going to act on it, but I was having suicidal thoughts. I didn't look her in the eye—I said it like it was nothing—and, I felt ashamed. The day was January 16, 2012. My daughter was five months old. It was the first time I had ever felt that way in my life, and it scared the heck out of me. We were on the phone to the clinic that day, and the extra dose was stopped. We would experiment with other medications, but in the end, I would spend the next six and a half years taking a drug that was never meant for long term use … and it kept me alive.

By the end of January 2012, I had attended the intake interview for the Anxiety Treatment Centre. Since I was battling two different kinds of anxiety, I was assigned to a private counselor rather than a group. I had lost four more pounds and was preparing to begin cognitive behavioral therapy (CBT). I would make the drive to Hamilton, weekly, for the next seventeen weeks. We discussed the anatomy of anxiety and listed everything that I avoided doing or had difficulty with because of it. My "coping cards" listed positive affirmations that I read to myself in every situation. I had coping cards for everything; anxiety, irritable bowel syndrome, nervous shakes, even coping with my mother-in-law while my mom was away. We also began monitoring my anxiety and panic every day and would review my notes for inconsistencies and misbeliefs. A big part of my recovery was differentiating between anger, anxiety, and excitement. As I learned what that looked like, the monitoring changed to thought records that had me adapting my anxious responses to something more realistic. The second entry on my sheet was about money. Just as I was seeing the light at the top of the depression sinkhole, unexpected debt in the tens of thousands meant that we would have to sell our investment property. For the first time, it was no longer anxiety. It was anger, hurt, distrust and resentment. I now understood the difference.

My first homework assignment was small but big at the same time. I was to go to the community center with my mom and both kids and take my daughter into the thirty-minute library group–alone. I cried a river just thinking about it. I cried when I got there. I cried through the entire thirty minutes. But it got a little easier each time we went, and by the end of the six weeks, we were quite comfortable. By March, my doctor awarded me with a tiny toy looking glass—to symbolize how distorted thinking affects reality—and it still serves as a reminder on my dresser today.

My first daily "exposure" to my daughter was for half an hour in the morning. All I had to do was get her up and change her diaper–it terrified me. Over time, I worked my way up to half an hour several days a week and eventually, more time and even feeding her a bottle. I kept an affirmation card beside me, and I journaled my thoughts and feelings after every exposure. By the end of May, I was spending a full day a week with my daughter without assistance. This was the greatest gift, and that doctor was my savior. I left his care on June 25, 2012, armed with thought records, coping cards, knowledge, and a cue card full of questions that helped me assess my cognitive distortions.

In the background, while I worked on the postpartum depression and anxiety, we set out to discover what was causing all the weight loss. I had lost another seventeen pounds in the first six months of the year, and by my daughter's first birthday, I weighed one-hundred-thirteen pounds. I was wearing clothes that I never thought I would wear in my lifetime. I struggled to find size zero and often-times ended up in the children's section to find something the correct size. I could read the concern on people's faces when we met. The pediatrician thought I had cancer, my uncle hugged me like it was my last day on earth, and a co-worker who never embraced anyone hugged me tight and told me to get better. I had begun with thyroid testing with my family doctor in January, then on to the gallbladder and kidneys. I started vitamin D supplements and prepared to have urine cytology and cystoscopy to rule out cancer.

By the end of May 2012, as I was learning that the tests were non-resultant, I was hit with ten days straight of severe diarrhea. I had managed to drive myself to Hamilton for my checkup at the Women's

Health Concerns Clinic, but I went severely downhill while I was there. I attended the emergency room at St. Joseph's Hospital and, although it was a horrible experience, I was referred to a gastroenterologist at the McMaster Digestive Diseases Clinic. Before I even made it there, I went on a gluten-free diet. I cut out all sugar and red meat, and I only ate cooked fruit and vegetables; anything that I could do to make it easier for my stomach to digest what I was eating–while I spent the summer with a local gastroenterologist undergoing more testing.

On August 8, 2012, my daughter turned one. The theme of the party was Angelina Ballerina, and she was dressed as a beautiful little ballerina with her curly blonde hair. There were ballet slipper cookies, mouse kisses, ballerina cupcakes, pink punch and Rice Krispies squares, and an Angelina cake. Family and friends from far and wide gathered to celebrate her first year. And as I stood to thank everyone for coming, I was brought to tears at the outpouring of love in the room. We were not just celebrating her first year, we were celebrating survival. She was a healthy little girl. I was alive, strong, and kicking the depression and anxiety to the curb a little more every day. There were more good days than bad days, and my tiny, precious girl had been raised by a village. Although the journey was not complete, we had won!

Three days before my daughter's first birthday, and right after the party, I began eating gluten again so that testing could start for Celiac Disease. I was sick as a dog for the next two months while other test results were becoming available. I was highly lactose intolerant and had Oral Allergy Syndrome. I had been on maternity leave and was due back to work at the beginning of September. I couldn't afford to be off work without pay, so I made arrangements to go back to work with strict accommodations so that I could be close to a restroom at all times. Between the stress of working, the gluten, and preparing for an upper endoscopy, I made the decision to go back off work within just six weeks. It was only then that I discovered that I could have applied for disability benefits and should have been on disability for the entirety of my illness. It was October 22, 2012, when my gastrointestinal healing journey began. My most recent test results were all rolling in, and I was officially off gluten for the rest of my life. The result was Irritable Bowel Syndrome (IBS), which is what they say when they have exhausted every other possibility. The road to recovery would become all about my diet and exercise.

I was put on a waitlist for a dietician at McMaster, and I began a boot camp style workout class with another mom who was suffering postpartum depression. The physical activity was incredibly healthy, and it was good to get out of the house. I returned to Burt and his yoga classes and found solace in that practice. Burt became a listening ear and often gave me profound guidance. I recall so vividly sitting down after class one day and telling Burt how lost I was. He told me of an elder who once told him to take the next step. I didn't know what the next step was, and he said: "it's right in front of you." First, you will get up and walk to that door, then you will get in your car and drive home. You will go to bed and get up tomorrow and just take the next step, whatever it is that you need to do, just keep taking the next step. That conversation is so vivid in my mind whenever I feel lost and alone. It makes me stop and remember how truly small the steps to recovery need to be sometimes.

I had begun counseling sessions with a psychologist in March, and within a month, it had turned into couples counseling as well. I would go on my own for a session and then attend with my husband. In those early months, we learned a lot about each other, and I learned a lot about myself. Those sessions would eventually uncover the deeply hidden suicidal thoughts that were running through my head. My medication had been stabilized, but I was still dealing with anxiety and trying to fix my marriage at the same time. My husband and I struggled tremendously in these sessions with trust, finances, and communication. It was a whole new level of exhaustion and pain. I would leave the sessions torn right down to nothing and hurting inside. Hurting so severely that I thought my family would be better off without me–and, one day, pulled to the side of the road on the way home, looked him in the eye and told him that he made me want to die. It was awful and hurtful, and it would take years before I realized that those words were so unfair to him. It would also take years before I forgave him for not begging me not to do it. All I needed was for someone, anyone, to tell me how much I was loved and how much it would hurt if I were not there with them.

I worked through all those thoughts and feelings and on December 4, 2012, I said "no" again. I placed payment for the session on the psychologist's desk, and I said "I'm done. I can't do this anymore." It was the realization that the counseling was tearing me down, rather than lifting me up that saved me again. The psychologist warned me that our marriage would never survive on the unstable ground that it was on, but I chose me. I could not be there for my family if I did not take care of myself first. The most profound thing that I have ever heard about suicide is that it doesn't end your pain … it passes it on to those you leave behind. I knew that I could never leave that pain behind for my family to endure.

By June of 2013, the postpartum depression was behind me, and I was living life again. I was finding joy in volunteering at my son's school and in being a stay-at-home mom. Life was abundant, and I felt free of the dark shadows of the past. I had finally been matched with a dietician who was well versed in Low FODMAP diets. FODMAPs were a new concept in the IBS world, and the trial led me on a new healing path. I spent eight weeks on an elimination diet, journaling thoughts, feelings, and symptoms, and was slowly able to add foods that were tolerated back in. In time, I had built a list of foods that would become my staples, and I found freedom in being able to eat outside of my home again. The treatment marked the end of my healing journey and the beginning of my steady rise back from one-hundred-five pounds.

I returned to work in March of 2014, stronger than ever and stress-free. With the help of workplace cognitive behavioral therapy, I found my place again in society and in a daily routine. It was there that I tested the limits of my recovery as I gradually returned to full-time hours. The entire journey that I had been through had given me the belief that, beyond every challenge, a new story was waiting to be written. I felt buried, unable to climb from the deep hole, alone, cold, and dark, but I harnessed all the positive energy and abundance around me, and a new day began. I continue to wake up every day and give thanks for the blessings in front of me and the opportunity to begin anew.

Using the same proprietary process that I used, you too can navigate your way through depression and anxiety. Inside my Cornerstone of Growth, you will navigate five ironclad elements that will lead you to overcome your adversity and grow. These elements include keeping a positive mindset, finding your strength & courage, maintaining a social support network, maintaining a professional support network, and advocating for yourself.

THE CORNERSTONE OF GROWTH

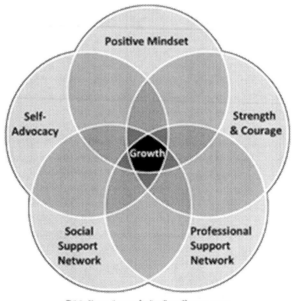

©Melissa Anne | rise2wellness.com

POSITIVE MINDSET

We all know that it's hard to find the silver lining when we feel like we have been beaten down by everything in life. Having a positive mindset doesn't mean that you forget those things are happening. It means finding the positive in every adversity, focusing on the lessons you've learned and finding the humor in adverse situations. I invite you to start concentrating on the positives by sitting down each evening and notating three things that went right that day. This can be done with your partner and can be anything—no matter how big or small—write it down. Maybe you're happy that you got out of bed and showered, or glad that you ate a meal with your family. After you've done that, reflect on those three milestones. I ask you to do that every day for a week and then the next and notice what starts to happen. Your focus will shift from judgment to gratitude for the little joys that we often overlook. Before long you will see that your thoughts will take you right to those happy moments without having to think about it. Your mindset will change, and you will live in the present moment focusing on all the abundances in your life.

We often speak of people being stuck in "victim mentality." This refers to those who always seem to have something bad happening to them and who take pleasure in the attention they receive. They could be experiencing the happiest time of their life, and they still describe it with negativity. The challenge is to recognize that you are in that state of mind before you can begin to take small steps to change it. You cannot change something that you are unaware of. With depression, we often shift into "victim mentality" without knowing it. If you find yourself there, it's time to shift from victim to survivor. I invite you to begin speaking with intention and then with awareness. You will soon find yourself trying hard not to say anything negative or complain, which is difficult for a lot of people. This will allow you to be mindful of your thoughts, but it isn't sustainable in the long term. It takes a lot of energy to censor yourself in that way. It is when you shift to an awareness that you will begin to see real progress. You will start to catch yourself in a non-judgmental way when speaking to others about your experiences. You may still recount those events, but you will find yourself softening the lines.

Affirmations are short, positive phrases that we repeat over and over to ourselves that help us to overcome negative thoughts. They eventually shift our thinking and the world around us. They are deeply personal and, therefore, we use the two most powerful words, "I am." Find the things that are truly personal to you and affirm them every morning when you get up. The trap that we sometimes fall into is thinking that our affirmation is positive when it's not. For example:

	Negative "I am"	Positive "I am"
You are not alone	I am not alone	I am surrounded by love
You are not a failure	I am not a failure	I am successful
It's not your fault	I am not at fault	I am strong
This is just temporary	I am temporarily sick	I am a work in progress

The right affirmations will become significantly powerful for you. In a particularly difficult time for my kids, I began affirmations with them. They were four and seven at the time. We started with "Today is going to be a great day" to overcome the negative emotions and tantrums that were happening in the morning rush. We soon discovered the power of "I am" and added in "I am calm" and "I am peaceful." My kids took to this idea, and three years later, this is our morning ritual on their way to grade two and grade five every day:

"I am peaceful. I am calm. I am brave. I am strong. I am patient. I am ready. I am love. I am loved. Today is going to be a great day."

One of the best ways to keep your positive energy flowing is a celebration! Celebrate everything. Did you hit a goal or reach a milestone? Maybe you managed to brush your teeth or have a shower. Whatever it is, celebrate it. Celebrations don't have to be big, elaborate events. It could be a special dessert at dinner or a book you've been longing to read. Maybe it's quiet time to sit down and start reading. I chuckle writing this because I have toasted, at the dinner table, brushing my teeth that day. Whatever it is, make sure that it feeds your soul and affirms the significant progress that you are making. In other words, don't eat a special dessert if your goal was weight loss or buy expensive items if your goal was saving money.

STRENGTH AND COURAGE

Strength and courage come in many different shapes and sizes. The definition of courage is "strength in the face of pain or grief." Courage is demonstrated in getting up every day and taking the next step, however big or small it may be. For many people facing depression, it can be hard just to get up in the morning. We see ourselves as lost, and we retreat into darkness because we feel everybody would be better off without us. I know how hard it can be to move from that place and this is an opportunity to ask for your partner's support. For a long time, it was an effort for me to get up every day and I made the conscious decision to "live" each time. But you make that decision every day until you don't have to anymore. What I mean is that it will seem like a chore, a difficult thing to decide. Yet, as you begin to heal and change and grow, it becomes a little less difficult. Soon, it will become a mindset and not a decision at all. It will be a joy to live your life to the fullest with love and passion. I say this to all of you now and know that if it speaks to just one person, it made a difference. Choose yourself and do whatever you have to do to survive because it's the deep pain that you really want to end, not your life.

Deciding to live is a lot easier when you know your reasons for doing so. What or who is your reason for living? Who supports you the most? Who surrounds you with positive energy? There is always a reason to live, and this is where a supportive spouse is essential. Now, I live for myself, but in the beginning, I couldn't do that. I lived for my kids. The fear that stopped me at every thought of suicide was what will happen to my children if I am not here to raise them. The answer terrified me, so every day I got up for my children, and I survived for my children. Maybe your reason is the rewarding work you do or the difference you make volunteering somewhere or the friends that stand by you through thick or thin. Whatever it is, own it. Write it down. Remember it. I want you to know deep inside you that your life has so many beautiful gifts worth living for. Recognize those gifts and make them your daily affirmations of joy. Find the strength deep inside you by finding yourself and celebrating that this moment in time will not last forever and there will be light where there is now darkness. Declare it to yourself and those around you and remember your intention every time you find yourself in that deep dark place.

Often, it's hard to confide in those around us about our darkest moments. It's not that we don't trust them with our innermost thoughts and feelings; instead, we don't want to hurt them with the darkness within. It's hard to admit that those are our true feelings during that time in our lives. To heal from the darkness, we do need to confront it. Journaling is an excellent process to explore your thoughts and feelings deeply. It allows you to evaluate and reflect on your thoughts without worrying about structure or recording events. It is known to ease anxiety and depression and to help you to focus on your recovery. Choose a time in your day when you can find solitude and make journaling a part of your practice.

Living in the past or the future takes away our enjoyment of the present. You can never wholly live if you are dwelling on something that you can't change or worrying about something that may or may not happen. Anxiety at its very core is worry and what ifs. It robs us of enjoying our lives now and in the moment. This is where practicing mindfulness can help. Smile and enjoy whatever you are doing, whether it be work or your own activities. Fully appreciate precisely where you are today and what you are doing.

SOCIAL SUPPORT NETWORK

As I lay in bed, my biggest supporter was building a social support network for me without even knowing it. My mother would be the first person to tell you to find joy in life. She would be the first person to make you promise not to do anything drastic if you are feeling like life has beaten you down. So, it was fitting that my mother started the process of making calls and making sure that I was face to face with the right people. Whether it was longtime friends, my aunt who volunteered on the patient advisory committee at St. Joseph's Hospital, or public health nurses and support groups, I was on the phone or visiting with someone.

Helping to build these supports is something great for your partner to do in support of you.

While it's lovely to connect with people over the telephone and by text, there is nothing quite the same as face to face interaction. It brings feeling and emotion to your conversation and body language that wouldn't otherwise be seen. There is something about talking with someone and experiencing a touch of the arm, a hug, or a hold of the hand. True deep emotion and sincerity are conveyed in face to face interactions. I understand that it can be difficult to achieve with our busy lives and schedules, yet I invite you to make an effort to interact with someone in person once a week. During that time, share your story. Talk about what you are going through. If you are at a support group, listen and learn from the stories of those around you. Ask questions. Be present and mindful. Sharing our experiences with others makes us feel included, accepted, and useful. You may find that the person you shared your story with needed to hear it more than you needed to share it. We all struggle in life, and it is in sharing those struggles and adversities that we help each other navigate and grow.

I once sat in my car in the snow for hours and purged everyone in my life that did not align with my energy. People that had not been there for me or whom I had not heard from during my most happy or most difficult times. People who I only ever heard from when they needed something or who betrayed my trust. A friend of mine called it weeding your garden. If you did not rid your garden of the weeds, your plants would suffocate. The weeds would steal the water and vitamins from the soil, and the fruit of the plants would never grow. It's the same in life. To grow and realize your ambitions, you must weed your garden. This can be done in many ways ~ review your Facebook friends list or close off relationships that have been hanging in the balance. It can be as simple as recognizing in your mind that someone came into your life for a reason and being ok with seeing them go when the time comes.

Everyone comes into our lives for a reason. Some are there to teach us, some to love us, some to support us, and yes, some to use us. Begin to recognize why people are or were in your life and align yourself with those whose energy aligns with yours. Energy never lies, and you will feel the connections when you are around those people. You will feel understood and at ease when you are with them. Find your tribe and stick with them, for those are the people that will support you. That doesn't mean that you never let anybody else into your circle. Instead, now you are aware that they are in your circle for a reason and they may not stay there. The people in your circle should cheer you on and celebrate you! Build a social support network that includes a strong circle. Always remember that there are plenty of people in your life who love and respect you. You don't need to hang on to those who don't.

Swallow your pride and accept any assistance that is offered, no matter how big or small. Let others be strong for you until you can be strong for yourself. Ask your partner for help and allow it to come. Receiving aid does not make you weak, and it does not take away the control that you have over your life. It's temporary. It's time to be selfish with your self-care. Allow people to step up and show you why they are in your circle because, one day, you might be doing the same for them. Think of it this way, you would do whatever you could for a friend who was in the same position as you, right? Recognize that you deserve the same kindness. Know that your friends and family are just as happy to do for you as you would do for any one of them.

PROFESSIONAL SUPPORT NETWORK

I am the first to admit that I overwork myself and when I am not working to my fullest potential, it feels as though I am letting people down. I am also living proof that sometimes you must slow down and allow people to help. I understand how hard it is to accept the kind of support that you truly need right now. It feels like a defeat, failure. For me, finding assistance was more comfortable than receiving it in some respects. I had help right in front of me (my husband, my mother, my friends) and it was taking that help that made me feel guilty and shameful. In fact, I didn't reach out to friends who probably would have helped if they had been given a chance. When it came to professional help, it was a challenge for me to both find it and accept that I needed it. I was in denial that I could be so broken that I needed so much professional help. It was a full-time job to work with all the professionals that I had partnered with. Yes, it was a partnership in that we were both accountable for my progress. I had to do the work to heal and so do you.

I invite you not just to accept the help that comes your way but recognize that this is a time in your life when you need professional help. Professional help includes those both in and outside of the medical profession. It includes religious leaders, yoga and meditation instructors, personal trainers, natural healers, and more. It's essential to nourish your body, mind, and soul for a full recovery. How we think affects the way we feel. Find out what is offered in your area and decide what will work for you. If you are full of anxiety and the jitters, maybe you need cognitive behavior therapy and yoga, rather than meditation right now. Set yourself up for success in whatever you choose. That doesn't mean that you never move to a meditation practice. It just means you do other things for now.

Finding the right professional support can be overwhelming if you don't have a plan in mind. Write down your goals for recovery and rank them in importance. Do you want to take a more holistic approach, or do you want to stick with medical professionals? These goals and preferences will help you to figure out where to start in your search for professional support. Remember, you are building a network of people around you that will partner with you in your recovery. In the beginning, they will be mainly guiding you while you can't lead yourself. As you grow and strengthen, you will take on a more significant role in your recovery. If you're not sure what that looks like yet, that's okay. Taking small steps towards recovery can mean starting with one or two services and adding more as you heal. You don't have to do it all at once, have it all figured out or do it alone. Take the help as it presents itself and continue to revisit your goals. Maybe today your goal is to get dressed, but a month from now your goal is to take a walk outside with your infant without worry. Remember to celebrate those milestones as you hit them.

SELF-ADVOCACY

Self-advocacy means understanding your strengths and weaknesses, developing personal goals, being assertive (meaning standing up for yourself), and making decisions (BrainLine, 2009). Self-advocacy also means communicating your needs and making decisions about the supports necessary to meet those needs (Martin Huber-Marshall, & Maxon, 1993; Stodden, 2000). I am asking you today to advocate for yourself–as strongly as you would stand up for your loved ones. You are surrounded by love and friends and family who support you, and they will stand up for you when you can't stand up for yourself. Once you find the strength, it's time for you to step in and advocate—that doesn't mean that you'll lose all of the support that you already have; instead, it makes your position even stronger. The further help that you put in place will come from your own passion and conviction. You are your biggest fan, and you know what you need more than anyone else. As you grow and heal, you will find that inside yourself again. It will just happen one day. You will wake up and say today is the day that I take control and get what I need.

Remember that depression is not just sadness. It has many faces and affects how you think, feel, and act. Anxiety is your body's natural response to stress. It's when that reaction is intense, sudden, and repeated that it is debilitating. Both anxiety and depression are real medical conditions. With that understanding comes the ability to not only navigate yourself through it but to educate others about it. Advocating for yourself includes explaining to others what you are feeling and why. That includes explaining it to your partner. It takes time to get there yourself and to understand what is happening, but you will get there. To grasp what you are experiencing, read about it. Educate yourself on the symptoms and everything that you can do to aid your recovery. You will be able to help yourself heal quickly, and others understand more fully when you are knowledgeable. Talk to people wherever you are–tell the stranger at the grocery store what you are experiencing. Suffering in silence will not find you solace. Break the stigma because talking about your experience may put you right in the path of someone that can help to save you. One day, your knowledge and all the adversity that you experienced may help someone too. You have control. You always did. You just let it go for a while to allow yourself to heal and allow others to hold you up in the process.

OVERCOME

Whether you're almost there or you've just begun, you will overcome this illness. Believe that within yourself and affirm it every day. Take your time and accept all the help that you need to heal. In the beginning, others will make plans for you. They will find you the support you need and make your appointments with doctors, and natural healers and whomever they think will help you. As time passes, you will begin to take over your recovery plan and really voice what it is that you need in your recovery. Now is the time to develop your self-care plan. This includes what you will do for you and not as a mother or a wife or a sister or an aunt. What will feed your soul and bring you back into alignment? Write it down. Develop your plan and add to it as you grow.

Improve your sleep and eating habits. I understand that you may be sleeping a lot, and, with a newborn, sleep may be at a premium. Try to ensure that the quality of sleep is there. Go to bed on a set schedule and limit distractions in the room. Remove television and other electronic devices that emit unnatural wavelengths. This doesn't mean that you will always get the best sleep of your life, but it sets the plan in motion. It trains your body to know when it should be sleeping and what a good rest feels like. Improve your eating habits—try to eat less meat and reduce sugar, alcohol, and caffeine. All of these can affect your mood, your health, and the quality of your sleep. Reduce your stress, and you will reduce your anxiety. Reducing stress often has the bonus of elevating your mood as well, helping with depressive symptoms. What do you like to do to reduce stress? Work out at the gym, swim, run, take a yoga class, meditate. Whatever it is, plan for it, schedule it and follow through with it.

All the physical activities that you may take part in to reduce stress will also help to reduce anxiety. Although there are many facets of anxiety, it is best overcome by confronting your fears, or whatever it is that is making you anxious. Avoiding those situations will only affirm in your mind that you should not be doing those things or going to those places. Skills can be learned, such as those through cognitive behavioral therapy, to reduce the effects of anxiety. Anxiety is mostly exaggerated worries, therefore consider identifying and challenging those worries. Ask yourself, what is the likelihood that my fear will come true?

Relaxation and breathing techniques are essential to not only a healthy recovery but a healthy life. We all could benefit from practicing controlled breathing and relaxation techniques to reduce the physical symptoms of daily tension. This can be done on your own or as part of a structured yoga class. Most yoga classes comprise of breathing, yoga poses, and relaxation. Consider also taking up meditation if you have never done it before. Meditation is turning your attention to something, whether it's the breath, the body, or a mantra. It helps in making a permanent shift in your mindset. There are many forms of meditation and mindfulness is one of them. Mindfulness is being aware of where you are and being fully present in what you are doing. There is no judgment, just awareness.

Start by being mindful in your day to day living and work your way up to a more formalized meditation. There are meditation classes that you can attend and recordings that you can listen to and be guided through some inner work. In fact, there are even meditations that you can practice that will help with sleep. Dr. Joe Dispenza talks at length about re-wiring your brain and reconditioning your body. He has recorded many meditations with a focus on remembering and living your future. In this way, you free yourself from your past and live in the present moment. I invite you to read his blog "Let Your Past Life be a Past Life." It is incredibly eye-opening.

THE BENEFITS OF COGNITIVE BEHAVIORAL THERAPY

One of my cognitive behavioral therapy homework assignments was to take my daughter to swim lessons. I didn't always get in the pool with her, depending on my gastro situation that day, but I always made it there. I was having an especially bad day this particular day, so my husband took her in the pool. I felt awful, ridden with guilt that I couldn't spend the time with her, and my husband had to go in. I imagined that he was angry with me for being sick. I failed to see the positive, "I always made it there," and she was happy! He snapped a photo of us together and, to this day, my daughter keeps that photo at her bedside. It's her favorite picture of us together. Just days ago, she asked me to recreate it. I share this with you as a reminder to you that you can survive anything. This picture brings me tears of joy, and I hope that it brings you all hope and strength to grow.

GROW

You've overcome your depression and/or anxiety, and you have made your way back into regular life. The dark cloud above you is gone. But you're not done yet! Now is the time to grow from your experience! Find what feeds your soul. Use this experience to find your true purpose in this life. I know—this seems like a big task, doesn't it? You don't have to have it all figured out, and you don't have to turn your life upside down. It could be that you are doing what you love and what feeds your soul. It could be that you just need more self-care in your life. Whatever it is, you owe it to yourself to learn from this experience.

Spend time in nature and in the sun. Being in nature has been proven to alleviate stress, boost your immune system, and fight depression. Being in sunlight alone nourishes our bodies with vitamin D and elevates our mood. Whether you are healthy or ill, nature is a great way to feed your body and reset your mind. It is a place to be away from chaos and think about the present. Remember during your journey that it is one thing to look happy outwardly, but quite another to be truly happy inside.

You may have spent a lot of time looking happy during your recovery, but now is the time to ensure that you are joyous in your life. Being present, meditating and spending time in nature are the beginning steps to discovering what may be holding you back.

Developing an attitude of service will help you to shift your focus from within. Often, we find ourselves and our true calling when we are helping others. You have overcome your illness, and rightfully so, you gave all your energy to your self-healing. Now is the time to step away and help others. Volunteer at your child's school or at a soup kitchen, spend time with distant family and friends, talk to the quiet person at work that nobody talks to, live life in aid of others. You will discover what your gifts are and how you can share them with the world. You felt buried, unable to climb from the deep hole, alone, cold, and dark, but you harnessed all the positive energy and abundance around you ... now grow!

Melissa Anne, BA, Certified Coach Practitioner, Certified Master Coach Practitioner

Mindset Coach, Personal Development Speaker and Founder of Rise2Wellness®

With twenty years' experience in the field of yoga and mindfulness, Melissa is a leading authority on healing and growth. As a leader, Melissa has tamed numerous wild Canadian children with meditation, breathing, and relaxation. As a speaker, coach, and author, she works with a wide range of individuals inspiring and empowering them to navigate their way through stress, anxiety, and depression. After helping her son navigate anxiety at an early age and spending time in the classroom with so many children, it became Melissa's biggest passion to help parents with children who are navigating anxiety, bullying and positivity. In Melissa's opinion, coaching is the single most powerful tool that an individual can use to be successful. Melissa is a best-selling author, an award-winning speaker and entrepreneur, a 200-hour RYT, a 95-hour RCYT, as well as a proud mother.

Connect with Melissa:
www.rise2wellness.com
melissa@rise2wellness.com
www.facebook.com/Rise2Wellness
www.facebook.com/speakermelissa
https://www.linkedin.com/company/rise2wellness
https://www.youtube.com/channel/UCfuIQXAM-B_
3M3kl9ghhTyg/featured

Seven Beliefs of the Indestructible Human *by Rod Macdonald*

B uddhist teachings suggest that life is suffering. The notion that life is suffering appears to be opposed to the more light-hearted popular idea that life is bliss (or awesome, wicked, fantastic, or some other adjective). Can it be both suffering *and* bliss? Most would agree that it most certainly is both and more.

As people go through life, they have a vast array of experiences. The average person will interact with tens of thousands of people before the end of their lives. While we become who we are in part due to genetic predisposition, much more of how we show up in the world is a result of the programming instilled in us by those around us.

In addition to the human interactions we have, consider that in the developed world, adults will spend fifteen years of their life watching television and seven years listening to the radio, on average. As if that wasn't enough information being processed, the average person reads over one-hundred-sixty books and one-hundred-twenty magazines in their lifetime.

All those person-to-person and person-to-information-source interactions produce massive amounts of data that the brain processes. As best as we understand the brain, it takes in information and attempts to categorize it with neuronal connections in an effort to make it easier to navigate life. Those connections sometimes empower us, and in other cases, limit us.

When information comes in that introduces a new way of thinking or behaving, or supports an existing way of thinking or behaving, those connections may become habitual ways of showing up in the world. The more powerful the experience, the more likely it will lead to a long-lasting part of our identity.

When trauma is added to the mix, those connections can be even more deeply etched into our lives. For example, if a dog attacks us the first time we interact with one, we may expect danger the next time we see a dog because a belief may be formed to protect us in the future. If, on the other hand, we had years of *positive* interactions with dogs, being attacked would seem out of the ordinary. It may still create a negative belief, especially if it was traumatic enough, but if not, it is unlikely the one attack will change how we feel about dogs after years of positive interactions.

While the dog attack is a dramatic example, what is even more relevant to us on a daily basis is the gradual adoption of limiting beliefs as a result of hearing negative messages from those we trust, as well as messages from our own inescapable self-talk. Because of the nature of human evolution, limiting beliefs are much more easily installed as they were required for survival for much of our history.

Today, when we pair the tiny but ongoing negative messaging with the occasional traumatic situation, people are ripe for "system failure" on a small or large scale. This might take the shape of failed relationships, bad habits, or the inability to hold a job. In its worst manifestation, it might take the shape of crippling anxiety or depression that seems to take on a life of its own.

IN MY LIFE

In my life, like most, I have experienced the spectrum of human emotion, from bliss to suffering. As is typical, I have spent more time paying attention to the suffering and not enough time appreciating the bliss. There have been times of darkness when it seemed like I was being torn apart and ground down in the jaws of a nightmarish beast. Often, just when it seemed to stop, I'd be spat out and chewed on again by something so vile that it consumed both light *and* shadow.

These darker times came and went, with varying frequency and intensity. I was never able to predict the appearance of the beast, partly because it always seemed to be there, lurking. I came to expect it, even if there was no reason for its appearance, making me doubt its existence altogether. Then, often with my guard down, it would again swallow me up.

In hindsight, the beast appeared more often in the poorly lit days of winter and seemed to pile on when other challenges occurred. Why, I wondered, would the monster appear when things were already tough enough? For a long time, I didn't know. What I did know was I grew to despise it; hating how it made me feel. It sucked my life energy from every cell of my body and made the things that would typically be enjoyable, appear colorless and dull.

I came to realize that it thrived on my pain, be it the loss of a loved one, the failure of a project, or upon rejection by someone for whom I cared. It always grew stronger in moments of weakness. If my body or spirit were vulnerable, it would jump at the opportunity to invade, like a hungry lion stalking an injured gazelle.

Eventually, I came to understand that all those manifestations were born of my imagination. Like dreaming of falling, the beast was only as threatening as my mind would make it. I discovered that while I could never be sure of its origin, what had started as a normal emotion, turned into a feeling. That feeling morphed into a mood. That mood eventually grew roots, first as one limiting belief, then another, and another. If I believed it was there, it was, and it was becoming an identity of limitation as all limiting beliefs can.

There was no one moment I knew things had changed, and certainly no lightning strike of enlightenment. To the best of my understanding, what did happen was a gradual awakening fed by the persistence of my curiosity and passion for understanding human behavior. This passion grew into my calling to become a coach. Coaching strengthened me, feeding me crumbs of determination that inspired a growing appetite for happiness.

I was clear about one thing; I would not, under any circumstances, become a victim of my mind. The truth was, there was no beast; it was always my mind that stalked me. However, I realized that my mind wasn't trying to destroy me; it was a mutated desire to protect me. My mind created a sick loop, trying to protect me from pain by holding me down, but the holding down became suffocation. I broke the loop by making a choice. A choice to become an Indestructible Human.

WHAT IS THE INDESTRUCTIBLE HUMAN?

The Indestructible Human is a concept of adaptability. We know that even when the body fails, there exists a human spirit that allows us to go on, even when it defies expectations. Take the renowned physicist Stephen Hawking as an example. Diagnosed with amyotrophic lateral sclerosis (ALS) at age twenty-one, he far exceeded the typical life expectancy of three to five years, living an additional fifty-five years; passing away at age seventy-six. In addition to the care he received, the reason for his much-extended survival has been hypothesized as having a purpose, another way of describing human spirit.

Becoming an Indestructible Human is about developing the self-awareness to recognize who we are now and choose whom we want to become, regardless of the life conditions we might face. The

Indestructible Human includes resilience but goes far beyond it to adaptation. Resilience is the ability to sustain stress and return to who you were. Adaptation, by comparison, is about sustaining stress and becoming better as a result.

To understand how we can become indestructible, it is helpful to understand from whence we came.

THE PROLOGUE OF MODERN HUMANS

For its four point five-billion-year existence, life on earth was simple until people appeared. To be fair to our oldest common ancestors, modern humans are the ones that made a mess of things. We are the only species on the planet that were we to disappear, the earth would be better off. Without us, the environment would heal, and billions of animals would live as long as their natural predators would allow. There is no question that humans have been the most significant blight on the earth, and yet here we are.

As a species, it seems we have gone too far down the wrong path. Depending on which source you use, about 3.5 million years ago, humans were driven almost exclusively by basic survival when we learned the benefits of coming together and formed the earliest tribes. However, even within increasingly sophisticated tribes, about fifty thousand years ago, there were still those of us with a desire to exert individual interests, at least until both boundaries and opportunities began to appear. About twelve thousand years ago, we became increasingly appreciative of innovation, including what we believe to be the earliest agricultural revolutions. With more predictability in our food sources came more innovation and growing hunger for competition and profit through early trade. Early economies grew, and through both trade and conflict, power supplanted survival for the "haves," while the "have-nots" continued to struggle to stay alive. Over the last thousand years, we continued the seesaw of power via force on one side and power via commerce on the other. During the previous 300 years, there has been a slow awakening, and most recently, a curiosity about what is beyond force, profit, or even power.

This awakening to curiosity has culminated in a global question. Can we come together and transcend a bloody, power-hungry history, or are we going to collapse under its choking, polluted weight? Time will certainly tell all, but as some have discovered, there may be another chapter in human history yet to be revealed that, should we get there, may be a bridge to an entirely new understanding of ourselves and a new role in the universe.

What will allow us to endure and get to that new role, and actualize the potential we have, are our deepest beliefs. Many feel they are powerless as individuals, already swept into the raging current of our turbulent life conditions. However, we are not powerless; for every country is made up of groups, every group is made up of individuals, and therefore, every individual matters. It is our beliefs that either help or hinder our ability to see common ground and therefore, our beliefs are where we must start.

THE PROBLEM AND THE SOLUTION: OUR BELIEFS

Many people in the developed world go through life lurching from day to day, year to year, from home to work, and back again. We do all this while experiencing ever-increasing stress coupled with ever-decreasing happiness, resulting in challenges to mental and physical health. Combine these with a lack of physical movement, a less-than-ideal diet, and a technology-fueled disconnection from self and others, and you have a potentially catastrophic collision that threatens us as much as war and famine did generations ago.

One might not be surprised to learn that the root of the problem is ourselves, or more specifically, our beliefs. Our beliefs are the sum of everything we have experienced and learned as individuals, created, and installed at a mostly subconscious level from a time even before we were born.

Our beliefs may be understood as a messy combination of DNA, education, experience, as well as the environment in which we find ourselves. Also, these beliefs were written into our programming because of either intentional or inadvertent installation by our parents, family, peers, role-models, and others. Just like bad programming in a computer, faulty human beliefs create chaos in our lives and the lives of those around us.

Consider if you will, the repercussions of a belief like, "people from X country are all criminals." That kind of belief would limit or even sabotage both personal and working relationships when those people are met. A belief like this may operate at a subconscious level until brought to the surface, where it is revealed as both inaccurate and ugly. However, it will persist if it is not addressed.

Likewise, a belief such as, "I am unworthy of love" will also limit or sabotage both personal and working relationships. The long-term result may include anxiety, depression, solitude, and a downward spiral to sometimes lethal consequences.

TIME FOR AN UPGRADE

By upgrading our beliefs, through the introduction of powerful new beliefs, what we could accomplish as a species would be impressive. For most of us, we are programmed with our initial belief system by our parents and caregivers from birth until we can formulate beliefs ourselves. Because parents are rarely trained in how to install empowering beliefs, they do the best they can. They are informed by their own beliefs, as a result of the experiences gained throughout their lives. In many cases, the beliefs they install in their children are contradictory, sometimes hypocritical, creating subconscious conflict in the minds and hearts of their children and the adults those children become. You can't blame the parents; otherwise, you'd have to blame *their* parents, and their grandparents, great-grandparents, and all those that came before them.

While there are many helpful belief systems from throughout the world in all cultures, we have spent the last 200 years getting further away from them and now find ourselves with what sometimes is a listless, lurching sense of right and wrong. The critical understanding then is to create one's own beliefs and install them in such a way as to overwrite the limiting beliefs that may have been getting in the way of living your best life.

Typically, we only begin to formulate beliefs about ourselves in our childhood and teenage years, influenced by, or independent of our parents or caregivers. Unfortunately for us, and in some cases for those around us, the prefrontal cortex of the brain, where we create strategy and analyze incoming information, isn't fully formed until sometime in our twenties. We spend much of our teen years formulating beliefs that are not entirely well thought out and, in some cases, dangerous or counterproductive to a satisfying life.

WHAT TO DO ABOUT IT

Some suggest that ninety-five percent or more of our lives are managed subconsciously, at a level below attentive thought. Our brains have managed to put many of our daily choices on autopilot because the brain as amazing as it is, is limited in how much it can process. The brain takes repetitive activities and creates beliefs that are filed away to be retrieved later without new processing power being required. These mental and emotional "shortcuts" get us quickly to what we believe to be desired results. For example, how you get out of bed in the morning, how you get dressed, and even the route you take to get to work, quickly become repetitive and no longer need conscious attention. These and thousands of other choices are moved into the subconscious where we can then act from without thinking. While we sometimes refer to these shortcuts as habits, routines, and practices, at the root are beliefs that led to the creation of these shortcuts.

Unfortunately, these beliefs can manifest as shortcuts to potentially damaging results, such as road rage in response to minor transgressions, reaching for unhealthy foods in response to boredom, or reaching for a cigarette to relax, amongst others. Our brains seek pleasure or avoid pain and therefore will try to find the fastest way there, even if that means something we wouldn't choose if we paused long enough to think about it.

What is most promising is that we can create new empowering beliefs and with enough repetition, can overwrite old, limiting beliefs. It is simple, but not always easy, because we are attempting to overwrite beliefs that have been there for decades and in the case of genetic programming, centuries. When you combine a conscious understanding of the process with repetition, you can influence or create subconscious beliefs.

WHICH BELIEFS?

There are many beliefs that you might wish to install, and you are encouraged to do so if they align with your values and lead to a better life. As a catalyst, I propose that amongst all the individual beliefs you might wish to install, there are at least seven universal beliefs that, when installed, will serve to elevate you in your journey of maturing consciousness.

These seven beliefs are inspired by a combination of ancient teachings (subtle energy found in the chakras, meridians, Ki, and others) and modern science (aspects of human psychological theories including credit going to Graves, Beck, Cowan, Maslow, and Erikson, amongst others). While you may be curious to learn more about these sources, one needn't know or understand them to learn and benefit from the seven beliefs of the Indestructible Human.

HOW TO INTRODUCE THE SEVEN BELIEFS OF THE INDESTRUCTIBLE HUMAN

We can employ the conscious mind to access the subconscious mind where beliefs exist. While consuming information and education through a variety of methods is helpful, and may introduce new or improved beliefs, the results may be haphazard or temporary. What has proven to be effective both in ancient and modern traditions is repetition. As simple as that sounds, you needn't look further than the mantras of ancient yogis or the repetition of expressions of love from parent to child. Repetition of the right belief can create an almost indestructible, positive outcome.

It is worth noting that the repetition of positive beliefs alone may not be enough. Just as taking vitamins but not washing one's hands may result in the acquisition of a cold, installing positive beliefs without protecting oneself from negative influences may result in weak beliefs, vulnerable in times of crisis. Also, worth mentioning is the value of strengthening other systems through proper nutrition, exercise, and the avoidance of toxins.

To install these or other beliefs, you may employ live or recorded repetition, as a form of *entrainment* (the synchronization of you to a rhythm, in this case, the repetition of your beliefs). Inspired in part by mantras, whose origins are speculated to be over three thousand years old, it is believed that the repetition of powerful sounds and words may imbue the user with a positive outlook, improved health, and in some cases, transcendent experiences.

Technique 1: Create your version of each belief and say each one silently or aloud, and then reflect on it. If you practice mindfulness meditation, this may be a time you leverage for reflection.

Technique 2: Create your version of each belief and record it at least once and as many as one-hundred-eight times. The number one-hundred-eight is said to have sacred properties in some belief systems. Repetition is required, so repeating the belief five to ten times will begin to be effective. This is in part, inspired by the technique taught by the Certified Coaches Federation's Level One Training.

THE BELIEFS

The following seven beliefs have been inspired in part by "the emergent, cyclical, double-helix model of the adult human biopsychosocial systems" (as proposed by Clare W. Graves and amended by Don Beck and Chris Cowan), the Hierarchy of Needs (as proposed by Abraham Maslow), as well as the widely acknowledged energy centers of the body (referred to by some as chakras, meridians, Ki, etc.).

Each belief is presented with an explanation, followed by what happens when it is weak or strong, what weakens or strengthens each belief, how one might respond when challenged, the physical location where it may be found, and how to integrate it into your practice.

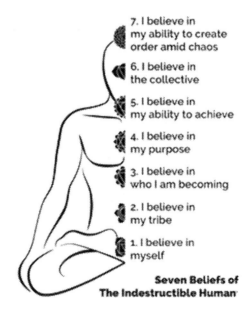

7. I believe in my ability to create order amid chaos

6. I believe in the collective

5. I believe in my ability to achieve

4. I believe in my purpose

3. I believe in who I am becoming

2. I believe in my tribe

1. I believe in myself

Seven Beliefs of The Indestructible Human

1. I believe in myself

This belief explained:

Belief in oneself is critical because regardless of *where* we are or *who* we are with, we are always with ourselves. From a psychological perspective, many mental health challenges are rooted in some aspect of what we believe *about* ourselves and at an even deeper level, whether we believe *in* ourselves.

What happens when this belief is weak:

The lack of belief in self can result in poor choices in relationships, work, and what we are willing to tolerate in general.

What happens when this belief is strong:

When we have, or develop, a strong belief in self, we can navigate the most challenging of situations. Without it, we will be limited in our ability to relate to others and our environment.

What weakens this belief:

This belief has connections to our most primitive needs encoded in our DNA from our most distant ancestors. When needs such as shelter, food, sleep, and basic human connection are threatened, this belief can be weakened as we try to survive. People or environments that threaten us will erode our ability to believe in ourselves just as a building built on sand won't be as secure as one built on bedrock. We must avoid or extricate ourselves from people and situations where our basic needs are threatened.

When challenged:

Should someone challenge your belief in self, you could counter with, "thank you for your input; I am looking out for myself, just as you are looking out for yourself. I hope we can eventually work together to help each other."

Ways to strengthen this belief:

Strengthening the fulfillment of our basic needs will create a safe space from which we can believe in ourselves. Beyond that, seeking mastery of life's basic needs through proper nutrition, vigorous physical activity, and supportive, loving relationships will create life conditions for belief in self to flourish.

The dark side of this belief:

The dark or unhealthy manifestation of this belief might be to only think of oneself, which is common in the most stressful circumstances. In this case, it might manifest as willingly sabotaging someone else to gain their resources, such as setting up a co-worker to fail.

Physical location:

While you may experience this belief in other areas of the body, this belief is most often found in the base of the spine. When this belief is stressed, it often manifests as tightness in the musculature of the lower back, hips, and lowest parts of the digestive tract and urogenital area, an instinctive way of protecting oneself, even if physical harm is not imminent. You can stimulate this belief with deep breathing and consciously relaxing the tension around the base of the spine.

Sample statements that reflect a strong belief in oneself:

"I believe in myself."
"I am strong."
"I am vibrant."
"I take care of myself."
"I am the protector of my body, mind, and spirit."

2. I believe in my tribe

This belief explained:

As young children, we rely on others for survival, based on bonds of love and trust. Once we begin to develop the ability to fend for ourselves, communicate, understand, and value these relationships with others, we form tribes. The earliest tribe most will experience is that of mother and child; beyond that, it will include other caregivers, grandparents, siblings, and other relatives. As we progress through childhood, we form new tribes that include friends, teammates, co-workers, etc.

These tribes, when healthy, are our earliest experiences of how to relate to others in the world and whether we feel accepted. In addition to the previous belief in oneself, this belief is the second most critical because we all require relationships as we progress in life. Without healthy tribes early in life, we form limiting beliefs around trusting others, or our belief that we can fit in and be accepted by others.

What happens when this belief is weak:

When the belief in one's tribe is weak, because we believe it to be so or because someone of importance has told us so, we can easily feel isolated. When we feel like we don't belong to a tribe as we progress through life (i.e., at work, at home, in a social group, or on a sports team) we often regress into having to rely on ourselves and not others, which is rarely sustainable. If coupled with a weak belief in self, it can be catastrophic for our mental health and ability to function appropriately in society.

What happens when this belief is strong:

When belief in one's tribe is strong, there is inoculation from the stresses in life. When we feel down, we expect our tribe will help. Complex challenges become more comfortable to take on, in part because we believe our tribe will assist with physical or moral support. When we face traumatic experiences, we are empowered when those around us help.

What weakens this belief:

If you participate in a tribe that is unhealthy or surround yourself with negative people, you will eventually suffer the consequences. It is often compared to being in a toxic environment, like a smoke-filled room. Being there for a brief time usually is not an issue, but constant, ongoing exposure will lead to complications eventually.

When challenged:

Should someone challenge your belief in your tribe, you could counter with, "thank you for your input; I believe in my tribe just as you believe in yours. I hope we can find common ground to collaborate and support each other's tribes."

Ways to strengthen this belief:

Surround yourself with positive people that believe in you and that you can believe in as well, allowing you to form healthy tribes. Consider the various tribes you have been part of in the past and how those tribes have been positive, negative, or neutral in your personal development. Then consider the tribes you currently participate in, including where you work, your family, your circle of friends, and so on. Spend less time with the people or tribes that don't serve to support your development, and more time with those that will support you and whom you can support in return. Also, consider the leader of these tribes to ensure he or she holds the good of the tribe at the highest level, rather than his or her gain.

The dark side of this belief:

The dark or unhealthy manifestation of this belief would be to insulate yourself so much within your tribe that you shut out the rest of the world. This insulation is where cults and gangs crawl in to take advantage of your desire to belong.

Physical location:

While you may experience this belief in other areas of the body, this belief is most often found deep in the abdomen, below the navel. When something doesn't feel right, you may have perturbations in this area that you refer to as a "gut feeling." You can stimulate this belief with deep belly breathing and conscious relaxation of the lower abdomen and back.

Sample statements that reflect a strong belief in one's tribe:

"I believe in my tribe."
"My tribe supports me."
"My tribe has my back."

3. I believe in who I am becoming

This belief explained:

This belief recognizes our ability to formulate our own identity, beyond the dependence on our tribe or others. This belief is detectable in teens when they begin to rebel against the family unit, in school, or early work experiences. This desire to create and then defend our identity is not about pure survival as with belief number one but about what we believe, what we stand for, as well as what we like or dislike. All humans, as their consciousness evolves, will develop ideas that they feel compelled to defend when they've aligned themselves with them. Belief in who you are becoming is positive when those ideas are constructive, such as someone who takes on the role of defender and stands up against a bully. Unfortunately, if the first two beliefs are vulnerable, we find ourselves in unhealthy tribes, regurgitating the same negative ideas that have gotten us to where we are.

What happens when this belief is weak:

When belief in who you are becoming is weak, you may create a weak identity, ripe for negative influences (i.e., gangs, toxic relationships, abuse, etc.) because it is easier to join than create.

What happens when this belief is strong:

When belief in who you are becoming is strong and positive, you seek out experiences that allow you to expand yourself, your knowledge, and find ways of sharing that with others. We must have faith that who we are becoming is an ever-improving version of ourselves, rather than a version of ourselves that is stagnant.

What weakens this belief:

The two greatest threats to the belief in who you are becoming are a weakness in beliefs one and two (a lack of belief in self and or tribe). When you hear people around you tell you what you *can't* do, rather than what you *can* do, those people are unlikely to support your healthy development.

When challenged:

Should someone challenge your belief in who you are becoming, you could counter with, "thank you for your input; I believe in the path I am taking. I hope you are as happy or happier with your path as I am with mine."

Ways to strengthen this belief:

Surround yourself with people that challenge you to be your best self, including friends that will call you out on your negative words or behaviors. As well, seek out work and other environments that value your individuality, as well as how you fit into the group.

The dark side of this belief:

The dark or unhealthy manifestation of this belief might include a sense of grandiosity or unrealistic sense of importance. The dark side of this belief may also manifest itself in violence or outbursts that are inappropriate or counterproductive to achieving your goals.

Physical location:

While you may experience this belief in other areas of the body, this belief is most often found in the upper abdomen, just below the arch of the ribcage. You can stimulate an elevation of self by merely finding that area of the upper abdomen, placing light pressure and lifting the rib cage slightly as you breathe in deeply. You are likely to experience an increase in confidence and clarity as a result.

Sample statements that reflect a strong belief in who you are becoming:

"I believe in who I am becoming."
"I am perfect as I am and getting better every day."
"I can overcome any challenge because of who I am."
"I am becoming the best version of myself every day."

4. I believe in my purpose

This belief explained:

As we continue to mature, there is an understanding that while we seek to create and protect our identity, we also understand the value in working hard. Not just for immediate reward, but for a reward that may be further in the future (i.e., a big promotion or retirement) or after death (i.e., heaven or reincarnation). This belief recognizes long-term relationships and goals that require an ongoing effort, even when times are tough. Having a clear and strong purpose can help fight against depression and anxiety because short-term setbacks (real or imagined) are less important when in perspective with the larger goal.

What happens when this belief is weak:

When belief in purpose is weak or non-existent, there is a much higher risk for despondency, depression, and meaninglessness. Some people never set big goals, because they prefer to play safe and small.

What happens when this belief is strong:

When belief in purpose is strong, we can push through challenging times, because there our purpose is like a light guiding us through dark times. For some, this may be a belief in a higher power or universal consciousness, or afterlife. Regardless of anyone's individual religious or cultural teachings, we all have longer-term goals, either internal (i.e., weight loss goal, intellectual goal, etc.) or external (i.e., being present at a child or grandchild's wedding, finishing a postgraduate degree, etc.).

What weakens this belief:

Having a poorly defined purpose or allowing others to question that purpose will undermine this belief. This belief must, in some ways, be impervious to challenge.

When challenged:

Should someone challenge your belief in your purpose, you could counter with, "thank you for your input; this is the purpose I've chosen. I hope you choose a purpose as equally inspiring for you as this is for me."

Ways to strengthen this belief:

As you define your purpose, spend time challenging it yourself to determine its imperviousness. The purpose must be big enough that there are multiple ways to achieve it, even in the face of the most significant adversity. For example, rather than have the purpose of being the best Mount Everest summiteer in the world, you might choose a purpose of being the best mountaineer *you* can be. This broader purpose centers the goal on you, rather than create a dependence on a comparison with others that you have little control over.

The dark side of this belief:

The dark or unhealthy manifestation of this belief might include believing your purpose is more important than another person's purpose. We must respect the purpose of others as we would expect them to respect ours.

Physical location:

While you may experience this belief in other areas of the body, this belief is most often found just above the level of the heart in the center of the upper chest. You can stimulate strength of purpose by placing one hand on the upper chest and breathing deeply.

Sample statements that reflect a strong belief in purpose:

"I believe in my purpose."
"My purpose grants me strength."
"Come what may, my purpose will see me through"

5. I believe in my ability to achieve

This belief explained:

This belief is about achievement, strategy, and the pragmatism required to succeed with even the most complex goals. In some ways, this is a more mature version of belief number three, ("I believe in who I am becoming"). While belief number three is about what you are becoming as an individual, belief number four is about how you can apply that strategically to a goal that may (or may not) include other people.

What happens when this belief is weak:

When your belief in your ability to achieve is weak, you will feel mired in doubt. You will doubt your ability to strategize about how to achieve your goals, and even if you have the right strategy, you will doubt your ability to execute it successfully.

What happens when this belief is strong:

With a belief in yourself, your tribe, your identity, your higher purpose, and a belief in your ability to achieve, it will seem there is almost nothing that can stand in your way.

What weakens this belief:

Like the previous belief, a weak belief in your ability to achieve will manifest as rarely taking risks, playing safe in most aspects of life, including relationships, career, and self-development.

When challenged:

Should someone challenge your belief in your ability to achieve, you could counter with, "thank you for your input; these are the goals I have set. I hope you have equally inspiring goals; maybe we can help each other achieve our respective goals."

Ways to strengthen this belief:

To strengthen your belief in your ability to achieve, build up your wins. Start with easier, smaller goals, and as you achieve these, your confidence will grow, and even goals that may have seemed impossible before will become achievable.

The dark side of this belief:

The dark or unhealthy manifestation of this belief would be to make achievement the most important thing, regardless of the rules or who may be hurt in the process. The belief may also manifest too logically and without consideration of the "human" costs of achieving, such as stress, burnout, or personal loss of relationships as collateral damage.

Physical location:

While you may experience this belief in other areas of the body, this belief is primarily found in the throat, often associated with our ability to speak up or share our commitment with others through the spoken word. You can stimulate this belief by expressing yourself confidently through speech or song.

Sample statements that reflect a strong belief in one's ability to achieve:

"I believe in my ability to achieve."
"I believe in strong competition."
"I believe I can win in any circumstances."

6. I believe in the collective

This belief explained:

This belief is about embracing the truth that together, with all the diversity we represent, we can be better together. This belief may mean defending the weak, holding those accountable that have done wrong, and speaking up on behalf of those that have not been heard.

What happens when this belief is weak:

When belief in the collective is weak, we either focus too much on ourselves in isolation, or we focus too much on the domination of one group over another, rather than seeking ways for all to prosper.

What happens when this belief is strong:

When belief in the collective is strong and healthy, you respond to the needs of others, even if there is no gain for yourself as an individual.

What weakens this belief:

Belief in the collective is weaker when we isolate ourselves or identify with only one group, to the exclusion of others.

When challenged:

Should someone challenge your belief in the collective, you could counter with, "thank you for your input; I see value in you just as I see value in all others. I hope you can see that value as well."

Ways to strengthen this belief:

To strengthen your belief in the collective, consistently look for value in individuals and groups, rather than looking for differences and flaws. Also, see the common ground we hold with others, whether it is seeking happiness, love, or safety. One key question to ask is, "What would I want if I was in their position?"

The dark side of this belief:

The dark or unhealthy manifestation of this belief would be to become paralyzed by trying to serve everyone, protect those that don't need protecting, or ignore individual needs in the false belief that only the group matters.

Physical location:

While you may experience this belief in other areas of the body, this belief is most often found between, and slightly above the eyebrows. This area referred to by some as your "third-eye." You can stimulate this belief by putting pressure or massaging the space between, and slightly above the eyebrows.

Sample statements that reflect a strong belief in the collective:

"I believe in the collective."
"The collective is made stronger by its diversity."
"I believe in our strength together."
"Our differences make us stronger."

7. I believe in my ability to create order amid chaos

This belief explained:

In Gravesian terms, this is a second-tier belief. That means that it integrates and transcends all other beliefs. That does not make it inherently better than the other beliefs any more than a sweater is better than its yarn. They are the same and, therefore, inextricable. While the whole appears to be more than the sum of its parts, it is essential to remember that it doesn't exist without these individual parts.

What happens when this belief is weak:

When your belief in your ability to create order amid chaos is weak, you will be overwhelmed by the chaos or lose your way.

What happens when this belief is strong:

When this belief is strong, you don't shy away from chaos; you move towards it. Much like a firefighter may run into a burning building, you will not fail in the face of adversity because you believe in your ability to create order.

What weakens this belief:

Too much chaos, over too long a period, will overwhelm anyone eventually. While you needn't be afraid of chaos, you should be self-aware enough to know if you have the resources to delve into the chaos ahead. If not, seeking assistance would be beneficial.

When challenged:

Should someone challenge your belief in your ability to create order amid chaos, you could counter with, "thank you for your input; I understand this situation is challenging. I am endeavoring to find the order within and beyond the chaos."

Ways to strengthen this belief:

As with all beliefs, enough sleep, proper nutrition, an outlet for frustration, etc. are essential to cultivating strength. In this case, focus on your ability rather than on the chaos, for the chaos is out of your direct control.

The dark side of this belief:

The dark or unhealthy manifestation of this belief would be to look for or create chaos so that you can be the hero that solves it. There is a risk that by relying on your desire to address the challenge you're facing, you may disregard others that may want to help or have the resources you need, thereby alienating them unintentionally.

Physical location:

While you may experience this belief in other areas of the body, this belief is most often found at the top, or crown, of your head. You can stimulate this with physical inversions (temporarily putting your head lower than your heart, such as a "downward dog" pose, headstand, handstand, or simply hanging your head and shoulders off a bedside).

Sample statements that reflect a strong belief in my ability to create order amid chaos:

"I believe in my ability to create order amid chaos."
"I each chaos for breakfast."
"Every chaotic challenge strengthens my resolve."

Putting it all together

Amongst other methods of conditioning the subconscious mind, the acknowledgment of these beliefs can, and will, begin the process of shifting your belief systems to be better aligned with who you want to become, regardless of who you have been.

While you can work on each belief one at a time or separately, here is a sample of what you can create, capturing all seven beliefs in one entrainment:

> *"I believe in myself and my tribe. I believe in who I am becoming, and I believe in my higher purpose. I believe in my ability to achieve what I set out to, and I believe in the value of all others. Most of all, I believe in my ability to see, find, and create order as I experience the world."*

I encourage you to put effort towards upgrading your beliefs consciously. The Seven Beliefs of The Indestructible Human may be your starting point, but you can examine and improve or replace any belief you have. When you begin to do this work, remember that this is a gradual process that takes time, dedication, and patience. It is a subtle process that works to gently over-write limiting beliefs and replacing them with empowering beliefs.

Depending on the length of your belief entrainment (see "How to introduce new or improved beliefs," earlier in this chapter), it will take approximately three to thirty minutes to listen to, providing a mild but effective reminder to your subconscious that you have empowering beliefs. Your belief entrainment can be used in conjunction with other practices including meditation and other activities to increase self-awareness and mindfulness.

It's been said that change is inevitable, and that is true. It is up to you to take back control of that change so that you can be in the driver's seat, deciding where to go, rather than a passenger in life, going places you never intended.

I wish you well on your journey of self-discovery and challenge you to make the world a better place, starting with yourself. May you adapt and overcome all obstacles you face, for regardless of your physical body, you are an Indestructible Human with an indestructible spirit.

Acknowledgements: I acknowledge and deeply appreciate all the teachers I have learned from, past or present, living or deceased, directly or indirectly, (listed alphabetically): Richard Bandler, Don Beck, Chris Cowan, Erik Erikson, Milton H. Erickson, Clare W. Graves, John Grinder, Daniel Q. Marisi, Abraham Maslow, Elizabeth Payea-Butler, Anthony Robbins, and Derrick Sweet.

Rod Macdonald, B.Ed., Certified Coach Practitioner, Certified Master Coach Practitioner, Licensed Master Practitioner of Neuro-Linguistic Programming

CEO Certified Coaches Federation®, Founder of Indestructible Human® Coaching

With over thirty years' experience in the field of wellness and self-improvement, Rod is a leading authority on personal and professional change. As a leader, Rod has helped numerous organizations to be their best both big and small, including not-for-profit national organizations and for-profit international companies. As a speaker, coach, and author, he has influenced hundreds of thousands of people to positively transform their lives and the lives of those around them, delivering his message on stages at events in the United States, Australia, New Zealand, China, and across Canada. In Rod's opinion, coaching is the single most powerful support mechanism an individual or organization can employ to be successful. Rod is a semi-retired multisport athlete, four-time Ironman competitor, cross-Canada cyclist, former competitive rower, 200-hour RYT yogi, as well as a proud husband, and father.

Connect with Rod:
www.certifiedcoachesfederation.com
www.facebook.com/certifiedcoachesfederation/
www.instagram.com/certifiedcoachesfederation/
www.linkedin.com/groups/157066
www.twitter.com/certifiedcoach

www.youtube.com/certifiedcoach
rod@certifedcoachesfederation.com

www.indestructiblehuman.com
rod@indestructiblehuman.com
www.facebook.com/indestructiblehuman
www.instagram.com/indestructible.human/
www.linkedin.com/company/indestructiblehuman
www.linkedin.com/in/macdonaldrod/
www.twitter.com/IndstrctblHmn
www.youtube.com/channel/UCAdgZmLgxFYx8TK6mRfYmgQ?

Less is Never More

by Blake Miles

E ach and every day of our lives we are led to believe that less is more. If we desire a healthier life, we are instructed to eat less; when we seek more wealth, we are advised to spend less; when we strive to have more time in our lives, we are conditioned to believe that the answer is to do less. We even treat ourselves with less respect in an effort to be more popular! We live every day with the understanding that acquiring, desiring, and even aspiring to less is somehow the path to bringing more into our lives. But what if the opposite were true...? What if less was, in fact, not more? Imagine a world where the key to greater health was not to decrease our food intake but to increase beneficial wellness practices, like physical activity and a positive mental attitude. Picture a society where the path to wealth was not paved with coupons and corner cutting, but with aggressive income building and intelligent investment. Just think of the lives we might be leading if we learned to make the most of the time we have and to use that time to transform into the best version of ourselves, even if it meant that other people would be critical of us! Obviously, that is exactly what we should be doing in order to lead rewarding, fulfilling, and abundant lives. So, why do we insist upon doing the absolute, complete, and thorough opposite?

Let's start by identifying why we choose to believe that less is somehow more in the first place. The truth is frighteningly simple: Less is simply easier and more comfortable. You see, having more, achieving more and even being more requires more work. Not only is there more tangible output - physical, mental, emotional - required in becoming our best self, but we also have to exert the effort required to overcome one of our worst fears: failure. A great many of us cling to the belief that the best way to sidestep failure, and all the shame, humiliation, and criticism that we expect to come with it, is to simply do nothing. If you don't attempt something, it's not very likely that you'll fail at it, right? Such is how so many of us lead our lives every day, claiming to want more, declaring that we deserve better, yet doing nothing differently and always looking for the most effective way to do, be, and achieve less.

For most of us, this counterproductive approach to life and the attitude that spawns it are the result of conditioning, sometimes started in early childhood, wherein we are taught not only to accept, but actually embrace, the scarcity mindset. That conditioning follows us throughout our life. We are surrounded by the delusion of scarcity and encounter it every day because it is a ruthlessly efficient tool for keeping us in control. Grant Cardone, in his bestseller "The 10X Rule", says "The idea that one would only have enough to be "comfortable or "adequately satisfied" is a concept that has been sold - by the educational system, the media, and politicians - to convince an entire population of people to settle instead of strive for abundance". We are conditioned to believe that either we shouldn't want more, we don't deserve to have more or that we are incapable of securing the means or performing the tasks necessary to procuring more in our lives. Therefore, we are left assuming that abundance is out of our reach and that it is, in fact, futile, even dangerous, for us to pursue it. We are told to be happy with what we've got, to count our blessings, to accept our lot in life. Further, we are warned that if we don't, we will encounter failure and loss, so we are better off - and safer - just taking what we can get. So, we avoid investing our money personally, instead entrusting our wealth to strangers and tolerating minuscule rates of return because the bank influences us with the threat of fluctuating interest and volatility. We follow a diet trend or buy into a dangerous health gimmick because the people selling these products influence us with the threat of failure and the guarantee that we couldn't do it on our own. We ignore and dismiss our goals and dreams, because everyone from our employer to our own family shrouds us with negativity, convincing us that we will never achieve our dreams - an argument based exclusively on their inability to do so. Some people believe they are helping you by preventing you from making the same mistake they did. Even sadder, many simply don't want you to succeed where they failed and take some twisted and pathetic solace in watching you give up on your dreams. Such is the sad state so many of us find ourselves in every day, leading the life we've been told to live and accepting our fate because we fear the consequences of pursuing our passion. We are so well controlled that we seldom, if ever, give a moment's thought to the consequences of ignoring our passion and living the rest of our lives without ever fulfilling any of our dreams!

So, how do we avoid living in this scarcity-based mindset and teach ourselves to believe in our own value, so that we might create the best version of ourselves possible, and share our gift with the world? The best, and most authentic, way that I can answer that question is to share my own experience with you. You will see the scarcity mindset and the "less is more" doctrine come into play as I tell you the story of my journey into, and out of, adversity. It began when the economic downturn of 2008 guided me to a low paying warehouse job, which I was quite fortunate to secure, given the economic climate of the time. I was overqualified for the job, which my manager recognized. As such, I was offered numerous opportunities to prove myself and to advance more rapidly. I chose to ignore these opportunities because of pressure from my co-workers, who resented the special treatment I seemed to be receiving. I turned my back on the potential to grow and succeed because I wanted to fit in with the crowd. I lost a great deal in my effort to maintain my standing amidst the status quo. While I allowed myself to lose opportunities, I did manage to gain one thing - weight. Poor eating and a sedentary lifestyle, at home and on the job, lead to me gaining over one-hundred pounds in less than two years.

It was at this time that we were taken by surprise with the news that we were to become grandparents. The otherwise joyful revelation was a mixed blessing for us since this development in our lives brought with it many challenges for which we were ill-prepared. The paramount of these was the fact that my daughter was still in high school when this happened, and she was building a promising future that my wife and I were not about to see her give up. My wife was earning significantly more than I was, so it made sense that I should be the one to leave my position and help raise our grandchild. Additionally, of course, as a result of the extra hundred pounds I was hauling around, I was unable to walk up a flight of stairs without pausing to catch my breath, and I had just been diagnosed with chronic hypertension. I was terrified at the prospect of attempting to keep up with the demands of a baby and, eventually, a toddler. To round it out, we quickly began to experience the financial setbacks of our circumstances. All of this escalated to create formidable tension and animosity in our home. Something had to change soon or things in our family were going to quickly unravel.

As I mentioned at the outset, the scarcity-driven, less is more mindset is conditioned human nature. As such, I immediately turned to that way of thinking to address my challenges at the time. I employed calorie restriction in my attempt to lose weight, I became even more sedentary as a result of hypertension induced headaches, and I made feeble attempts to cut corners financially but failed to actually keep track of our budget. I was reactive instead of proactive, negative instead of positive and I plodded on every day mistaking less for more. I had not yet built up the resilience I required to help me deal with the potential challenges of life, like those I was now facing.

I decided to build that resilience with a little research. I started by reading up on how to get out of debt, wherein I discovered my first mentor, and my reclamation began to take shape. I read an article by Warren Buffet in which he spoke about the stock market, saying that it was wise to be "fearful when others are greedy and greedy when others are fearful." He was reflecting upon the tendency that human beings have to make emotional and irrational decisions, spending in good times and hoarding in the bad. He had just finished doing the literal opposite, investing deeply in the heart of the economic downturn, while many people panicked and sold off their stocks.

I realized that the stock market was not the only place that this human tendency caused turmoil and ruin. It became very clear to me that this was the less is more stigma at its apex. People investing because everyone else was doing it, then losing everything because they panicked when the price of the stock dropped suddenly. A lack of knowledge and experience, combined with fear and unwillingness to admit that weakness, caused them to follow bad advice and make irrational decisions about their money. I was doing the exact same thing in my life, my home, and my family. I wasn't prepared to admit my lack of knowledge, to embrace my weakness, or to learn what I needed to know in order to make better choices in my life. That was the day I discovered that less is never more and began the journey that would lead me to a new mindset that changed everything.

I began by repairing our financial situation because that was the area in which I was currently doing my research. I had already created a very efficient budgeting program that we were following very faithfully in our home. It stretched our family income as far as it would go and identified areas where we could eliminate unnecessary spending to create a weekly surplus. Unfortunately, that's where the momentum ended. By the end of the month, most of the weekly surplus was gone. The reason for this was, of course, because less is never more - saving money is a potentially useful tool, but only if it is used to create income. We were simply saving, which is merely the act of redistributing current income, so we were only creating the illusion of growth. There were a few different ways in which we could have supplemented our income, but the most practical for our family at the time was to invest our weekly surplus to generate a return on our money. I did not invest in bank directed funds, which promised low rates of return in exchange for protection from volatility. I put our money directly into equities, using reliable company research to choose good, solid stocks in which to invest. I had discovered, through my research, that volatility is not an enemy when you are investing and is something to be understood rather than feared. That's the sort of thing the banks and financial advisors don't want you to realize when you're investing your hard-earned dollars. The want you to live in scarcity and fear. They don't want you to realize that less is never more!

While our financial plan was gaining momentum, I turned my attention to my health. I had already begun using portion reduction to restrict my caloric intake. Unfortunately, it had little effect on my weight, apart from making me feel hungry and tired. The reason for this was, of course, because less is never more - reducing calories and restricting food is not a sustainable method to help you to lose weight and get fit and healthy. Caloric deficit is an important factor in weight loss, but adding physical activity allowed me to achieve that deficit without starving myself or feeling deprived. By incorporating regular daily activity, my eating habits became a matter of fueling that activity, so I could eat more of the right foods and feel satisfied as well as fit and energetic! I personally chose to engage in fun and interactive physical activities that gently raised my heart rate. Two of my favorites were lifting weights and walking with my wife. Resistance training allowed me to visibly track my progress and achievement and journal ongoing results. Walking with my wife provided effective fat burning without the boredom of exercise. My wife has always had a pretty strong competitive streak and walking with her soon turned into a contest for speed, time, and distance, whether I liked it or not. We got so caught up in beating our best times or surpassing each other for distance traveled that I didn't even think about the aerobic effect. Next thing I knew, it was time to buy new clothes because the ones I was wearing were becoming way too baggy on me! My most effective results came from doing things I enjoyed and repeating those things consistently. I didn't worry about what I should be doing - I focused on the things I enjoyed doing. This resulted in me developing a more positive attitude toward everything in my life. Nowadays my favorite activity is trying to keep up with my kids and grandkids when they play one of their dance-based video games. I burn a lot of calories bringing joy to my offspring, who delight in laughing at my dancing style (or lack thereof)! The key is to create a lifestyle that you can sustain every day, doing the things you love. That's the sort of thing the people trying to sell you fad diets and quick fix programs don't want you to realize when you're creating your perfect wellness ritual. They too want you to live in scarcity and fear. They don't want you to realize that less is never more!

The next thing that was revealed to me was the power of progression and compounding. This amazing phenomenon is one of the best examples of how more is more, and it is applicable to many aspects of our lives! Each day I would progress a little more in my weight loss and fitness efforts - a few more reps, a bit heavier weight, an extra five minutes walking or walking faster - and each day I would see quicker and more profound results. The same effect appeared with our financial growth, through compounding, allowing just a little investment at a time to grow steadily into sizable results. Soon, I began to apply the power of progression to everything in my life. If I was struggling with something, I applied myself to it a little every day until I was succeeding. Once I was succeeding, I continued to put in a little extra effort each day until I was excelling. Then I would keep building on my success, by constantly improving in whatever way was appropriate, until I had achieved a level of success that left me feeling satisfied and abundant and brought joy and prosperity to my family. You always need to do more, but it doesn't have to be an impossible amount of more. That's the sort of thing small minded people who are struggling with adversity in their own lives don't want you to realize when you're trying to become the best version of yourself by growing a little every day. The want you to live in scarcity and fear. They don't want you to realize that less is never more!

All of this brought me around to the most profound realization of all - that the greatest example of growth through progression is demonstrated by the accumulation of knowledge. We all know that knowledge is power, but not everyone realizes why. It's because less is never more, and less knowledge may be the greatest plight that our society faces today. By staying informed, educated, and enlightened, through reputable sources of reliable information, we can take possession of the single most powerful tool for personal growth and development available. Before becoming informed, I fell for every gimmick in the book. I opened myself up to scarcity, fear, and indolence. That allowed the world to make me believe that less is more, and to take advantage of me, and it will do the same to anyone who doesn't keep themselves properly informed. Once I sought out the knowledge to formulate my actions, I was able to create meaningful transformation in my life and open the door to limitless abundance and fulfillment!

Before long, the people around me began to reach out and ask me how I had accomplished this transformation in my life. Many of them were the same naysayers who had tried to discourage me months earlier. I quickly realized that the next logical progression for me would be to help others to overcome their adversities by showing them how to embrace the Less is Never More mindset. One of the first people that I mentored told me that their greatest obstacle was the belief that it was too late for them to change and that they were overcome with a sense of futility every day. I asked them to consider the result if they had made just a small amount of progress on each of those days that they had opted not to take action and, after making a few quick calculations in their head, they were moved to tears when they realized the opportunity they had missed. After collecting themselves, they asked me, in a somber tone, if it was still too late and, at that moment, I knew what my ultimate purpose was, and what I would endeavor to teach people from that day forward. I shook my head adamantly, and proudly declared: "It's Never Too Late."

After establishing my company, N2L (Never 2 Late) Transformations, I set about encapsulating the Less is Never More mindset into a process that people could follow to guide them to success in any undertaking. The result was "Less is Never More - Mindsets and Habits for Abundant Transformation," my signature program. It consists of seven rules, combined with three daily rituals to follow, which will help you put those rules to work in your life. The outcome is an ongoing progression, leading to the achievement of your goals, the fulfillment of your dreams, and the attainment of your desired life.

RULE #1: KNOW YOUR WHY

Let's get the most important reality out on the table right off the bat. You will not stick to your goals unless you start by knowing *why* you want to achieve them. When we embark on a goal, large or small, the first thing we usually ask ourselves is *what* or *how*. But the answers to these questions take us in the wrong direction in a number of ways. Firstly, asking *what* and *how* invites a lot of outside input, much of it unsolicited and unhelpful, including misinformation, manipulation, and ridicule. By first asking *why*, we solidify our goal with a solid purpose, which will shield us from being misled or discouraged. Secondly, *what* and *how* put us on a path toward a final destination. The aim here is not to get from Point A to Point B, but to create a new lifestyle for ourselves that will fulfill our desire for the rest of our existence. Understanding *why* you are trying to create that lifestyle will inspire constant daily actions to maintain it. Thirdly, it will prevent us from derailing ourselves in our efforts, because knowing *why* you want to accomplish something is more motivating and inspiring than being sure that you are doing it the right way!

RULE #2: MAKE INTELLIGENT CHOICES

Once you establish your *why*, you can properly explore your *what* and *how*. That means conducting sensible research and seeking out the most qualified people and trusted resources to help you make your choices about your transformation. Don't forget that your methods should also suit your desires and preferences, otherwise they won't be sustainable. Make your passion and joy part of your research. At all points along the way, take an intelligent approach and don't allow scarcity and doubt to cloud your judgment or steer you into the path of misinformation. Remember your *why* throughout the process and use it to keep you focused on the sustainable lifestyle you will soon enjoy. This will prevent you from adapting the "endgame" approach that will make you susceptible to scams that promise shortcut methods to quick results.

Your intelligent strategy will keep you on course toward a permanent lifestyle change

RULE #3: SET YOUR MIND TO IT

Most people approach a life transformation with a should do approach, meaning they intend on trying to accomplish their objective. The truth is that when we say we will try something; we are expressing our expectation to have it fail. It's as though we are saying: "I don't expect this to work, but I will give it a shot anyway." It's a powerful message we send to our brain, like drawing up a contract with ourselves, then slapping an escape clause into it. The can-do approach really isn't any better, as we are just trying to talk ourselves into seeing it through. Our assertion that we can is nothing more than a dash of upbeat talk sprinkled onto a plateful of good intentions. It does not create a new environment in which we have now suddenly ensured our success. You must have a "will-do" mindset, which is achieved by focusing on where you are headed, as opposed to where you want to start, focusing on your *why* while applying your *how*. That mindset will stay with you every day, creating new attitudes and habits that will create a sustained and progressive change that will endure throughout your life!

RULE #4: TAP INTO WHAT DRIVES YOU

You need to figure out what moves and enthuses you so that you can build a process that will keep you engaged, motivated, and inspired. Too often we blindly adopt someone else's blueprint for success and expect it to work for us. But the key to creating our own transformation is not achieving someone else's success, it is the result of designing the lifestyle that inspires and excites us. If you want to live a life that is filled with certain activities and habits, in which you look and feel a certain way and participate in and achieve certain things, then why would you attempt to create that life by following someone else's steps, in an opposing direction, doing opposite things, participating in contrary activities, leading to a different outcome? It doesn't make much sense, does it? Yet, so many of us do exactly that, then wonder why we lose interest so quickly. The first step in achieving the lifestyle you desire is to start living it! From day one, begin living that life as much as you can, then build on that momentum, progress a little each day, and keep being that person, doing those things and living that life until it becomes second nature and, eventually, reality!

RULE #5: TAKE OWNERSHIP OF YOUR LIFE

As I discovered, the power to transform our lives is within us - it is not the responsibility of anyone else, nor does anyone else have the power to transform us. We can, and should, seek help from nurturing people that create a support circle for us, but it is very counterproductive to cling to the belief that anyone else owes us anything or that they would come good on that debt even if they did. Many people waste precious hours blaming others for their struggles. I have always believed that the day you can prove, without a doubt, that all your problems are caused by someone else is the day you have relinquished all control over your happiness. If someone else truly holds the power to guide the events and decisions of your life, then they also hold the power to prevent you from ever knowing true joy or satisfaction. Once you can embrace that you are responsible for your struggles, you can become responsible for your empowerment and truly start to transform your life!

RULE #6: WORK WITH A MENTOR

Once you accept the responsibility for creating lasting change in your life, you will be able to identify the people that can truly help you in your transformation. Surround yourself with like-minded, nurturing people who can recognize your motivation and desire for change. Study the words, actions, and lives of those who are already living the life that you seek. Don't copy their processes, but emulate their mindset and attitude, and absorb their positive energy into your own life. Reach out to a coach who has overcome struggle and adversity in their own lives and allow them to join you in your exploration of a new and abundant lifestyle. It's never too late and you never have to face this alone!

RULE #7: GET STARTED

With all of this in place, you can turn your attention to *when*, and *when* is now. Don't waste an excessive amount of time planning. Establish your *why*, formulate your *how*, then get on with it! Less is never more, and that applies exponentially to taking action: Less action will never equal more results. Remember that the purpose of establishing *why* and *how* is simply to help your transformation remain sustainable, but to put that to work you have to get going on the actual development of your new life. It only takes a small step every day, but you must take the step, so that you can take two steps the next day, and so on, until you have achieved your objectives. "You don't have to be great to get started, but you have to get started to be great." -Zig Ziglar

To remember these seven rules, just remember the acronym **W.I.S.D.O.M.S.**:

Know your **Why**,

Make **Intelligent** Choices,

Set your mind to it,

Tap into what **Drives** you,

Take **Ownership**,

Work with a **Mentor**,

Get **Started**!

The three daily rituals that will help you to integrate these rules into your life are very simple and quick to perform. Five to ten minutes in the morning should be sufficient. As you grow, you may choose to spend more time on these to further empower your transformation. For now, find a quiet place, close your eyes, and meditate on these three things, and speak them aloud. You may also choose to write down a record of them in a daily journal.

RITUAL 1: GRATITUDE

The scarcity mentality would have us believe that gratitude means considering yourself lucky for what you have and not wanting more. The Less is Never More mindset shows us that gratitude is an assessment of what we already have in our lives, so we don't waste time desiring those things we have achieved. By taking an honest and thorough inventory of what we have, we will know precisely what to invite into our lives.

RITUAL 2: AFFIRMATION

The scarcity mentality would have us believe that affirmation is the act of telling ourselves that we are nice and that we deserve good things in life. The Less is Never More mindset shows us that affirmation is positive self-talk that reminds us of our plans and purpose. By affirming our mission and reminding ourselves of the qualities we possess to achieve that mission, we empower ourselves to invite exactly the right tools into our lives that will see our mission realized.

RITUAL 3: INVITATION

The scarcity mentality encourages us to invite objects and achievements directly into our life. The Less is Never More mindset expands our viewpoint to see the greater value of things like strength, health, freedom, time, focus, wisdom, friendship, courage, and forgiveness. By inviting these powers into our lives each day, we achieve the state of mind needed to acquire those things that will create the life of our dreams.

Start each day with these three rituals. It may feel strange when you start - I used to wake up really early, to ensure that nobody caught me doing them! Now I do them early in the morning because I find it so exhilarating to start my day by reflecting on my gratitude, affirming my strength, and inviting wisdom and abundance into my life! Don't underestimate the power of these rituals. Performing them each day, and using them to remind yourself of your *why*, re-align your mindset, explore what drives you, and empower yourself to take control of your life, will keep you on the path to your transformation and the life you desire!

Our existence is linear, but our lives are a series of events that cycle along that line. We must ensure that those events unfold in a cycle of positive action, growth, and abundance. Otherwise, we fall victim to mayhem, get swept up in turmoil and become a slave to adversity. Our desires become a challenge from outside of ourselves, demanding us to give an uninspired response and try to fulfill them through a set of incoherent steps. Eventually, we begin to believe the lies around us, because it affords us an explanation for *why* and *how* we have allowed our lives to get so far out of our own control! By applying the Less is Never More mindset, positive actions compound upon one another to create growth in our lives. We recognize something good in our lives, we identify the powers that we have at our disposal to nurture that thing, then invite more of those powers into our daily routine. In this way, everything we desire to achieve becomes an invitation from within ourselves, awaiting an enthusiastic response through an inspired plan of action. Through this chain of events, sustainability and ongoing inspiration are ensured and success is guaranteed.

It is my sincere hope that embracing this mindset, by putting these seven rules and three rituals to work in your life, will create the cycle of positivity and abundance that you've always dreamed of. Be patient with yourself, and the process, as you begin today. Remember that it is never too late to create positive change in your life. It's also never too soon to get started on that fresh mindset. As you go to bed this evening, in fact, I invite you to reflect on how good it is just to be alive, then build on that abundance when you wake up tomorrow, and for every day thereafter.

Blake Miles Certified Coach Practitioner, Certified Master Coach Practitioner

Freedom Coach, Founder of N2L Transformations®

Blake is a leading authority on creating abundance out of adversity. Drawing from his own life experiences, along with training and certification in numerous coaching and wellness practices, he helps people to embrace their deepest desires and transform their goals into reality. Blake is also an accomplished confidence and elocution coach, having taught those disciplines for many years in his previous role as a performing arts teacher. He has spoken and performed in venues across Canada, including a prestigious two-year tenure as Guest Master of Performing Arts Studies at the Royal Conservatory of Music. A proud husband, father and grandfather, Blake now fills his hours inspiring people to go for their dreams and live the most fulfilling life possible, when he's not hanging out with his two beloved grand kids.

Connect with Blake:
www.n2lblake.com
lifecoach@n2lblake.com
905-781-1584
www.facebook.com/blake.miles.925
www.instagram.com/n2l_ufc/
www.twitter.com/N2LCoach
www.linkedin.com/in/blake-miles-40879129/
www.youtube.com/channel/UCjEqFR8xruiw65_kSd2KNUw

Values-Based Parenting

by Sandra Kosor

As far back as I can remember, I have always seen myself becoming a mother. Like many little girls growing up, role-playing with dolls and my Easy-Bake Oven, and the imagination of becoming what I saw my own mother do was part of my childhood. I haven't linked it to anything specific that happened to me, but the desire to nurture, protect, love, and raise children was always strong within me.

My life has been blessed with rich layers of perspective on parenting; however, I am not in any way a parenting expert. Similar to the approach I've taken to most things in my life, I strive to be an enlightened person and believe in spiritual purpose, and things happen for a reason, and that each of us came into this life with our own unique gifts and talents meant to be discovered and shared. I also believe in the effectiveness of values-based parenting.

As our children grow and change, I have been very happy to grow right along with them. My evolution as a parent and a human being is rooted in learning, mind-wellness, and the degree to which I understand and honor my values. Whether they are values I was raised with or those that have developed through life influences, values have been essential to my life's journey and have framed my life as a mother.

I've never taken for granted what it takes to develop and maintain meaningful relationships with any child. Like anything worthwhile and valuable, it takes an investment of time and attention on ourselves, and on our kids. It is never too late or too early to start. Relationships with our children change and mature with the ebb and flow of what happens in our life, and our words and actions have a powerful impact on what shapes them through those times. The first step is being clear on what my values are, what is important to me. Then, making a constant, mindful effort to align my priorities and actions to those values.

In today's world, taking time to unhitch from all the tech to reflect on your values, what you stand for, and what really matters will help you not only reaffirm and be mindful of your values, but it will also help you see if you are doing anything, or planning to do anything that may be in conflict with the answers to those questions.

I have an insightful collection of memories that capture the joyful rewarding moments as a parent, as well as stumbles and mistakes I made throughout my twenty-six years as a mother. When I take the time to reflect, I can identify the patterns of behavior and decision-making that were either aligned or misaligned with my values.

Values-based parenting relies on us doing regular maintenance on our mind-wellness through the process of keeping self-care areas in practice; understanding ourselves and being self-aware, having the ability to see and understand other's perspective, being self-assured, and showing genuine humility. These self-care practices frame values-based parenting and as we work to develop them, they in turn keep what is important to us at the forefront as we navigate the parenting journey and understand the impact of our actions on our children.

The unexpected thing was, the spin-off for me in working through these practice areas, I also gained insights into the complexities of my relationship with my own parents. Being the child and seeing the importance of these the self-care practice areas helped me understand even more so the impact on our children when these things are not understood or ignored.

PARENT AND CHILD

I was adopted as an infant in the 1960s and raised by my mother and father, who were married in the late 1950s. After a long engagement allowing them to save for a down payment for their home, they started their life together and registered to adopt. They brought me into their life and two years later, a second child for them and sister for me. My parents have aged into their eighties now, and they are still married and living in the same house, the childhood home I grew up in.

Typical of that era, my father was the sole breadwinner and worked his entire career with one company from the time he was in high school until he retired. My mother had to leave her job as a bookkeeper to stay home full time to raise us. She dedicated her life to our family of four, taking care of my father, and keeping our home in order. I have never thought of her as anyone other than my mother. Ever. I loved her very much as I grew up and I appreciate that she taught me many things continue to resonate with me.

My father was there for everything I did growing up. He called me "princess" for years and years, and our bond felt strong enough to last through anything. I carry a lifetime full of memories that are examples of how I felt loved and as secure as any child could or would want to feel.

Conservative family values were at the core of our home, and through the years, the influence my parents had with me to please them was unwavering. All the conservative clichés were my playbook for growing up and in place to ensure a harmonious household and defined us to the outside world as a close family.

I remember how much I loved my parents as a child. No question, no conditions. They were everything to me, and I was devoted to pleasing them. I became a high achiever throughout grade school and high school years. I can best describe the feeling of their approval as intoxicating, and I realize I was hooked on the high of every fix. Pleasing them made them happy, and when they were happy, I felt their love. Following the rules brought harmony to the family, and seeking their approval became my roadmap to happiness.

When I was an older child, I liked to look at old family photo albums. I marveled at the ancestry of my family, and I wanted to know who everyone was. It helped me connect myself to where my family came from and feel a real sense of belonging. I collected old black and white photos from both sides of the family and yearned to feel part of that history.

I remember being about ten years old when I came across a photo of myself in an antique-looking frame, and it looked like I was about two or three years old. I was wearing an odd-looking toddler outfit and thinking about all the blonde curly hair I had even at that young age. There were several photos of my sister and me around the house, and I wondered why this one was not out on display. With grins on their faces, they told me I was not the child in the photo. It was a photo from the 1930s of my father when he was three years old. Sharing such distinct characteristics with my father was thrilling, albeit an incredible coincidence. The discovery was one of the most impactful memories for me, and I carried that photo with me for years. From that point forward, the adoption label had even less significance for both of us.

THE FALL FROM THE PEDESTAL

Unbeknownst to me, the pedestal upon which my parents placed me was inching ever higher with every achievement, agreeable decision, and moment of pride and every obedient choice I made. Little did I know just how fragile and unstable that pedestal was, and how oblivious I was to the painful fall from that pedestal that was in my path.

The topic of my adoption was a fascinating topic to my friends, and inevitably, the question came up whether I would ever look for my "real" mother and father. The term "real" usually irritated me because they weren't real to me at all. I already had real parents, and I was far less interested in finding out who they were than others seemed to be. So, I simply referred to them as "birth parents." There were times during my teenage years I remember being curious, but for the most part, I didn't think about it much, and I had little desire to complicate my life by searching for them.

However, as life tends to do, my path led me there anyway. When we were in our twenties, my sister confided in me with the news, she was actively searching for her birth family. Her experience with our parents growing up had been very different than mine, and she struggled to earn her own pedestal. As her big sister, my nurturing instincts took over, and I took on a protective role with her throughout our childhood. She was having an extremely difficult time coping since I had left home and she wanted to connect with her biological roots with the hopes of finding family with whom she believed she would feel more like she belonged. She asked for my support, not knowing if and how she was going to break the news to our parents or how they might take it. She had also brought a set of forms for me to fill out to start the process for myself, hoping we would both get lucky.

I was dating seriously at the time and I decided it would be practical for me find out what I could about medical history before I married and started having children. I filled out the paperwork and sent it in, with little thought of anything turning up, and I never gave it much thought again after that. Yet, it was to become the decision would lead to my biggest life change and cause me to question everything I believed was truth in my life.

That visit from my sister triggered a five-year chain reaction of circumstances that created a case file and led to my reunion with my birth mother, and my two half-sisters. I was thirty-one years old, moved across the country, married, changed my name, and just returned to my career after maternity leave when I received the call in my office. I was completely stunned.

Twenty years later, my relationship with my birth family is strong, and has developed over time into something very positive and loving. It was a surreal experience, and I am so blessed and grateful we found each other, and I am astounded sometimes at the odds that we overcame. I am one of the lucky ones, as many government-adopted children from that era seldom find the answers they are looking for, and even when they do, happy endings are rare. As stunning as all that was, it was not nearly as stunning as the reaction from my mother and father, and the loss I experienced as a result.

Telling my mother and father was never in question. We were close and I wanted to tell them, and I didn't feel I had anything to hide. To say it was a surprise getting that phone call in my office that day is an understatement, and so I had little doubt it would be a surprise for my parents as well. But in my wildest dreams I never thought I was doing anything wrong, let alone see it as a betrayal towards my parents. I was not capable of abandoning my life with them, as I had proven to them my entire life that I loved them unconditionally.

Not long after I told my parents about meeting my birth mother, our relationship changed. It took my head years to catch up to understand what that change would mean, and my heart lagged for two decades. My whole life, I felt that I made an effort to honor them, protect them, show compassion, and offer understanding towards them. Our relationship altered, nonetheless.

After this happened, I questioned a lot about myself, especially whether I could trust my beliefs and values. I discovered that things that I thought couldn't change, could change. That revelation had a deep impact on my perspective on many things for a long time.

As times passed and I worked on dealing with the aftermath on a therapist's couch multiple times, I was able to sift through the pain and secure my sense of self. After some hard work, I was able to see those changes as positive. I gained a renewed commitment to what I believed in and what I valued based on the truth I know exists.

The process of making sure my values stay front and center throughout my life have become guideposts for me as a parent. I vowed to ensure my own child would grow up knowing love. I have not had contact with my mother and father for nearly two decades.

MINDFUL SELF-CARE

There are a few things I have found that need regular, mindful attention for me to continue to evolve as a person and offer my best as a parent. Spending time on ourselves is not easy these days, yet I know how important my values are to my feelings of success and happiness on my relationships with our kids, so the work on myself must be done.

Rooted in values-based leadership principles, there are a number of self-care areas that get my attention that help keep my values in check, such as understanding myself and what I do through self-reflection, develop and improve my self-assurance, acknowledge my weaknesses and my strengths, admit when I'm wrong, acknowledge I don't know everything, ask for help when I need it, and maintain gratefulness for everything that has happens because it shapes who I am and what I believe.

SELF-ASSURANCE MATTERS

Self-assurance and inner strength are important components of values-based parenting. Self-assurance means you accept yourself and who you are, with your weakness and strengths. It is an outward expression of appropriate self-regard. It also means being able to comfortably ask for help without feeling weak or out of control.

This is not easy, and even though this is an important area of mindful self-care, it can be one of the hardest things to develop. This was true for me and still is a conscious challenge. It is hard for me to admit those kinds of things, especially being raised that strength and high achievement and looking good to the outside world matter so much.

For me, there is a lot of fear of judgment and people thinking less of me if I admit these things out loud. But it is a myth. Just because you don't say it, doesn't mean people don't see it anyway. As a parent, we can sometimes feel pressure to do everything right, say everything right, and the thought of admitting to the world, and your children you don't do or say everything right, and that you are weak is unthinkable for some. How can I admit I was wrong, have weaknesses, and need help? Won't that put me at a disadvantage and make me less effective? Won't they think less of me?

As parents, we tend to think this way for what we think are all the right reasons. But if you think about the ability to influence and guide your children in the same context as leadership, aren't we usually influenced more so by people we can relate to, and whom can relate to us? It's the same principle with our kids.

I strive to be a self-assured parent. This is difficult for me, and it is a conscious effort. A parent who has inner strength, is self-assured, with the ability to admit to their children they don't have all the answers and who can comfortably admit when they are wrong. They look for help and assistance as well as delegate and work on areas they are not as strong. And the irony is, most of the time people who know you, love you probably already know this about you, but it doesn't mean they love and accept you any less because of it.

The goal with self-assurance is to gain credibility and affect positive influence over our children's behavior, as a responsible and competent parent. One of the ah-ha moments for me was the realization that the myth that I had to know everything and never admitting when I'm wrong was rarely the advantage I thought it was in terms of parenting our kids successfully. When I let go of those myths, I experienced better outcomes and I appeared a little more relatable to them, and ultimately gaining future credibility.

What I learned in my career in employee development is when we share our mistakes, we create teachable moments. When we are transparent about our own personal growth, it inspires growth and learning of others. When we admit imperfections, it becomes ok for others to be fallible. People connect with people who share their imperfections. With our kids, we become more human, more relatable to them, and build trust in the process.

THE CORNERSTONE OF UNDERSTANDING SELF

Self-awareness is our objective evaluation of ourselves and leads to understanding ourselves and how we relate to others and the world. And as we become more self-aware, we become better at self-control. When we focus our attention on ourselves, we evaluate and compare our current behavior to our internal standards and values.

I have been married twice. I was in my late twenties when I married for the first time, and we deeply wanted to start a family. For us, it was not as simple as we thought it was going to be. I experienced several devastating miscarriages and was told having children was not likely to happen. I can still recall the sting of that news, but we turned it around knowing we were both willing to consider adoption and began looking into that possibility. The doctors continued with tests and treatments to help determine a cause of miscarriages, and it was during a battery of routine monthly tests that they told me I was pregnant again. As I was high risk, I didn't think I was going to be able to handle the emotional stress of another loss and was terrified the entire pregnancy. I was referred to a doctor who was a specialist in high-risk pregnancy, and I saw him every four weeks while in his care. During what would be my last monthly office visit with him at twenty-nine weeks, he checked me directly into the hospital from that appointment. Things had worsened, my body was shutting down and the baby was in distress. For two weeks, the goal was to keep the pregnancy going as long as possible to increase the chance the baby would survive. At thirty-one weeks it was determined our baby was in jeopardy and an emergency C-section was ordered. When I woke up in the OR, it was eerily quiet, and I soon came to the realization I was no longer carrying the baby. As I placed my hand where the bump used to be, I was overwhelmed with fear and dared not to ask. Relief came when a nurse came into the room, she told me my daughter had been born – and a tiny little girl who weighed less than three pounds was in the neonatal intensive care unit doing just fine. It was astounding to me at the deepest feeling of love that emerged instantaneously, and how intensely my life could change in that moment of knowing I had become a mother.

As I had hoped since my childhood dreams, being a mother was true joy. However, our marriage was not meant to last. After seven years of struggle, we divorced when our daughter was four. I became a single mother prepared to raise my daughter alone and did so for a while until I found my forever person.

I married my second husband a couple of years later. He was a single father raising three girls full-time, and we instantly became a two-parent, blended family starting off our marriage, raising four girls together all under the age of eleven. We have been deeply happy in this marriage for twenty years.

Striving for greater self-awareness was, and continues to be, a cornerstone to our successful marriage and relationship with our children. It is a work in progress that we have improved on over time. If we know ourselves, we can lead ourselves, and if we can lead ourselves, then we will be able to successfully parent (and lead) our children.

This a significant principle for us. For several years we had all four kids full time in our home, and like many divorced families, they spent every second weekend with their other parents. Over the years, we struggled with the relationship between us and our exes, with multiple legal actions along the way, as our children grew up. We weighed the impact on the kids, family, resources, and sometimes we conceded and moved on quickly to more important things. Other times we chose to address the issue head-on. Those situations were upsetting and unnecessary, but they could not be ignored. What kept us together and united was our constant reflection back on our behavior, our values, and what we stood for. We asked ourselves questions that helped keep ourselves in check, such as, "Did we stay true to ourselves?" "What did we do that we are proud of?" "If the kids were watching us, would they be proud of us?" "If God was standing beside me through all of that, would I have chosen differently?"

When we chose poorly, either wittingly or unwittingly in misalignment with our values, we usually felt it. We discovered our "tells" when we made parenting decisions or acted in a way that drifted away from our values, either wittingly or unwittingly, making the situation harder to deal with in the long run. I liken those "tells," to the rumble bumps you experience on the highway when you drift too close to the shoulder or the on-coming lane. Over time and through our experience, we figured out our 'tells' emerged when we chose to be indifferent, or didn't give due care to the situation, or when embarrassment and fear of judgment keep us from asking for assistance when we didn't know what to do. Our tells also emerged the times we gave in to apathy and side-stepped our values because it was easier and gratifying for the short-term, like giving out a meaningless punishment in anger because it was easier than taking the time to create a worthy teaching moment. However, once we learned from those mistakes and uh-oh moments, we had much better results and ultimately learned how to avoid them in the future.

Self-reflection feeds growth. We pass this along to our children by helping them be self-reflective, self-aware, and learn self-control. We've learned from our mistakes as parents that by practicing this ourselves, we have a positive impact on our children's own personal growth. It comes from a place of support, rather than anger, punishment, or humiliation.

The years of raising children in a blended family were happy with a lot of "messy" mixed in as we tried to figure it all out together. As we went along, my husband and I talked a lot, and chose our course of action together, in agreement, with the best of intentions for our family given the circumstances at the time. We were tested and challenged by our outside world on a regular basis by life in general and those who either wanted us to fail or unconvinced we could pull it off. What kept us moving forward was not only our unwavering commitment to each other and our family but our aligned values, which worked well for us most of the time and when it mattered the most.

When we met, we were drawn to each other right away, and our connection was strong very quickly. We took the time to talk long and hard about our own personal values, and alignment was non-negotiable to the decision to get married. A lot was at stake, for our relationship and for the lives of our children. This proved to be the right approach, as it got us through some extraordinarily tough situations, as well as regular life that comes with raising four children.

While the excitement of finding each other, falling in love, and planning a wedding was buzzing in the air, like many couples it was tempting to get caught up in the "getting married" activity and pay less attention to what it was going to take to actually "be" married, after the party was over. Since we were single parents, getting to the point of being a stable, married couple was our priority. For us, being married meant being clear about expectations and having strength as a couple, and as a parental team.

I SEE YOU, I HEAR YOU, I UNDERSTAND YOU

"Seek first to understand before being understood" -Stephen R. Covey

Gaining perspective and understanding others is the ability to see situations from multiple points of view to gain a much fuller understanding – it means that you ask questions, consider opinions with an open mind; taking time to understand *all* sides of the story.

Due to advances in social media, we are inundated daily with a litany of points of view on hundreds of topics on a global scale. What issues do you have strong opinions about? What are your views on parenting topics, such as whether to spank or not to spank a child? Give children an allowance for doing chores? What age is appropriate for giving a child their own cell phone?

Whether or not your values align with giving your eight-year-old a cell phone or not, the value of handling your eight-year-old son's request for a cell phone means gaining an understanding of his eight-year-old perspective on the issue in order to communicate your message to him and have it understood.

Another myth we overcame is that just because you seek and gain understanding, it doesn't automatically mean you agree. Understanding merely provides a perspective that will help you do the right thing in alignment with your values and what is important to you. The biggest gain we found was that we were able to avoid presumptions and biases that could have skewed our decision in the wrong direction. Perspective improves the quality of the decision as well as our ability to communicate that decision clearly while keeping the responsibility to make the decision in your hands. Keep in mind that parenting really isn't a democracy when it comes to issues that impact your values and what is important to you. You are the parent, and decisions ultimately rest with you. Simple democracy is just voting, and while you will find yourself counting votes in some family-vote situations, your role is not merely a vote counter. Family input is effective when voting for simple, low impact decisions like which movie to watch or what type of pizza to order. You have the life experience, and in the appropriate circumstance, this will carry more weight, but still including them and weighing their perspective is positive. The time you take and the knowledge you gain gathering opinion and perspectives will guide you on how to handle it when there is opposition.

As we improve at this and take the time to understand the child's point of view, even on trivial issues, we became better equipped to decide whether a) to agree or disagree with them and b) what we want to do about it and c) how best to frame the response so they understand it.

Our goal was for our children to understand and believe that we were truly focused on doing the right thing. This is a critical guidepost and applies to any issue, such as increasing their allowance, a broken house rule, poor report card, or sibling conflict.

Early in my parenting journey I was influenced by my studies in behavioral psychology, business leadership and several parenting authors on the subject, and in particular Barbara Coloroso's books about our roles as parents. I remember reading her books and being inspired by how much her messages aligned with my own values and beliefs on the responsibility and stewardship of actively shaping the hearts and minds of our children. My experiences over the decades have reinforced my belief that when you gain perspective, and provide your kids with your decision, you create your ability to frame the message in a way that leaves kids with their dignity intact, and they hear positive messages from you such like "you are listened to, you are cared for, you are important to me, you can handle this."

The pairing of gratitude and humility are values my husband, and I share and hold special within our experience as parents. While driving in our neighborhood recently, we noticed a church with a sign out front that read, "Humility is not thinking less of yourself – it is thinking about yourself less." It made us smile, and we realized that was the perfect way to articulate humility for us. To some, it might seem that the quest for self-assurance as a parent can be in at cross purposes with the value of humility. How is it we value a strong sense of humility and still be in charge as parents? It's all in how you define it and how you show it to your children.

Showing humility for us has been in simple everyday actions such as listening to our children; really being present and listening to them, not just waiting for our turn to talk. Also ask them for input into things and being willing to accept they might be right and change our course of action when something isn't working. The thing about humility is that you realize you are doing what you do for the good of your children and your family, and less about ourselves. Practicing humility is understanding the important role our children play in the overall success and harmony within the family and being open and self-assured enough to allow them to influence things in age-appropriate ways.

Humility as it pertains to values and the focus on what is important to us as parents is even more simple than that. Humility helps us make it about them and not about us. And we acknowledge that children matter by treating them that way. It means to recognize and accept what it is that we're all made of; a mix of gifts and skills, weaknesses, and faults. With this, comes the reality that we are all made of the same "stuff" as every other person on the planet. None of us is better than anyone else. We are all gifted and beautiful, faulted, and broken in our own ways. It is not an end state; it is something we practice and strive to demonstrate each day. It is taking a step back so that they may be brought forward.

I am not advocating that values-based parenting is the right way. It is one way but not the only way. There is no one right way to parent effectively. I am sharing values-based parenting and the effect on my experience as a mother, and the roots of this perspective from my childhood. It continues to evolve as my parenting story enters a new chapter with our grown adult children and their children to come. Whether this approach is relatable to you, there will always be a way through the challenges and joys of being a parent. If you are already a parent or planning to be in the future, I invite you to take the time to reflect on your values and what is truly important to you, align with your parenting partners and commit to keeping your values as reliable guideposts for your own humbling, awakening, joyful, loving gift that is parenting.

Sandra Kosor, B. Sc. Hon, Certified Coach Practitioner

Sandra Kosor is a proud wife and mother, born and raised in Calgary, Canada. She has also called Halifax and Vancouver home and is now a Canadian living in Houston, Texas. With nearly three decades of experience, Sandra began her career in Human Resources after completing a B.Sc. Honors degree in Psychology from Dalhousie University. She is an accomplished HR professional in learning and organizational development with expertise in enterprise leadership skill development programming. Sandra has been privileged to have partnered with clients in a wide range of industries and corporate environments to develop customized learning aligned with company vision and values. Sandra has international and overseas experience, authorized to work in Canada and the USA. Sandra is a dedicated coach committed to empowering others' success. She views coaching as a calling, leadership and parenting a privilege and deeply values family and human connection.

Connect with Sandra:
sandrakosor.htxus@gmail.com
www.instagram.com/sndrksrhtx
www.linkedin.com/in/sandra-kosor-16185823

Five-Steps to Brilliant Breakthrough Solutions: Overcome Barriers and Leap to Your Destiny

by Kennedy Barasa Wanyonyi

S ome things choke your progress and cause you to stagnate or get stuck; I call them barriers. Obstacles are inevitable; they're part of life and personal and growth development. Overcoming them is like for digging of gold; it is a lot of hard work, and there are no guarantees, but when you strike gold it's great.

Obstacles can bring the best out of you if you have a mindset that is open to seeking opportunities in adverse situations. They can make you wise if you are free to learn from your mistakes and failures. The question is, "How can you be at your best when you are facing formidable contrary forces? To answer this question, I designed what I call "The 5-Steps to Brilliant Breakthrough Solutions", solutions based on character, communication, relationship, wisdom, and learning. See the diagram below.

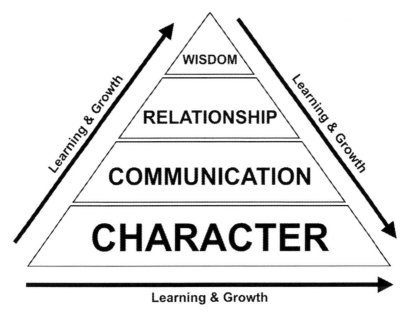

The 5-Steps to Brilliant Breakthrough Solutions Pyramid

STEP 1: CHARACTER

The character of an individual is the foundation; it tells who you are; it represents your destiny and determines the beauty of the outcome and excellence of success. The character for brilliant breakthrough solutions helps to bring the best out of your personality and launch you on a path to develop the right attitude for success.

DEFINING CHARACTER

When I am asked to describe character, my simple definition is what differentiates me from others including my siblings even though we may look alike, or share the same family name, or traits. Though my brother and I might have inherited similar qualities from our parents, nevertheless, we may differ from each other remarkably. We may all be tall, afro-hair, and athletic like, but when it comes to the academic subjects, we excel in, my brother good at mathematics and I at biology. Again, my brother might be patient, and persevering, I, on the other hand, might be eager and scrupulous. Physical appearance, intellect, and behavior amongst other things describe what character is.

An individual's character also encompasses his philosophy of life. Philosophy includes a person's attitude, viewpoint, thinking, values, beliefs, and way of life. Other terms used to define a person's character are the mindset, the frame of mind, will, personality, self, and identity. It is worth noting that these terms are often used interchangeably.

One thing that gives significance and value to an individual's character is his life experience. Life experience is connected to events, situations, and circumstances a person has encountered in the course of his life that molded him into who he is or is becoming.

CHARACTER AS THE HINDRANCE

Sir Thomas Browne said, "Every man is his greatest enemy, and, as it were, his own executioner." Character cannot become an obstacle until it is perceived as such by the mind and turned into action and behavior.

a) Physical appearance

It's hard to see the relationship between physical appearance and barriers. However, on close examination, you can observe underlying issues that make physical appearance a significant impediment to advancement in life. Some of the problems relate to stereotypes, stigma, shame, rejection, guilt, and self-blame, particularly birthmark, overweight, stature, infirmity, disability, and racial profiling that might make people despise themselves. People with these issues may face discrimination in the workplace, educational settings, and be denied significant socio-economic opportunities including medical and healthcare.

They might encounter negative societal attitude and could be labeled as lazy, or unhelpful. Consequently, their self-esteem might suffer; they may feel neglected, abandoned, or marginalized. The negative attitudes and beliefs arising from prejudice can build up into significant obstacles, which most of those affected may find it hard to overcome.

b) Negative mindset

Someone with a negative mindset has a tendency to see the worst in situations, to be panicky, worried, stressed and discouraged, to grumble and complain, accuse and find fault, malign and backbite, to see threats in situations instead of opportunities, escalate matters into a crisis instead of finding solutions, to seek sympathy and pity, and to play the victim.

Somebody with a negative mindset also exhibits a propensity to believe that he can't make it because he isn't smart enough, everybody is against him, the thing he is attempting is impossible, or people don't understand him. He uses excuses as a reason for not doing what he could do.

c) Negative self-talk

Negative self-talk is a constant bleak talk and thinking you carry on about yourself. Examples of self-talk may run like this; I failed, so I'm not good enough, I have no friend because I'm are ugly, and so on.

d) Negative thoughts and emotions

Negative thoughts are associated with feelings of fear, discouragement, anger, hopelessness, pessimism, frustration, and disappointment. These feelings may undermine your ability to think objectively; they might make you lose hope and be hard on yourself whereby you blame yourself unnecessarily or find yourself guilty of even petty things. These thoughts and feelings could lead to loss of self-confidence, self-doubt, or giving up on your dreams.

e) Negative attitude

Negative attitude includes cynicism, dishonesty, indifference, irresponsibility, jealousy, pessimism, prejudice, pride, resentment, revenge, sadness, selfishness, skepticism, suspicion, thoughtlessness, intolerance, greed, cowardice, and so on. These attitudes might cause a person to respond to issues unfavorably.

f) Bad personality traits

Bad personality traits include self-indulgence, apathy, selfishness, being self-seeking, self-centeredness, egotism, grumbling, complaining, ingratitude, averse, deceptive, and so on. Bad personality traits may well cause someone to deny himself, be obsessed with perfectionism, or reject criticism.

g) Experiences

Failure, rejection, abuse such as rape, violence or bullying, discrimination at the workplace, discrimination because of race or gender, or discrimination because of disability, infirmity or stature are some of the powerful forces that might hinder you from moving forward.

THE CHARACTER FOR OVERCOMING BARRIERS

I consider the following character features solutions to surmounting the obstacles including those discussed above.

a) Positive self-talk

Continuous cheerful, friendly, and promising talk and thinking you carry on about yourself. Positive self-talk ignites the passion that speaks to the womb of your spirit, which can lead to the leap of faith and imagination of unlimited possibilities; imagination is the heart of creativity and innovation.

b) Positive mindset,

It is a state of mind that is open to possibilities, that welcomes change, learning, and growth.

c) Positive attitude

Exhibiting positive attitude can bring about positive thoughts and feelings that could improve your mood and emotions, which might make you more calm, peaceful, joyful, happy, and lead to hope, boost confidence and self-esteem, and motivate you to aspire to do well.

d) Good personality traits

Examples of good personality traits are self-control, integrity, determination, commitment, pleasant, calm, grateful, keen, reliable, driven, and so on. Demonstrating these qualities may help you take control of your life, take responsibility for your actions, adapt to change, relate with others well and win new friends, be committed to what you are doing, etc.

STEP 2: COMMUNICATION

Communication helps you express yourself and understand what you want to achieve in life, know and manifest your dreams. Communication for brilliant breakthrough solutions takes you to underscore the potency of language and words for success.

DEFINING COMMUNICATION

The two words that aptly describe communication are message and convey. Communication is about transmitting a message. Message expresses the thoughts, feelings, beliefs, and behavior of a person. You communicate to yourself and others. Messages are delivered to inform, to arouse interest in something, to choose, judge, and decide, to trigger action, to create awareness, to draw attention, and so on.

Three critical things underline a message. They're purpose, nature, and tone. Purpose refers to the intention of a message. Nature of a message concerns the kind of a message being relayed. Tone relates to the feelings, mood, and the spirit of a message.

Words are fundamental to communication. The Oxford English Dictionary defines a word as a single distinct conceptual unit of language, comprising inflected and variant forms. Words have meaning, and each definition conveys something you wish others to know. Words form a language, which is the system we use for communication.

Time, tone, and location are significant in communication. Certain time and location depict historical, cultural, and religious significance people attach to them. For instance, people gather on Sunday at a set time in church to worship God. A date is set in Canada for the Governor General to deliver "Speech from the Throne" at Parliament to the nation. Effective communication requires among others right timing, right location, and proper tone.

COMMUNICATION AS AN OBSTACLE

a) Words: Toxic words. These are words that can disrupt your success without you knowing. They are can't, try, if, but, could have, might, would have, should, maybe, someday, why, and try. (From the CCF L1 Training)

b) Tone: Tone projects your feelings. Tone can tell whether you are approachable, likable, or not. A harsh tone can be a major obstacle to communication, because it may project you as an angry person. Anger turns away people.

c) Time: Message delivered at a wrong time; it is stale. The old message bears these characteristics:

- Old therefore irrelevant.
- Lacks energy and ideas and has no variety.

- It is boring, suffers overuse, and has no life.
- It has lost its effectiveness and force due to the lapse of time.

d) Location

A wrong location and negative environment can be a drawback to communication.

COMMUNICATION AS THE SOLUTION TO BARRIERS

a) Words that inspire, motivate, persuade, and influence. These words break resistance, they uplift your spirit, because they transmit high energy; therefore, they generate unstoppable momentum. These words are easily, naturally, aware, experiencing, realizing, unlimited, expanding, before, after, because, now, abundant, possibility, create, and visualize. (From the CCF L1 Training)

b) Time - here I'm talking about a message of the moment that speaks to the heart of your audience. It's current and expresses hope, it's energetic, and spiced with inspiring and diverse ideas, and thus, active, and forceful.

c) Tone - a message delivered in a way that connects you with the audience, building rapport, eliciting interest, satisfaction, and approval. You may have come across the advice to smile when you are talking to someone either face to face or on phone. A smile radiates friendliness, warmth, confidence, enthusiasm, and fellow feeling, which draw people toward you. Tone includes being gracious, authentic, sincere, honest in your speech. It also involves speaking with dignity and having a message that's suitable to the occasion and beautifully presented.

d) Engage and demonstrate active listening.

STEP 3: RELATIONSHIP

Relationship is the nucleus of life. It is at the center of every man's enterprise. Albert Einstein said, "that man is here for the sake of other men." The relationship for breakthrough solutions is intended to help you explore fundamental relationships that will help you fulfill your destiny, investigate necessary connections that will get you out of where you're stuck, and consider and finally decide on who to take with you to your destiny.

Thomas Merton said that, "No man is an island." Naturally, people are inclined to contact, to belong, to the community. These three things are critical to the relationship, which are choice, reason, and behavior. Bond is a choice, a decision made after careful consideration because of the value it adds to your life and profession. You relate to someone for some reasons. Most relationships are founded on need and motives. Lastly, behaving respectfully, friendly, courteously is essential to building and maintaining a healthy and beneficial relationship.

TYPES OF RELATIONSHIPS

1. Valued relationship

The valued relationship is a relationship where people value each other. They put a premium on the relationship. Because of this, they nurture, protect, and advance the relationship.

2. Opportunistic relationship

Opportunistic relationship is driven by selfish intent. People in this kind of relationship look for an opportunity to benefit themselves.

3. Covenant relationship

Covenant comes from the Latin word con venire, meaning a coming together. It denotes two or more people entering into a contract in which they agree on promises, stipulations, privileges, and responsibilities. A covenant is binding on the parties. It has rewards and penalties; rewards when either party honors the agreement and sanctions when either party violates the relationship.

4. Contractual relationship

The contractual relationship is a legal relationship between contracting-parties evidenced by an offer, acceptance of the proposal, and legal and valuable considerations. A signed contract is binding on the contracting parties.

5. Peer relationship

Peer relationship involves a group of people with similar interest, age, background, or social status.

6. Acquaintances

These are people who slightly know each other. They are people you have met or met for the first time, but you don't know them very well. They could be colleagues, associates, allies, neighbors, churchgoers, and so on.

7. Intimate relationship

Intimate is a close friend who may be the person you share your heart with when you are in difficulties. He could be a person you lean on in hard times.

8. Blood relationship (kin)

These are your family members and next of kin. They share a bloodline with you.

9. Spiritual relationship

Spiritual relationship centers on the relationship with God and other divine beings as per your beliefs and faith. My faith in God and Jesus Christ is the basis for building a deep devotional relationship with Him. This relationship is extended to those who share a similar belief with me and even those who don't. In this relationship, I see God as my helper, as the One who could aid me overcome barriers.

10. Father-son relationship

The father-son relationship goes beyond biological ties. Here I am alluding to the responsibility of a father. A father takes the position of a teacher, instructor, tutor, mentor, or coach. He molds the other person's thinking, feelings, beliefs, behavior, expectations, vision, and perspective aiding him to be who he desires to be. There is knowledge transfer, imparting and fusion. There develops a strong connection between the two even as becoming one. This fruitful relationship leads to the formation of the desired personality. The power of knowledge changes the individual.

RELATIONSHIP AS THE HINDRANCES

It is worth noting that the relationship per se is not a hindrance. The following might make affinity an impediment: motive, attitude, behavior, emotions, and mood. Words and tone of communication could cause a relationship to be an obstacle. Words and tone have the potential to hamstring relationship if you can't use them correctly.

RELATIONSHIP AS THE SOLUTION TO OBSTACLES

Again, relationship is not a solution to barriers, but a catalyst to overcoming limitations. We should not see relationship as an entitlement or a right, but instead, as a privilege. Projecting a positive attitude, mindset, and personality, and behaving well towards others can make those whom you are in a relationship with treat you favorably and help you.

THE PEOPLE YOU MAY NEED ON THE JOURNEY TO YOUR DESTINY

a) People who give and give sacrificially, and they do it out of a willing heart, and not under compulsion or selfish motive.

b) People who forgive, they are ready to forgive no matter how deep you've hurt them, no matter how you've messed up your life, you don't merit it, but love makes them accept you, value and validate you.

c) People who extend a helping hand to you when others abandon you in your worst moments.

d) Encourager - a person who stands with you when you face threats or when others deny you.

STEP 4: WISDOM

Proverbs allude to wisdom as the principal thing, and because it is the primary thing and getting it leads to understanding, therefore, it is essential to get it. Wisdom for breakthrough solutions challenges you to explore and discover the right knowledge to surmount barriers.

People often ascribe wisdom to sages. Nevertheless, the writer of the book of Proverbs hints that wisdom is all around us and is calling out to us; the problem is that we hardly pay attention.

DEFINING WISDOM

Wisdom is to know what to do, doing it right and doing it well. It's worth to note that wisdom consists of knowledge, understanding, prudence, and discerning. Even so, knowledge is fundamental; it is the structure that supports the other elements of wisdom.

KNOWLEDGE

Knowledge is a noun, and as a noun, it denotes a thing. Examples are treatise, facts, data, theories, truth, intuition, news, notice, information, experience, and feelings.

Knowledge likewise is used as a verb, which denotes know. Know means to be aware of something through observation, personal experience, to be acquainted with something or someone, to be mindful of something. As a verb, it also means friendship and sexuality. Seeing it in terms of conception, it alludes to an idea, a thought, a discovery, or a concept. Incubation of ideas is part of the creative process that often leads to solutions.

Just as sexuality can lead to the birth of a child; likewise, conceptualization of ideas leads to invention, product, design, and solution.

From the fourteenth century, knowledge has been used to mean the capacity for knowing, understanding; familiarity; fact or condition of knowing, awareness of a fact, news, notice, information; learning; organized body of facts, or teachings; sexual intercourse as from circa 1400. The origin of the verb knowing – the old English meaning of knowing is perceived a thing to be identical with another; to be able to distinguish; see or understand as a fact or truth; know how. From circa 1200 meaning to experience, live through. Most of these definitions are still in use today.

The elements of knowledge include:

- The act, fact, or state of knowing,
- The range of information,
- All that has been grasped by the mind,
- Learning,
- Awareness,

- Being familiar with something or someone,
- Distinguishing one thing from the other,
- Experience as known by a person or group of people,
- A body of knowledge, stored as memory, soft knowledge, hard knowledge, or informal knowledge, which can be retrieved at any time when there is a need for it.

Most of the stored knowledge is unprocessed. This knowledge must be processed into a form that can be readily applied. We do this using the tools of interpretation, explanation, analysis, inference, insight, perception, and experience, which are the domains of understanding.

UNDERSTANDING

Understanding is to know the meaning of something. You can understand something by perceiving and interpreting its intended purpose and significance. You can do this through direct observation, participation, and by being familiar with something as a result of studying it and experiencing it. Interpreting something involves explaining it in depth. The intent is to make the meaning clearer and tell its significance.

Empathy is another definition of understanding, which is the ability to understand and share the feelings of other people.

Etymologically, understand is carefully compared to the Greek word "epistamai," which means, I know how. The old English meaning of the word understand is examine, investigate, and consider under certain circumstances, which implies that understanding is the act of questioning, studying, scrutinizing, and finding facts, theories, news, notice, information, data, truth, experience, and feelings. Knowhow entails practical knowledge, capability, knack, ingeniousness, and so on.

In summary, understanding refers to:

- Knowhow - the practical knowledge and ability to do things in a well-reasoned manner,

- The ability to examine, investigate, scrutinize, consider available knowledge to make it more meaningful and useful,
- Interpret knowledge to give an informed and sound opinion, also to provide options,
- The ability to learn, judge and make decisions,
- The ability to distinguish things to provide them with real meaning,
- Show empathy,
- The capacity, skill, and power to see deep into nature of things, situations with accuracy to distinguish and select the right knowledge to solve the circumstance you are facing.

PRUDENCE

Prudence is an act of exercising caution and sound judgment. It is giving much more attention than you would usually do. It is weighing something carefully and giving more thought and attention intently to avoid mistakes. Examples of prudence are exercising restraint, discipline, and patience – virtues essential for moral and ethical conduct.

DISCERNING WISDOM AS "OBSTACLE."

I am putting the word obstacle in quotes to show that as much as wisdom is regarded as a solution, it might in some circumstances be a hindrance. I am using wisdom collectively to mean knowledge, understanding, prudence, and discerning. I consider the following barriers:

- Ignorance, not just lacking knowledge about a subject or situation, but having false knowledge, superficial knowledge, or being ill-informed about something or someone. Ignorance destroys and it is one of the greatest limitations people face.
- Distorted knowledge characterized by bias and generalization.
- Apathy.
- Ineptitude and incapacity.

- Being wise in your own eyes, that is, in your estimation, which is self-conceit. Merriam-Webster dictionary defines self-conceit as an exaggerated opinion about one's abilities; it is one of the vanities. Having this mindset is indeed a limitation. The profound truth is that no one has a monopoly of knowledge.
- Rejecting advice and correction.
- Unsound wisdom comprised of bitter envy or jealousy, selfish ambition, confusion, evil fruits, wavering between two opinions, hypocrisy, wickedness sown by strife/competition, open favoritism, insincerity, and disingenuousness.

WISDOM AS A SOLUTION TO BARRIERS

- Foresight or forethought – the ability to respond favorably to unpredicted situations and the unknown.
- Insight –this concerns the ability to have a sharp, profound, and occasionally unexpected understanding of a complicated problem as well as the ability to see and clearly understand the inner nature of things.
- Know how, that is the knowledge of the methods or techniques of doing something, either technical or practical.
- Empathy, developing the ability to understand and share the feelings of other people.

STEP 5: LEARNING

Learning maximizes a person's ability to face life's challenges. It's an integral part of growth and development. Learning for brilliant breakthrough solutions launches you to "Personal Self-Development Plan," a blueprint that outlines your journey to your destiny, how to get there and what you need to get there successfully.

Learning is an integral part of developing and growing, also known as self-development. Self-development involves developing your talents, gifts, potential, and capacity. It also consists of increasing in personality, communication, relationship, wisdom including knowledge, understanding, prudence and discerning.

WHY LEARNING IS VITAL TO OVERCOMING BARRIERS

Learning is important because of the following reasons:

- To build continuous improvement into your daily activities,
- To make excellence your lifestyle,
- To develop the capacity to adapt to change,
- To discard old bad habits and develop new healthy productive habits,
- To build a winning culture, and
- To reinvent yourself.

ELEMENTS OF LEARNING

Learning entails the following:

- Meditation, reflection, confession, and affirmation,
- Feedback which includes counsel and correction,
- Classroom teaching, tutoring, mentoring, and coaching,
- Experiential learning - including experience, apprenticeship, and discipleship.

LEARNING AS THE SOLUTION TO OBSTACLES

a) Learning gives you knowledge, which is essential to grow and progress in society.

b) Acquiring skills that are imperative in using knowledge to produce services and products.

c) Developing the ability to find the proper knowledge for innovation, invention, and creativity.

d) Acquiring and enhancing the capacity for critical thinking, which enables you to filter biased, distorted, and generalized information so that you have a balanced and objective perspective on issues.

THE LEARNING YOU NEED ON THE JOURNEY TO YOUR DESTINY

I consider the following critical learning you might need:

a) Reflection, this is where you build learning into your daily work and life.

b) Making continuous improvement in your daily activities and experience.

c) Creating the capacity for an honest in-the-moment feedback.

d) Learning that helps you build a winning culture.

e) Learning that positions you to make excellence your lifestyle.

6. EXECUTING ACTIONS TO MAKE LIFE BETTER

I translate the steps I have discussed in this chapter into action to make life better for the clients I work with as follows.

The first thing I tell a client when we meet either for the first time or for every session is, you're the best, so we are working together on this project to bring the best out of you, look at yourself, smile and tell yourself, I'm the best I ever dreamt about myself. Look at the obstacle you are facing as a gold mine. Gather your tools and yourself and get to work, blast that barrier and take the precious gold that was hidden from you. See you have the gold; celebrate yourself.

I do this to awaken the spirit in the client, to ignite the fire and energy that might have been dampened by the effort that did not yield the expected results or which could have been crushed making it look like it is impossible to advance any further. I do this also to fire up his imagination and challenge him to visualize himself at his destiny, as having overcome the barrier, and then I ask him, "how did you do it?" I get him to work on his mindset, to renew his mind and be transformed into a champion, into a winner, into the best he ever thought about himself, thus, to learn and develop this new mindset, a mindset of brilliance. A brilliant mindset is a mindset in which your unique self makes you shine and do better.

Another thing I do is to tell a client that he is a driver of a bus called Zola if this is his name. I ask him to imagine himself driving this bus, and I ask him questions. What're the most important things a driver must do? Why are you going to this destination and no other? What will you do to arrive at your destination safely? A driver must know his destiny to understand the purpose of going there. He must prepare well for his journey making sure that tires are properly inflated, engine is sound, brakes are excellent, cooling system is good, have a GPS in case he's not familiar with the route, stock enough supplies of food and drinks, be mentally, emotionally, physically, and spiritually fit for the journey.

I use the metaphor of a driver to emphasize to him that he determines the outcome of what goes on in his life, that his choices, judgment, and decisions matter a lot. He as a driver is in control of his bus and must take full responsibility for his behavior and results.

Building on the above, I reiterate to the client that you're the best, the best self. Then I ask him a question, "What does be at your best mean to you? What features of your character will make you be at your best and help you overcome the barriers you are facing?"

To be at your best might mean being wealthy, that is, financially, spiritually, physically, healthy, habitually, and emotionally. It may mean changing to fit and operate optimally in a fast-changing environment. You cannot use Galaxy S4 to solve today's technical issues, because its systems are obsolete; all you are to do is acquire the very latest smartphone available.

Language matters. Words transmit energy and vibrate, so they have the power to create or destroy. Nothing is done without energy. I ask the client, "What energy gets things done?" Different energy is required such as financial, physical, emotional, spiritual, health, and habitual. I follow up with another question, "Seeing yourself obstructed by a barrier and are stuck, what energy would you require to break through and advance to your destiny?"

Then I remind him that energy refers to the words he is using to describe his situation and how he sees himself. I challenge the client to develop a language that speaks to his dreams, to his destiny, to frame a language that's aligned to his future and fill his mind with it till it directs his steps. Such an expression is made of up of words that generate unstoppable momentum.

Finally, I urge the client to speak kind, generous, loving, gracious words to himself, and to be honest with himself, to be authentic and not lie to himself, or appease himself. And to speak the language of a wealthy person, of a champion, of a conqueror, of an overcomer.

As human beings, we are connected. Our destiny is linked to others, to the environment, and the Divine. Divine refers to God for those who believe in Him, and other spiritual beings. It also applies to the state we strive to attain, such as bliss, exquisite, love, pleasing, godly, great, excellence, good, righteousness, beauty, and so on. After this brief, I ask the client a question, "What do you say about relationship regarding the hurdles you are encountering? Is the relationship a factor? Explain. I follow up with another question, "Do you have the right relations that could help you overcome the obstacles you are facing and, more importantly, help you attain your destiny.

Knowledge is power. You need the energy to overcome the barriers keeping you away from your destiny. I ask the client the question, "Looking at the barriers, do you have the right knowledge to overcome those barriers and advance to your destiny?" To have this knowledge, you must know your barriers explicitly well. I ask him to describe the barriers. After that, I ask him "What those barriers mean?" The intent is to help him investigate, examine, and explain the issues and select meaningful and relevant knowledge that could solve the problem he is facing wisely.

Learning is the fundamental tool required in developing the capacity to be at your best. It may require you to be versatile, implying being a lifelong learner. Learning permeates every facet of your life. It's an embodiment of growth and development, and accomplishment. Overcoming barriers and advancing to your destiny is a learning process.

In my approach, I use questions and explanations. Questions to help a client dig deeper beneath the issues, involve the client in the search for solutions and design solutions specific to his situation and thus, own the process and solutions. I use explanations to clarify what I am presenting to the client so that he has a clear picture of what I'm saying. Therefore, my primary role is to clarify, facilitate, and be a thinking partner and encourager to the client.

The 5-Steps to Brilliant Breakthrough Solutions is a holistic approach. It involves the client and put the client at the center of his destiny. Character defines your destiny. Words create destiny. The relationship gives you the connections to make it to your destiny. Knowledge empowers you to realize destiny. Wisdom helps you live your destiny. Learning is like a feed. It gives you the strength to make it to your destiny.

Destiny is lifelong. It goes beyond life. It's like DNA that you pass on to the future generation. It lives after you. It's a gift you give to the next generation. It's a leap to your desired future, and the 5-Steps to Brilliant Breakthrough Solutions will empower you to leap to this future.

Kennedy Barasa Wanyonyi, BA, MA, MAL, Certified Coach Practitioner, Certified Master Coach Practitioner

Founder of Brilliant Breakthrough Solutions©

Kennedy is passionate about helping people overcome barriers and leap to their DESTINY. He strongly believes that people have good intentions to make it the best in life, often the reality doesn't match the intentions. Either knowingly or unknowingly, they get in their own way creating barriers to their destiny. However, there is a deep cry in each one of us to be our best. Kennedy designed "The 5-Steps to Brilliant Breakthrough Solutions," as an answer to this deep cry. He has helped many people find their inner strength and voice to reach their full potential by overcoming what they thought was insurmountable. He has led changes turning non-performing departments into high performing units. He has been involved in complex international projects, advised senior-level executives, thus bring diverse viewpoints to issues.

Connect with Kennedy:
kennedy.wanyonyi831@gmail.com
www.facebook.com/Brilliant-Breakthrough-Solutions-334134347343230/
www.instagram.com/brilliantbreakthroughsolutions/?hl=en
www.linkedin.com/in/kennedy-barasa-wanyonyi-08019546/

Informal Coaching: It Can Happen Anywhere. Are You Ready?

by Pennyjane Murray

The focus of this chapter is to examine the thought that the world is rich with opportunities for personal growth, and the prospect to assist in the growth of others. Some approaches are formal and sought out; others are informal and land in our lap as gifts from others. You may be reading this because you are not sure about how coaching can fit into your life? Or, you might be looking for some specific approaches, resources or techniques that would meet your current needs. Potentially, you are looking to assist someone else. Regardless you are interested in exploring coaching with a wide lens so you can move forward with new ideas.

People look for a coach to find or fine-tune their perspective and their plans to move forward to find success - personally, within a family or social circle or in their professional life. As you consider coaching, it is essential to note there are standard features for all coaching regardless if formal or informal. What may be different is the approach. We recommend that you find a method that works best for you and your needs the moment and as they evolve.

If you are looking for a guide to assist you in a structured, scheduled format, there are many options available. To answer what will work best for you: explore the internet where you will find links to coaching associations and federations that profile or provide contacts for coaches. Most also provide contact information so that you can contact them directly to gain further insight. Another option is to ask trusted professionals in your network such as medical practitioners, spiritual leaders, guidance counselors, business networks, and friends or family who have shared they have utilized a coach.

It may also be the time to ensure that what you are looking for is coaching and not therapy or professional consulting. It is possible that coaching and therapy are confused. At a high level, coaching is embraces moving from today into the future. It is very results-focused. Asking questions like, "Where are you today?" and "Where would you like to be?" Discussions and actions look at goals and the steps to move forward. The coach acts as a guide and assists in identifying and setting-up checkpoints for milestones. Therapy works to achieve understanding and emotional healing by exploring past issues and exploring root causes that may explain current circumstances, acting as an expert in such areas as physical, mental or psychotherapy. A professional consultant provides insight and advice in a broad range of specialty areas. Consultants draw from a full range of experience and knowledge (e.g., finance, law, architecture, human resources).

As modern learners, people rarely rely on one type of input; instead, people search for information through a variety of data points such as those listed above, and such virtual resources as YouTube, Podcasts, websites, and television shows. Value can come from many places, to get the most out of these methods start a Learning or Self-reflection Journal. Use this to chronical your journey. Make notes with notations to capture thoughts and insights. Flashes of inspiration can occur when presented something the first time, or sometimes in the review of older records when some new experience or perspective is shared. So be sure to reference sources and dates. As you progress, there are times you might find it interesting, to return to sections and re-read. Depending on your outlook at the time of review, you may see your thoughts or needs have altered, and you will think differently about where you are and what you need.

In my experience, I have met or worked with many people who have expressed they felt coaching was a mysterious process available to executives or for those people who were lucky enough to have the money to afford the luxury to be coached, or work for a company that provides it. They did not see coaching as an accessible option. When prompted for more clarity as to why they could not access coaching, they described coaching as taking only one form, and that was a structured and formalized process. Their impression was that that coaching could only occur in an official capacity. Overlooked entirely were the many informal coaching opportunities that they may have had in their lifetime to have been in a coaching situation themselves or the times they may not have realized they were coaching others.

Considering the thought that informal coaching opportunities are plentiful if we are open to them and discussions with people that highlighted the perception that coaching was out-of-reach, I was inspired to reflect on my life experience to determine why the nature and value of coaching is something so fundamentally part of how I think people interact. Professionally, as an educator of children, in later years as a facilitator of adult learning and as a member of multiple management teams I have seen coaching integrated powerfully in many ways. Often by people who didn't even realize they were coaching. What is striking is to think of how much more valuable the informal coaching could have been if people had been aware of what they were doing.

Conversely, I have seen and participated in poorly executed coaching. Typically, when this occurred, it became evident that the foundational components of coaching were side-stepped or ignored. Instead of coaching to forward personal growth, the trap, was the shift from coaching to teaching or consulting. What occurred was confusion when the coach switched mid-stream from conversations that posed questions, provided a mirror to what was being said to stimulate reflection on important and the steps toward the creation of a plan, to one where they were teaching or advising. This switch in focus confused the coachee (person being coached). What was shared, is that in most cases both were considered valuable, and could work well together if it was clear which frame-of-mind or approach they were using. What was critical, is the alignment with an individual's needs and outcomes.

The purpose of the next few paragraphs is to inspire you, through the lens of my experience, to see what opportunities you may have had where you have been coached or may have the chance to provide the power of coaching to others. With the unlocking of this awareness, you will more be more mindful, so you can fully embrace future opportunities.

This intellectual journey started for me on an actual flight. I was seated on an airplane completing some coaching notes before a young woman took the seat next to me. For confidentiality, I closed my folder and put away my papers. She apologized for interrupting me. I said it was no problem and that I had used the last few minutes to review records from a coaching session while the information was fresh. Reference to coaching sparked a lively discussion from Ottawa to Toronto. She was very interested, and we discussed our various encounters with coaches. As we unpacked experiences, it became clear that some of our first opportunities to where we were coached began as far back as our school guidance counselors or teachers, and then later "advisors" as part of post-secondary programs or work. As we discussed the things, we had valued most about these people she began to share how blessed she'd felt to have had a grade eight teacher who fundamentally provided group coaching to her entire class every Friday afternoon. In the last thirty minutes, they were to work with a different partner each week and take turns to share a goal for the future. The classmate's role was to ask what they had learned or done this week that might assist them in moving forward and how they would put this to work. They then wrote or drew a summary in their Personal Log. She then would meet with them privately, at her desk, once every two weeks to share and discuss anything that they could do together to move goals forward. She had never thought of it from the perspective that they were learning how to coach and be coached, but now realized why she still had lingering respect and many fond memories of this educator, and how this experience had colored her current management style.

This chance discussion caused me to think about the many other times in my past when people had taken an interest in the growth or success of myself or my friends. Looking back from the vantage point of being in my sixties, I reflected on how fortunate I was to grow up in a community with access to insightful: parents, grandparents, aunts, uncles and countless other family and community friends. There were many opportunities to discuss and explore life's challenges through the lens of the wisdom uniquely shared over a pot of tea or coffee around a kitchen table. The intimate nature of this experience created a safe and friendly setting to assist in transitioning from the general discussion about life, self-awareness, focused exploration, and action.

During the teenage years of self-discovery, my peers and I were surrounded by people whose approach to life was practical and steeped in broad life experience, plus they shared an essential need to look after each other both mentally and physically. Likely the case, because those who provided this source of support to us lived in rural settings during the early 1900s and had to be self-reliant. Even in the 1960s and 1970s in rural Ontario, the formal resources found in city centers were either not available or provided on an itinerant basis and therefore not regularly available. Although this is rarer today, it is still possible, depending on where you live, that this is true for you as well. As costs rise, access may be shrinking due to community budgets and focus.

What repeatedly struck me was that they had different ways of imparting "things to think about" in a way that was non-threatening and practical. Skilled conversationalists, they would weave well-thought-out questions into discussions that would provide an individual with something to ponder. The gift granted to the individual was the opportunity to contemplate the question or statement and determine for themselves how relevant it was and what mental journey it would take them.

However, as with many of us, at the time we might not have fully appreciated the wisdom or the generosity of this support. Both my grandmothers we extraordinary women. In many ways, way ahead of their time. My paternal grandmother found herself a young widow. In a time when few women worked in business, she not only worked but with a friend started a business. When asked how she did it, she would say, "You just have to have a big enough picture and the ability to break it down into steps. Then it isn't so big. It works for almost everything." So, whenever my brother or I went to her with something, she'd ask for us to describe the big picture. She would then ask, "What do you think is the first step? Now let's break that down." My maternal grandmother was a farmer's wife. She raised her own six children and through a very active role in the church and community, influenced many others in her quiet way. She was used to being practical and all about getting the most out of everyone and everything. My grandfather was well-read and clever, so between the lessons of church and from literature they would often say things, that at the time seemed obscure. It is only through reflection afforded by time and distance I can see the artistry that they and many of their contemporaries used to, in my maternal grandmother's words, "Bring someone along by having them think about and take ownership for their choices and decisions."

For example, sometimes dialogue would start with a statement, that at the time, may or may not have been perceived as directly relevant. For example, "Rivers have no borders, only humans make borders – so what borders are you putting in the way of what you want to accomplish?"

Rather than rush you on, they would let these thoughts sit for a few minutes allowing time to ponder. They never seemed to hurry or impose their timelines on you. Sometimes they would not go back to the statement, other times they'd use it to open discussion to probe your specific issue. Either way, most often you would go away thinking about it. The sayings would roll around in your thoughts and usually a day later; it would cause you to question how the ideas might be relevant and how they might prompt a solution to your dilemma. The power of this approach was that if often worked like self-coaching. Once the seed placed it caused people to think, ask themselves questions and link to next steps. To this day, there are frequent reminders of these funny little sayings and how they fit different challenges.

As early as I can remember, thinking for yourself started at the kitchen table. It was a family value that my mother, father, and younger brother would meet at the end of our day to have dinner together. What I realize now, is this was a choreographed move to provide time to seize, what I would now call, coachable moments. The whole process of assisting my mother in setting the table and preparing for supper, provided time for small talk creating a relaxed, conversational setting. It was a time where we shared funny or upsetting stories from across the day, and what of our after-school chores were complete (or more likely not). It also created topics for some well-placed questions that often would come up again during dinner as she shared stories of the day with my father. We sat at a round table which formed a circle prompting a discussion of equals, rather than someone being at the head and in charge. As we passed food around the table to reinforce family expectations related to etiquette, mom or father would reflect on either an international, national, or local news item, or something from discussions of what happened during the day. Somehow, they would zone in on something that we would benefit from working through, and that would be the dinner focus. Inevitably we'd be asked what we thought and why that was important.

What strikes me now, is how they modeled the power of listening. It was clear both parents were listening, because of the questions they asked or the way they responded. In the end, they would typically give the highest compliment of all by validating the importance of talking things through, determining how our thoughts could influence what we could do and ensuring we understood that we had accomplished something significant – thinking for ourselves! They would say things like, "Well that was a good talk." I often think back to the days sitting at the Arborite table with turquoise plastic chairs with fondness and with a sense of accomplishment. As we aged, the discussions dealt with more complex topics, and then as we entered our teenage years happened less and less as we all got busy with part-time jobs, dating, and other friends. Learning in this way was very organic and never felt forced. I often think about how this approach was such great parenting. They planted the seed early and built a foundation of how to work through challenges and opportunities.

There were times when the coaching was very personal and purposeful. A long-lasting memory was sharing with my mom one evening that the kids at school had been mean to me, teasing and excluding me from some activity at school and I was trying to figure out what to do. Being left out was a big deal when you went to a one-room school. With so few people, once shunned, you were alone. Of course, I shared with mom expecting sympathy. Instead, she pulled out one of those sayings, "It is better to be looked over - than overlooked." At ten, this was not the response I had been expecting, nor did I at first understand it. I am sure I looked confused. Without missing a beat, what mom did next was to explore what it meant and leveraged that to assist me in determining my next steps. I won't replay the whole conversation; however, I will recount the path of the discussion and the richness of it. Rich, because fifty some years later I still remember it, and draw from the experience often. To me, this supports the value of informal coaching and the fact that people who wouldn't define themselves as a coach, can, in fact, coach because they believe that people have the power to find their success.

She let the saying sit for a few minutes. Then she asked what I thought it meant. She inquired what it would be like if no one ever noticed you at all, and why at least being noticed was a good thing. We acknowledged that the type of notice I had experienced was not the type I desired. Her questioning forced me, every step of the way, to consider what I might have done or said to direct their attention negatively and to explore explanations for their actions or responses. The shift came when we discussed going to school that next day and how I could react. We examined the notion that we can't control what people think, but we could think about how I could choose to respond, what was my biggest fear, and what could I do if that became a reality. By the end of the discussion, I felt in more control. I had been heard, and I had some real ideas to move forward. Most importantly I felt supported as I worked on strategies to navigate my life challenges.

I refer to these stories to stimulate you to think if you also have had the good fortune to have had people in your life that had or have demonstrated the ability to take everyday conversations, or stories and turn them into a precious opportunity to get and give coaching. Alternatively, you can reflect on times when you provided this support to others. As you reflect were you ready? Did you take full advantage?

Informal coaching can have benefit whether you are the coachee or if you find yourself with the opportunity to coach others. Both roles provide you the opportunity for growth. In the position of coaching others, you begin to develop or increase your intuition or mindfulness. The goal is to become fully present and aware of what you are doing, where you are starting and on what or where you will be focusing. Being mindful provides the ability to trust your instincts and use the ability to understand yourself and others without relying on conscious reasoning.

If you choose to engage in informal coaching to enhance your life plan the following are some things to consider so you get the most out of the experience regardless of the role.

Watch for or create opportunities to take advantage of just-in-time coaching to gain new perspectives and ideas for moving forward.

If you meet someone and you believe their insight would benefit you, or you are aware that someone has switched into a coaching role seize the moment.

Informal coaching is not a passive activity you need to advocate for yourself. You have a responsibility to yourself to set the stage for success. Be prepared to ask to be coached, or if you feel someone has begun coaching if you could continue to build on the inquiry-type approach. Ensure to establish a timeframe for the session, so there is a natural end for summary and for planning the next steps. Also, make every effort to ensure you are in a comfortable setting and that you feel safe.

With the focus on being an active participant, and assist in shaping the experience, articulate as clearly as you can what is on your mind, or what you are trying to contextualize or solve to propel yourself forward. Ensure your informal coach knows you are not looking to them to fix things for you, however, that you would welcome if they would listen and act as a mirror to your perspectives and ideas and if they would ensure you look below the surface by asking questions to stimulate deeper thinking.

As they relax into listening and asking you thought-provoking questions, let them know you appreciate this exploration. In the end, if they have not already done this, request they summarize what they heard and what next steps you identified. Let them know this summary will allow you to reflect and confirm or add details. In the end, it is up to you to make a note of future actions and set a time to follow-up if you think it would be valuable and they are willing.

If the informal nature suited you, be sure that you continue in this format. If working with them, is a fit, but you would like to have this be more structured ask for that as well. Be prepared that if the person does not feel they are the best person for you, they might recommend someone or suggest you look for a formal coach. Either way, you have the next step and can act.

If you find yourself in the role of an informal coach, keep central throughout your conversation that the focus should be on the person. If your measure of success is that they come to their own conclusions, then that is what will occur. Do you worry about what to ask to keep the conversation going? By maintaining your intention entirely on them, and actively listening it will make it easier to ask questions as they will follow intuitively. Don't over think your questions or responses. Stay with versions of the "Five Ws" you learned in school: what, why, when, who and how.

To start, ensure you are clear what they want to discuss, if it is a big topic, you may need to use your questioning right away to get them to focus on just one thing. Ask the coachee to tell you what they would like to get out of the conversation. For example, are they looking to formulate a solution or next steps to solve a problem, or are they looking for a different perspective that they can consider as they continue to think through a problem or challenge? It may be necessary to pause and sit in silence as they ponder, as they may not have a response immediately. Respect the process and give them some time. As referred to above, if it becomes apparent to you both that there is an opportunity to gain some additional knowledge or skill, be sure that they request or are open to the appropriate instruction, training, or consulting. Verify if it is part of the same timeframe or a request to happen separately. When ready, to resume coaching, ensure they are clear you're your focus has changed.

With a map of where they want to go, it is now like driving a standard car. Many people worry about having the right questions. Relax into the process and don't worry too much about what you will ask, or you won't be authentic, and it will restrict conversation. Listen intently to responses and let questions flow naturally from the point of inquiry. If you find yourself providing your perspective to relate and find common ground or to challenge their thinking, be sure to identify it as your perspective and that the purpose of sharing was to stimulate their response not impose your ideas. Like shifting gears in a standard vehicle, sometimes the shifts you make are smooth, other times they are a bit jerky and need rephrasing. This ebb and flow are a normal part of dialogue. As you journey through the conversation, it is appropriate to validate or endorse the ideas they create.

Be sure that when it is clear the conversation is at a close, that you review their summary, including what they have identified as the next steps. It might be appropriate to thank them for trusting you to take the journey together.

Be clear of the scope of your skillset. Remember, that if you feel that you or someone that comes to you is looking for support for a medical issue or advice in a professional area that is outside your training or experience, that you will be acting with integrity if you refer the coachee to find a consultant, therapist, or doctor.

If you took the suggestion to start a Self-reflection or Learning Journal, by now, your notes will be full of references and ideas garnered from your experiences and research. These notes and reflections will support you on your journey. Harness the power of informal coaching as a strategy and enhance your personal growth and success.

I hope this chapter encouraged you to notice how abundant the opportunities for growth are. To be thankful for those that have coached us in the past and watch for the occasion to harness new experiences and gain new perspectives.

Pennyjane (Pj) Murray, M.Sc., B.Ed., Certified Coach Practitioner

Passionate4Potential Human Coaching®

For over thirty-nine years Pennyjane has been passionate about assisting people to liberate their potential. First as a teacher, then as a formal leader across multiple sectors Pj has assisted numerous individuals of all ages to realize small and large goals. As a speaker, and as a corporate and life coach Pj has had the privilege to work with people in both formal and informal coaching scenarios. In Pj's opinion coaching provides the opportunity to provide people with a window to shine the light on what is possible and unleash creative thinking. Pj grew-up working in a small business assisting amazing parents, brother, husband, stepdaughter and host of other family and friends to run a resort and marina. Life continues to bring new joys as a grandmother to two incredible and active grandsons.

Connect with PJ:
passionate4potential@gmail.com

Mindset Modulation

by Brett Skrupski

Think for a moment about creating growth, abundance, and success in your life. What is your experience of those thoughts? You may sense an empowering desire to forge ahead, championing yourself and those around you to new heights. Alternatively, you may have a pervading sense of anxiety, stress, or overwhelm. As a coach, I've witnessed a significant trend towards more negative experiences in the clients I have worked with. The good news is that when you find yourself chained to that limiting state-of-mind, you are not alone. The even better news is that you possess the ability to unshackle those metaphorical chains and achieve anything you set your mind to.

Creating a mindset of your own design—one energized by the desire to move forward, succeed, and achieve—is not something that can be completed with a figurative snap-of-your-fingers; as with all good and worthy things, it takes time, patience, and persistence. The destination is most definitely worth the journey, however, and you grow with every step you take in your preferred direction. Before you begin taking those steps, it may be of great assistance to have a map to guide you; you set the destination, and the way by which you get from point A to point B is key.

Ancient Chinese philosopher Laozi is credited with the famous quote, "The journey of a thousand miles begins with a single step," and it's so important to remember that any path you choose to walk is a series of steps–not one massive jump from beginning to end. One of the most powerful strategies I work on with clients is helping them both understand this concept and put it into practice. To help facilitate this, I've developed my own five-step process to begin crafting your mindset for success. Weaving throughout the steps are four themes, as well, which represent crucial elements for creating lasting, positive, and impactful change. As I elaborate more on my five-step process, I'll highlight the importance of these elements—awareness, agency, action, and accountability—and the role they play in assisting you in creating a mindset that best serves your intentions moving forward.

STEP 1: AWARENESS

Both a step and one of the elements I mentioned, awareness is most definitely the beginning of mindset creation. Awareness itself is a moment of realization—of your actions, thoughts, beliefs, intentions, and values—which constitutes a pivotal shift in personal growth and development. While it may seem a given, the absence of awareness in your life may surprise you; I know that it certainly surprised me when faced with it.

In the movie The Matrix, Morpheus famously enlightens his protégé Neo with the line, "Neo, sooner or later you're going to realize . . . that there's a difference between knowing the path and walking the path." The quote carries a great deal of significance, as it delves directly to the heart of awareness: knowledge and understanding. Before you can walk any path to change, you need to become aware that change is needed in the first place; you need to know the path to tread.

That knowledge can come as a gentle awakening, or a swift slap in the face; it all depends how far your head is under the proverbial blanket of obliviousness. To help illustrate what I mean, I'll pull an example from my own past and share it with you. I grew up with the habit of lamenting or complaining about many, many things. It was a common practice, and I did not realize the negativity wrought by the behavior, or that I was even doing it for the most part; that is, until my best friend from grade school brought it to my attention one day. He matter-of-factly stated that I was a complainer, though did not do so in a way that was malicious or hurtful; rather, I believe it was done to make me aware, as I was most certainly oblivious to it. The realization was rather shocking and humbling. I hadn't known that my consistent behavior was affecting others, as well as myself, in such a negative way; I mean—who wants to be around someone complaining all the time? It revealed a lack of awareness about myself and my actions, but also an avenue for positive change. It allowed me to discover—or know—the path I wanted to take and granted me the insight to change something about myself that I didn't agree with.

The programming you carry with you from childhood has a tremendous impact on your subconscious, and how you live your life. It provides a detailed roadmap from all your previous learnings and knowledge, and a "default" set of beliefs, values, and ideas. You had no power over how you internalized that programming growing up because your brain biologically was not capable of doing so; without a developed filter, all the experiences you had were taken in as true—in whatever form you interpreted that truth. As those patterns and programs were employed repeatedly, they became habitual, and exist inscrutably from your conscious mind. It's moments of awareness—like my personal example—that truly reveal how you, as an adult, can become very much aware of how oblivious you've been to certain behaviors, beliefs, and actions that may be incongruous with the kind of mindset you want to develop.

As hard as these moments are to experience, they are phenomenal moments of personal growth. You've become aware that something isn't quite right; something in your life isn't serving you; you're struggling to make sense of how you see things, and how the world is presenting itself to you. No matter how you phrase it, you're acknowledging and accepting that change is necessary. Even more powerfully, that you need to change in order to accomplish your goals and find success in your life.

If you're not lucky enough to have a friend metaphorically slap you with a wake-up call, you can bring about such moments on your own. Begin by asking yourself some (potentially) tough questions: Does this behavior contribute positively to myself and others? Do my actions bring me closer to my goals? Are there things I need to let go of in order to live a more fulfilled life? What stories am I telling myself that are no longer or were never true to begin with? In what ways am I holding myself back, and limiting my potential?

The answers you discover—and the steps needed afterward—may be difficult, but only because you've become used to the way things are and tend to avoid 'uncomfortable' levels of uncertainty. However, if you're willing to commit yourself and become aware of what you want to change for the better, you'll be on the right track—or path—to building the kind of mindset that enables you to succeed.

STEP 2: A DESIRE TO CHANGE

At first blush, the difference between awareness of wanting to change and a desire to actively change may appear almost indistinguishable; after all, if you're aware that a change will benefit you now and, in the future, why wouldn't you desire to make it a reality? A valid question, no doubt—yet one that many of us defy on a regular basis. This became apparent to me after a very thought-provoking discussion with a colleague involving mindset creation, and the process of moving from moments of awareness to action. We found ironic amusement in the fact that, for as logical as you and I are, we can make some startlingly illogical decisions, and often not engage in changes which serve our best interest. The thinking is not so black-and-white that we purposefully do things which harm or do not serve us, but rather, how infrequently we act in order to better, expand, and improve ourselves.

To explore the irony of this perspective, we discussed an example regarding physical fitness. As rational beings, we know how important it is to eat a well-balanced diet and exercise, yet the majority of the population (in North America, at least) neglects to do so. It's not as if any of us are incapable of making changes; we can easily walk or run instead of driving everywhere, and even if we lack the means to eat a fully organic diet, eating fast food is not the only alternative. This example very much speaks to the differentiation in The Matrix quote from before—that there is a distinct difference between knowing the path and walking the path. If you know what will improve your health and well-being, yet neglect to do so, you are actively choosing to remain dormant, rather than embracing positive and progressive change. If that's your choice, there's nothing wrong with it; this is no place—and I am in no position—to cast any kind of judgment over your choices. However, it exemplifies the basic idea that if you lack the desire to change, you won't. Change is an active process; one that requires you to embrace agency in your life and take responsibility for the choices you make. Even if you are clearly aware of a path to personal success does not mean you will walk it. The question raised in my colleague was, "If we're smart and know what's good for us, why don't we just do it?" A powerful and thought-provoking question, indeed.

We chatted more with the intention of discovering the 'missing link' between awareness—of ourselves and what is in our best interest—and taking the necessary action to move in a more positive and rewarding direction. The answer is ambiguous, as there isn't a singular reason why we know but do not do. If the first thought to pop into your mind in answer to this is laziness, you wouldn't be alone; it's very easy to write inaction off as laziness, though I believe the level of comfort we live in plays a much more significant factor. When we're comfortable, we possess less inclination to make changes and rock our metaphorical boats. It's shocking what we can become used to, given time, and without the pain of discomfort, we lack a real desire to change.

That desire plays a huge role, as it's the spark that lights a fire of action beneath us and drives us forward. All kinds of fear and limitation can hold us back from acting; it's different from person-to-person, and from situation-to-situation. The common thread, though, is that if we lack the desire, drive, persistence, or determination to set out on a journey of growth and improvement, we will find myriad excuses not to, and remain set in our ways.

To discover the 'missing link', I found that going back to one of Tony Robbins' basic principles shed light on an answer. He maintains that humans either seek pleasure or avoid pain, and when put to the ultimate test, will choose to avoid pain before pursuing pleasure. This speaks to my observation that our desire to change correlates inversely with our comfort level. Unless we can associate pain with what we do not want—in the case of the fitness example, feeling slow, sluggish, lethargic, or generally unhealthy—we will not move to change. If you are comfortable—whether you're telling yourself or not—with not achieving your goals, you'll not make the necessary changes in order to reach them.

So, what is my advice, you may ask? Learn to buck comfort and become uncomfortable. If you have a goal you want to reach, yet you lack the desire to take decisive and massive action towards it right now, ask yourself what is holding you back. Search for what's making you feel comfortable in a place, mindset, or state of being that does not agree with your awareness and desired direction. Once you've identified the culprit(s), work on associating pain with it (them) to such a degree that you become uncomfortable existing in that way. Use that discomfort to really understand what you don't want, and then shift your focus to what you do: the rewards from achieving your goal(s). Through a mixture of avoiding the pain you've created with your current situation, and a desire to move towards the pleasurable state your new goal(s) will bring about, you'll be in a much more motivated place to take the action that aligns with awareness of yourself, and where you want to go.

STEP 3: EMBRACE WHO YOU WERE SO YOU CAN BECOME WHO YOU WANT TO BE

As a coach, I have the privilege of learning my clients' stories; it's so fascinating to discover where they've come from, and how they've become who they are. Equally intriguing is exploring every client's relationship with their story. Some have a positive relationship, others negative; so, the question I have for you: how do you feel about your own story?

You, like everyone else, have choices, moments, and experiences in your past that you've considered alternative outcomes for. In fact, you may have significant traumas you wouldn't wish upon your worst enemies. Equally, I'm sure you've experienced amazing highs and successes which you remember fondly. Every one of these moments has contributed to the person you are, and who you want to become.

Knowing your story—and more importantly, owning it—is so incredibly empowering. Even if you hold onto regret or wish you could do things differently, it's important to remember two things: the past cannot be changed, and you are who you are because of who you were. Re-writing beliefs and limits that no longer serve you is entirely within your power; how they've affected you in the past cannot be changed, however, so it is crucial to frame the way you think about these experiences in a positive way. Depending on circumstances, this may be difficult to accomplish; when you've lived through real trauma, it can be tough to put a 'positive spin' on it.

You can achieve this level of acceptance and positivity by owning and learning from your past. Accept that which you cannot change and choose to learn and grow from the experience. It doesn't mean you accept wrongs done to you, or no longer care about any hurt you may have caused; rather, it's about not creating the artificial weights of blame or guilt which keep you from moving forward in your life. Owning your past and accepting responsibility for it can allow you to free yourself from the burden of guilt and shame. You may be who you are because of your past, but that history need not define your future. Only you can decide how you want to feel, what you want to pursue, and what kind of person you become. The choices you make right now do not need to align with who you were—especially if these choices lead you towards who you know you are and are willing to grow into.

The story of you is unique because no one else can experience it. You may have been born with every opportunity imaginable or required to move mountains for every inch you gained. For these, and every place in between, you have compiled a unique story from which to draw from. Learn from your mistakes; be humble in your achievements; expand; grow; own who you are. Only when you've come to terms with your past can you truly draw strength from it. And once you do, you're ready to use that strength to become the person you ultimately want to be.

STEP 4: PLAN BACKWARD AND PROBLEM-SOLVE TO THE BEGINNING

Have you ever put the effort and focus into planning a road trip? You know your starting point and destination; you map out which routes you'll take, and what stops you want to make along the way; if you're prone to the occasional bout of over-planning, you may also focus on making it the most "efficient" path possible. This process works well enough for trip-planning that you've likely used it in your goal setting, too; your goal is the destination, and an action plan serves as your map. If you've found success in this way, that's fantastic; it means you've little trouble stepping out of your comfort zone and embrace—or are at least comfortable with—uncertainty. If your results have been mixed, however, or leave you feeling overwhelmed and anxious, know that you're not alone. More often than not, you're going to find yourself feeling overwhelmed or anxious when thinking about your goal, and have difficulty defining your next step forward.

If you take a moment and think about completing a goal, compared to where you're currently at, there's a good chance you perceive that distance as a large gap and, worst-case-scenario, close to impossible. This fear and negativity stem from focusing on your current state of goal in-completion, and the perceived mountain you've got to climb in order to reach your goal finally. I make it sound rather ominous, but that's how it really appears to a lot of people—no wonder they have difficulty achieving success!

Instead, I like to suggest my clients to take a reverse approach. Once you have identified your goal, I encourage you to place yourself within the experience of achieving it. You're no longer mentally in the here-and-now—square one—but at the point of completion. After you've embraced the success of having achieved your goal, I ask you to take steps backward, and outline how you got there. Were there other people who helped you along the way? What skills did you use which enabled you to get to your point of success? Did you learn anything new along the way that aided you in your journey?

While not a revolutionary mindset shift, changing the direction you plan your goals in can have incredibly powerful impact. Instead of planning in the traditional way of start to destination, I like to use this strategy with my clients when creating action steps and plans. Beyond the mental jog that thinking this way coaxes the mind into, I find beginning at the goal and working backward elicits more creativity and positivity than starting from where you are now.

By positioning you in the mindset of having already completed your goal, it diminishes or removes the fear of failure, and actually promotes logical and positive problem-solving, because you've got to put a plan in place that links your perceived success back to your actual starting point. Every client's plan comes together differently, yet the results remain the same: approaching goal setting from this perspective reduces the anxiety and overwhelm they experienced previously and makes for a much more enjoyable and creative process. Try it for yourself, especially if you're having a tough time getting after your goals!

STEP 5: TAKE ACTION... NOW!

We all know the old saying about snoozing and losing, right? Well, it has a lot of truth (and a little neuroscience) behind it, even if it's a little on the blunt side. There are even multiple angles we can explore it from—including the literal notion of punching the snooze button! What really fascinates me about it, though, is the impact that snoozing—or hesitating—has on our actions and success.

We're all capable of immediate, decisive action in order to achieve a goal. For example, if we see a child drowning, there's little if any hesitation at all to run in and save them. Yet, for all we're capable of doing in an instant, why do we often find ourselves procrastinating when setting off to achieve our goals? This is where some of that neuroscience comes into play.

In the instant we're responding to the child drowning, our brains are running in the emotional, 'gut' response mode. There's no overthinking or analysis: we see an objective and act immediately to achieve it. The immediacy is key here, as acting right away is crucial in goal achievement and success. This is all well-and-good, but where does the 'snooze' part come into play?

When we're presented with a work project, a school essay, or a desire to change our situation to what we want, often we find ourselves drifting or stagnating off the start. Typically, it's because our logic brain has entered the equation, and is assessing things. If stress is encountered around a particular objective, our brains will seek to 'protect' us from it and put off or avoid the stressful situation entirely. Ever had the intent of doing or becoming something, only for your brain to produce a litany of reasons why you can't? That's the overthinking and procrastination of stress coming into play. We're pressing the figurative 'snooze' button on our lives.

The unfortunate, and damaging, language our mind uses inwardly in these moments is one of can't as opposed to won't. The brain is seeking to keep us safe from harm and trauma, which it often perceives stress as. When we're avoiding a stressful task, we're making the choice not to pursue it—we won't take part in the action because it causes us stress. However, the language is twisted inside of us and often comes in the form of can't instead. Allow me to provide a short example:

You want to run a half-marathon. You need to train for said marathon. How do you train for it? You run. Now, how many people actually enjoy running? There's no judgment here—but I know the number of people who dislike running will very likely outnumber the number who do. So, if you don't feel like running on a particular day, you're confronted with a decision. It causes you stress because if you don't run, you may fall behind on your training; and if you fall behind in your training, you're lagging even further from your goal. But you really don't feel like running today. Instead of saying, "I won't be running today...", we end up saying, "I can't run today...", and fill in the rest with some kind of excuse. We're so much more unfortunately accepting of a perceived inability (can't) over a choice (won't), as though it's grossly offensive we could choose not to do something.

This language leads to all kinds of difficulty for us; instead of empowering ourselves by making and owning choices in our lives (won't), we reinforce negativity and limitation by claiming inability (can't). It's this language that perpetuates our hesitation when we're going after something we really want. We train ourselves to defeat any notion of success so readily before we even take one step towards it. It's an ugly habit, to be sure, but when we're aware of it, we can work to break it.

Mel Robbins, author of "The 5 Second Rule", proposes a very intriguing pattern-interrupt for when we get stuck in these situations. Decide in five seconds or less and act. Now, it's not necessarily the best decision-making platform for all your major decisions in life, but what it does is motivate you to act—and act now.

Immediacy is the key takeaway from all of this. We know our brains will work to subvert our intention if met with stress. Stress is often encountered in change, growth, and expansion of ourselves—at least to some degree. In order to not fall into the trap our overthinking minds lay for us, the important thing to remember is to take some positive action immediately. Speak with anyone who excels in their life, and they will tell you that when they set a goal, they start making things happen right away. This doesn't mean the first step needs to be enormous or ground-breaking—it simply sets the tone and builds momentum right off the bat. You're empowered by working towards your goal, and when you find stress along the way, the momentum carries you right through it to the end.

We all press the 'snooze' button on occasion in our lives. There are times when it may be helpful or needed, depending on the circumstances. When it becomes habit and keeps us from living the kind of lives we want, however, then it's a problem. The first step towards anything new is regarded as the hardest. From a goal accomplishment perspective, this may not feel like the case—there's often a lot of difficult steps along the road—but it really is. When we make the decision to act, it requires us to move outside of the norm; to take steps outside the certainty of our comfort zone, in order to be challenged and ultimately grow.

A very dear friend once quoted me, "Imperfect action is better than inaction." The power of this quote is astounding, as it tackles so many ideas in such a simple and short sentence. For many of us, when we look at taking action, we "snooze." Jumping outside of our comfort zone is, well, uncomfortable, and it's not a stretch to suggest that many decide not to act in the first place because of this. Many people also become wrapped up in the notion that everything they do, and every step they take, needs to be perfect; that kind of pressure is self-defeating, and very easily allows us to give up and not take action ("If I'm not going to do it right, I'm not going to do it at all!").

The power in the original quote stems from the simplicity of admitting that it is better to take action, even if it's not perfect, than be left to the doldrums of inaction. To act "imperfectly" suggests that you may make a mistake, you may screw up, you may feel like you are further behind than you were before—but all the while you're actually learning and growing. If we refuse to act, we hold ourselves back, negating the possibility of opportunity and success, for the (false) satisfaction and comfort of our regular routine. Action requires us to move forward—an integral part of growth and life—because if we do not, we stagnate. It's so easy for us to drum up innumerable excuses to not act, to convince ourselves that we are happy where we are, or that we're not capable of attaining the level of success that we are capable of. Well, all I have to say to that is, "You. Deserve. Better."

Don't be your own worst enemy and hold yourself back. Refuse to let the certainty and comfort of your routine be a warm blanket, all the while punching the "snooze" button any time you experience challenge or adversity. Accept and let go of the notion that every step forward must be perfect—perfect is boring and unattainable anyway! Learn, grow, challenge yourself, live, and act! You'll thank yourself for it down the road.

Creating a mindset that aligns with your truth and goals is not an insurmountable task. Taking these steps to heart can truly help you from getting in your own way and holding yourself back. Becoming aware of who you are, what you want, and the potential limitations standing in your way allows you to begin the process of change. Embracing agency and accountability in your life enable you to claim your power, re-write stories which no longer serve, and make the decisions necessary to pull you closer towards your chosen outcome. And finally, taking consistent action brings all these thoughts, feelings, beliefs, and values into your reality—moving you forward and building the positive momentum you need to carry through any obstacle or adversity on your path.

Brett Skrupski, BA Hons, B. Comm, Certified Coach Practitioner, Certified Master Coach Practitioner

Mindset Coach, Future Design Coaching Services®

Possessing a real passion for growth and self-development, Brett has found tremendous success in his career as a coach, speaker, and educator. As a coach, he has partnered with myriad individuals to assist in their empowerment and overcoming of self-imposed limitations by exploring habits, language, and fear. As a speaker, Brett has created and delivered online learning modules for a coaching community, and conducted numerous workshops for captive audiences, covering a variety of topics. Finally, as an educator, he has had the honor of training new life coaches—helping to give them the tools necessary to venture out into the world and help countless others.

Connect with Brett:
www.futuredesigncoaching.com
info@futuredesigncoaching.com
306-380-1526
www.facebook.com/brettskrupski
www.instagram.com/brettskrupski
www.linkedin.com/in/brettskrupski

Believe in Yourself - Change Your Life, Change the World

by Sandra Wrycraft

Y ou are in a familiar setting, surrounded by who and what you know and understand well. Whether at work or home, you are content in this place of safety and comfort. You may not realize you have been conditioned to live here; in avoidance of judgment, concealing your inadequacies, uncertainties, and personal limitations. Living within your shadow, you are missing the opportunity to truly experience the light of life's full potential due to an inherent lack of belief in yourself, based on a foundation of subconscious fear. By living authentically, you will overcome self-doubt and have the great opportunity to create positive and meaningful change for yourself and the world around you in ways you have never dreamed possible.

As a child, you are an invincible creature, living playfully in the spirit of life. Then the reality of life's challenges emerges as you embark on achieving your dreams. You struggle as you begin to acknowledge your shortcomings and start living in a mindset of comparison with a new-found need for approval to validate your worthiness. You have become afraid and uncomfortable with being who you truly are.

Paralyzed by these limiting, self-manifested thoughts and beliefs, you imprison yourself in a mindset of self-doubt. The heavy weight of these unnecessary burdens manifest themselves in unhealthy ways, leaving you with a languishing spirit.

Your lack of assuredness inhibits you from living authentically. You may be afraid of exposing your vulnerabilities and protect yourself from judgment by others instead of embracing yourself as a beautifully imperfect human. In self-defense, you quietly conform, holding yourself in an insecure place of stagnation which can be an empty and uninspiring place to live. From a place of ease, you follow the path laid rather than standing out with a unique or unpopular opinion. So instead of living true to yourself, you live as an ideological chameleon, superficially camouflaging yourself to blend in. Life is challenging enough, let alone to suffer in a place of insecurity and fear. Living as an imposter, constantly changing your colors to disguise the person within for fear of revealing your unique individuality is an authentic life lost.

In contrast to living small, a lack of self-confidence may manifest itself in the form of ego or perfectionism. Opposed to camouflaging, ego presents its arrogant self as an armor of protection for the voice from within saying, "I am fearful of people discovering that I am unsure of who I truly am; my strengths and my shortcomings combined." Like ego, tendencies of perfectionism empower you to pose as an exceptionally capable achiever by demonstrating your worthiness to others through the promotion of your accomplishments. These protectionist mechanisms safeguard you from exposing your inadequacies instead of embracing your shortcomings as a true human being.

In the spirit of protecting yourself, you play it safe to avoid failure and judgment, neglecting to recognize that success is often preceded by failure. Experiencing failure allows for an opportunity to grow and learn in order to ultimately achieve success; however, the fear of failure can paralyze your desire for action. When you are afraid, you become a defensive and artful victim of self-sabotage by the stories you tell yourself. You are your own biggest critic and in comparing yourself to others, you tell yourself you are inadequate. Through these self-limiting tales, you disable yourself from moving forward; holding yourself hostage to a mindset of inferiority.

As much as you may be afraid of failing, for some, the bigger fear is in finding victory. This is a counter-intuitive concept; after all, you've been striving for success and reaching for those very goals. Let's consider Mary, a Director at consulting firm, who learns she is being considered for a promotion to VP, a level she has been vying for her entire career. Initially, she is excited and flattered by the prospect but quickly shifts into downward spiraling self-talk. She is concerned about how others may perceive her taking on this prominent leadership role and certainly does not want to appear arrogant. Also, with this big title Mary will become noticed and have her performance scrutinized to a much greater degree. Though capable of conquering this opportunity, she admits she is fearful of the limelight and questions her own deservedness. She removes herself from the running to prevent being seen as the remarkably bright, capable, and talented woman that she clearly is. Believing those dreams are for someone bigger and better, she fabricates a narrative that leads to unfulfilled dreams.

Self-doubt is an apparent part of the human condition, resulting in self-limiting thoughts and actions, preventing us from living our best lives. We seem to be living in a state of comparison, competition, and living up to how society defines success, what is on trend, what we should be, and what we must want. This causes one to live in a state of disempowering inadequacy. We encumber ourselves to honoring our societal contract that defines standards of success. We are constantly striving for a title, promotion, house, car, power, prestige, and all the material possessions that prove to the world that we are successful, that we are important, and that we are enough. We set unrealistic and unimportant expectations of ourselves to avoid judgment and live according to the unwritten rules of society. The pressure we live under is heavy, unhealthy, and unnecessary.

Social media platforms and the invention of the "selfie" has primed the stage for further regression in self-confidence, perpetuating an already desperate human condition of self-doubt. The constant comparison to others, the fictitious positive and fruitful self-image others portray is wreaking havoc on society's psychological well-being. People feel inferior to the glamorous, carefully curated highlight reel of others' exciting and adventurous "edited best lives." Foolishly, we believe we are not enough and live in a state of envy of what is truly fake news. These captivating benchmark profiles of perceived perfection omit the bland normality of what constitutes the rest of the story. In the spirit of keeping up, we reciprocate and become obsessed with "likes" and reactions to feed our own ever-growing need to confirm our validity and subsequent self-worth. As a result, we compound an already prevalent material and judgmental society that is feeling empty, unworthy, and incapable of living authentically.

THE AWAKENING

The foundation of building and living a full life is believing in yourself; a birthright that takes time and effort to achieve. It often requires a provoking experience of loss, pain or suffering to realize you have not been living your best life; that you have defined personal behaviors, standards and expectations for yourself based on a societal norm you believe you must live up to. You may lack the ability to recognize the circumstances in which you are living until that unexpected moment when you read something inspiring, hear a story, experience trauma, lose a job or loved one, a relationship ends, or you come to a mid-life realization (or possible crisis). You are awakened by an alarm signaling an understanding that you have one life to live and it is starting to pass by in an inauthentic, underwhelming manner. You envision the end of your life, looking back at who you were, what you did, and how you lived. The rear-view mirror vividly reflects lost opportunity in all the things that could have and should have been. It exposes the value of life you failed to realize by focusing on the wrong things. You are distraught as you acknowledge the costly sacrifice of not living in alignment with your values and your true character.

You snap out of that reflection and realize the time is TODAY. The moment has come to wake up and stand into the great opportunity you have to live your best life! It is time to stop living by the self-limiting rules by which you've allowed yourself to be victimized. These stories and excuses have existed only in your own mind. Your unfulfilled life has been a plot of your own making. With this new awareness, you acknowledge we all have the same destiny. You are not guaranteed your time here and the only way forward is to optimize every minute and live with no regrets as the truest, most authentic version of yourself.

You acknowledge your unique capabilities and dreams and begin to define what you want from this day forward. This is your one life. Discover who you truly are, where you belong, and how you want to live each day. Deep introspection can be scary but living inauthentically in a lost place of complacency and missed opportunity is even more terrifying. So, grab hold of yourself, face your fears, embrace your brilliance, and embark on a journey of self-discovery and personal transformation. There is no time to waste; your true self is awaiting.

THE JOURNEY TO BEING YOU

Being you. How can something so simple be so difficult? The journey of self-discovery and personal development, can be emotional and challenging, requiring honesty, perseverance, and desire. Acknowledging, appreciating, and fostering your unique and ever-developing talents and capabilities while practicing self-love will enable you to embrace your whole self, transcend self-limiting beliefs and develop beyond your own expectations. Overcoming your previous limitations comes with incredibly high reward while avoiding it comes with an extraordinary high cost of lost time that cannot be recovered. Consciously, you will take one small, courageous step, followed by another, bravely edging yourself away from fear and self-doubt and closer to the person you were meant to be. With each step, you will build momentum to try again, each time becoming easier until self-assuredness is just your way of being. Confident, brave, and authentic; there is no more rewarding place to be.

Consider the journey of a woman who had a sudden and unexpected realization that through her childhood experience, she carried a self-deprecating mindset and belief that she was not deserving of love, respect, or a sense of self-worth. She embraced self-discovery and personal transformation and has reflected on her ongoing journey:

Before I had the courage to embark on my personal journey, I knew I wasn't being the person I wanted to be, the person I could be. To be honest I didn't even know who that person was. Despite having a strong marriage and a successful career I just wasn't happy, overall. I was confident in my capabilities; but that wasn't enough, I wasn't enough. I had a strong desire to belong, to feel worthy, and couldn't figure out what was missing. I didn't know who I could be, and I simply didn't know where to start to find out.

The self-discovery journey is not an easy one and certainly is a very emotional one. At the beginning, it was difficult to keep moving forward as I wasn't certain on the direction, but I persevered even through the exceptionally hard days where I questioned whether it was "working" for me. My coach allowed me space but still held me accountable which gave me strength and helped me realize consistency is the key.

This is not a linear path to an "end goal". It takes work and intense reflection, every single day. Even defining "who I want to be," is constantly evolving but at least now I have a clearer idea of that vision. In the last while, I've really started to embrace my growth and all the emotions that come along with it. I'm nowhere near my destination, but my happiness for today, belief-in-self, and my desire to continue along this path are both so much stronger. Now I know I can be that person: my authentic, better self.

LIVING AUTHENTICALLY

Authenticity is one of the most empowering values. It is a mindset of embracing your individuality while being unwavering in the alignment of your actions to your beliefs. Stand confident in knowing exactly who you are, what you like, your strengths, shortcomings, and passions combined. Being unafraid of who you are does not mean you are stubborn, inconsiderate, or inflexible. It does not mean you are not open to feedback or continual self-reflection and growth. It simply means you are confident in knowing the good, the bad, and the ugly that make up your true, distinctive character. When you can wholeheartedly live as your true self, it is a profound place to be; connected to your higher self (your intention, your conscience, your values, and your purpose). Living with integrity in its deepest, truest meaning is being true to yourself.

Living with a mindset of gratitude for today is an ideal place to be centered. To live in constant strife for achievement and success, you fail to live in the present, and miss soaking up all the joy there is to feel here and now. You believe tomorrow will bring happiness so you strive for further achievement and in doing so you self-inflict stress and suffering, spending wasteful time worrying about what you must accomplish next. As a result, you neglect to be present and proud of who you are and where you currently stand. When you choose to chase what society says you "should be" versus embracing authenticity, you are sacrificing your values and self-worth. Strive for future goals without foregoing the joy of today. Stand in optimism, eagerly anticipating the future while being fully satisfied and in love with what, who, and where you are today.

When you stop rushing to become someone or something else, you will see value in the amazing person you already are. At first, it is nerve wracking because you are lacking self-appreciation and fighting subconscious anxiety about what others may think of you. Your fears of judgment or rejection have built a mindset based on a series of stories you have told yourself. Overthinking how someone may critique you is a wasteful, vicious, and unproductive cycle. Re-channel that focus to embrace self-love and self-respect and surround yourself with people that accept you for who you are, value you for your difference, and expect the same from you in return.

While it is human nature to compare yourself to others, re-framing that mindset to focus instead on becoming the best version of yourself, comparing yourself only to your own progress, you will begin to redefine your priorities. In doing so, you will lessen the extreme pressure you put on yourself to keep up with what you believe is required to feel worthy. In putting less value on how others may judge you, you will absolve yourself from the death sentence of inferiority and live as your authentic self with ease, knowing that you are enough. Embrace who you are, and practice self-care with a focus on what brings you joy.

In striving for goals, remember we are all human and sometimes make mistakes, say the wrong thing, and regret our actions. We are constantly evolving learners who are growing every day. When we can have the modesty and vulnerability to admit our faults, we can welcome them and in parallel, celebrate our strengths. We are all a work in progress and must take a more compassionate approach to our own lives, make light of our shortcomings, and stop taking ourselves so seriously. When you wake up each morning, acknowledge you are facing many of the same struggles as everyone else and are no more imperfect or less human. Stand in confidence and recognize that those apparent flawless, successful others suffer in the same way, no matter their title, wealth, success, or appearance. Allow the imperfect you to embrace your differences and shortcomings as blessings that create your genuine identity.

When you courageously show up as your raw, unguarded self, rediscover the curiosity and playfulness of your youth, you can find and sustain a place of joy, define your own destiny, and live without limits. The journey to living in total and complete self-assuredness is an aspirational, lifelong journey of constant personal growth, complete with phases of advancement and setbacks. There will always be situations and moments of self-doubt. Give yourself permission to be imperfect and find strength and perseverance in living with a wholehearted intention of becoming your best self. Don't chase perfection and superficial happiness; perfection is impractical, and happiness is but a fleeting emotion, both driving the wrong behaviors. Instead, seek a life of growth, discovery, and personal fulfillment. There, you will find inner-peace and a life of vibrancy.

PERSONAL GROWTH

In stretching yourself to grow, do not confuse achieving your personal best with keeping up with standards and expectations of others. Whether it's society's pressure, family values, or individual personality, we tend to put a lot of undue pressure on ourselves and feel defeated when we cannot reach our ever-raising bars of expectation. In my own personal experience as a driven, results-oriented individual who flirts with perfectionist tendencies, I acknowledge I set incredibly high expectations for myself – part of it is my DNA, part of it is in my family value system, and the balance is because of what society has taught me over the years that I should do, should want, and should achieve. For years I've continued to push myself in that direction, forever seeking a sense of fulfillment by striving for the next level of accomplishment. Much of this has been joyful and filled with great personal and professional reward, enabling me to live with the confidence that I am capable and I am worthy; however I was recently inspired by Benjamin Zander's philosophy of "living into my possibility" instead of "living up to the expectations I was setting for myself" which had a transformative impact.

From a prior place of doing, striving, and accomplishing, I turned my energy from an external source of gratification to a deep place of contemplation and self-evaluation. Pausing to be still took every ounce of my strength but it enabled me to understand that my busy doing was a self-imposed obstacle, allowing me to avoid the tough introspection I needed to do. It took honesty and vulnerability, but it relieved a lot of pressure because I was no longer living up to an expectation of ever-reaching heights and achievement of perfection. I was relieved of unconsciously proving myself by reframing my mindset to striving for excellence with a tolerance for missteps in working toward my goals. I released my own bias of expectation, empowering and liberating myself to pursue my true passions and aspirations, opening a whole new world of possibility should I dare explore it.

As you pursue your goals, squash self-limiting beliefs, ignore judgment and embrace fear and anxiety as a means to stretch yourself. When you start to find an element of comfort in discomfort, you move from a place of complacency and stagnation to embracing courage in order to grow, learn, and discover your possibility. When you choose courage over fear, you will find the path to authentically living your best life. In learning how to be courageous, you will find yourself, move past fear, and find freedom. Personal discovery and growth start with a foundation of self-belief and when you look through your fear, you will be unashamed of the full, wholehearted YOU. Acknowledge your unique character and brilliance and courageously show up as that person every day. When you awaken yourself and create space to live into your possibility without hesitation, you will enable limitless personal growth and achievement, a sense of fulfillment and ultimate reward: inner peace.

As you progress and experience personal growth, you may experience resistance and the need to justify yourself to the naysayers. As you go against the grain of complacency, removing your barriers, finding your confidence, growing, and transforming through self-discovery, others may try to hold you back. It may cause them to feel uncertain about their own way of being which could manifest itself with opposition or resentment, create feelings of envy, jealousy, or intimidation. Be prepared for the possible urge to justify yourself but do not give valuable, wasted time to these anticipated reactions that have more to do with others' struggles and uncertainties than it ever did with you.

To use a real-life example; Bob is a senior leader in a prominent financial institution. His coworker was issuing complaints of bullying against him. Bob was dealing with a colleague who was intimidated by his confidence and transparency and was pushing his own insecurities onto Bob from a place of fear and inadequacy. Bob has characterized his strength and character as an ongoing "curse of competence" as threatened coworkers repeatedly react negatively toward his self-assured personality. His ability to confidently speak up with independent and creative ideas has plagued his colleagues with insecurity. Bob struggles to find equilibrium in being his best self and working in harmony with his coworkers; a truth he manages on an ongoing basis. Bob is steadfast in his need to be authentic despite the political challenges it often raises for him as a confident leader. He acknowledges that compromising his personal values is a greater sacrifice than professionally dealing with adversity. While maintaining his true identity, Bob proactively cultivates healthy workplace relationships by fostering a sense of trust and understanding. Though difficult, Bob challenges himself to live with compassion from a place of generosity in working with his peers who have not yet discovered exactly who they are.

SUPPORT PARTNER

In the pursuit of becoming your better self, your willingness to be vulnerable may be one of the most challenging obstacles (even when you acknowledge your desire for change). You can approach the challenge independently; however, working with a neutral, non-judgmental party who can support you in partnership through this mindset transformation can be extremely effective. It must be someone who is not threatened, but rather invested in your journey; someone reliable to encourage you and hold you capable of believing in yourself. A truth teller who is unafraid of flagging your excuses, challenges your thinking, and holds you accountable to your personal commitments in taking this leap forward. A partner can support you by provoking insights, emotion, and positive affirmations to thoughts and capabilities you currently doubt. They assist in removing negative, self-limiting thoughts, reframing them into possibilities; creating opportunities for you to see and understand what once seemed unreachable. Once you know and experience the lightness it brings to live in the ease of self-assuredness, it's very difficult to return to a state of burden, encumbered by living in fear and in fiction.

Consider the example of an incredibly bright and successful specialty surgeon. He has the profile one would assume to be confident and strong, yet he struggled with self-worth and a profound lack of confidence. After experiencing a medical issue of his own, he paused, questioned his purpose and way of being and embraced the journey of self-discovery.

He sought out a partner to support him and moved from a place of internal resistance to finding comfort in his unique identity, creating a shift to allow him to fundamentally believe in himself. It required courage and vulnerability to self-reflect as well as a strong willingness and desire to embrace the journey. Being kind to himself and embracing his new self-awareness has been transformative. He now lives each day with the spirit and confidence that he is enough. His reflection of his personal growth:

I've shifted to a growth rather than a fixed mindset. I switched from trying to uphold impossibly high expectations for myself and reflecting on any imperfection as shameful. In reflecting on my personal flaws, I learned to accept that imperfections are part of what makes us human and that they can be framed as valuable data from which to improve. I learned how to hold a comfortable tension between aiming high and the need for perfection while being kind to myself when making mistakes, and not squandering the opportunity to learn from them. I brought the questions "who and how do you want to be?" into the forefront of my mind and maintained them there through continued work with my coach who would provoke thought and help keep these questions in my continued awareness. With my intended changes in the circle of my awareness and the accountability within which my coach held me, I was able to sustain my effort in personal change that resulted in personal transformation. These entailed self-acceptance, self-kindness, valuing myself as I value those around me, and holding the continuous intention to apply a positive and growth-oriented mindset to my life.

BELIEF IN YOURSELF

A person's success in life is truly based on what they believe of themselves. It is difficult to show up purposefully (personally or professionally) without a strong sense of self. When you break your personal promise to be yourself, it creates distance between you and your truest self but when your body, mind and conscious intentions can live in alignment, you can transcend to a state of self-actualized inner peace. Living in a state of calm within your own mind, life becomes simple.

Confident in yourself, you can go about your days with ease. Freeing yourself from your own story and disabling your imagination from the spiral of fictional storytelling, you become capable. When you can stand in a self-assured place of knowing yourself, you can believe in yourself with ease. Believing shifts your behaviors to enable who you are, not discount yourself for who you are not. Believing is acknowledging who you may not be yet, but celebrating who you are today while striving to be your best. Believing inspires action and enables personal growth.

Know that you are enough and that your distinctive beauty, talents, and gifts were meant to vividly shine; to stand out in your unique individuality. Practice self-compassion and embrace your worth by celebrating all you have accomplished to bring you to today, then challenge yourself to take the first step of your journey to a confident place of self-belief. Regardless of your chosen path of self-discovery, the life-changing impact will be remarkable in every way: your state of mind, your personal life, work life, and the greater impact you will make on the world around you. This is a short and precious life where every day matters. You have no time to waste lingering in the mindset of suffering or being less than you are capable of being. With a strong sense of self, you can live to life's fullest potential, accomplishing and becoming the most you can be. Embrace your gifts and live with pride and confidence that you are worthy of the greatest life experience possible.

CREATING POSITIVE CHANGE

In your life: By simply directing your emotional energy on being your best self, the meaningful impact you will make on others and on the world around you is immense. Not unlike equipping your own mask first in an airplane emergency, intentionally putting yourself first by investing in discovering who you are and want to be from within will enable you to confidently enter the world in alignment with your true character. Living wholeheartedly as the raw, unguarded version of yourself will free you to just BE. To be vulnerable enough to expose your true self and live confidently without fear of judgment will create a path to living complete.

Believing in yourself gives you the confidence to live in support and service of others. Instead of living in rivalry, you can confidently strive to live out your own dreams while living in community with others, supporting them to do the same. This shift will evoke a change in all your relationships; personal and professional, where friends, family, neighbors, and colleagues alike live in a supportive place of one another. A positive, selfless world where everyone can focus on the good, laugh more, cry less, and live with ease and vibrancy. When life isn't a comparison but a true journey to living as your best and truest self, you can live in abundance, applauding others when they succeed, sharing in their happiness and supporting them when they struggle. There is no time for comparison, complacency, or skepticism when you have the opportunity to live as a mentor and role model with an open heart and an open mind. When you are confidently living your best life as your truest self, supporting and empowering others to do the same, the collective impact will be extraordinary.

At work: Evoking this mindset shift in the way we approach life will have an equally dramatic impact on how the business world operates today. Organizations are primarily rewarding short-term metrics and bottom-line performance. This misguided focus on numbers over people, combined with society's fundamental lack of self-belief, fosters environments of rivalry where politics abound and innovation and productivity flounder.

In today's increasingly complex and global environment, leaders simply cannot know everything or be everywhere. Yet from a place of insecurity, they attract "yes-men" and "yes-women" in a desperate attempt to obtain reassurance, disabling themselves from building teams of the best and brightest talent. Self-doubt creates unhealthy competition and behaviors of envy and resentment, a focus on self over team, and much time and energy wasted on concealing weaknesses and hyper-managing personal reputations.

Supporting leaders to know who they are will give them a mindset to succeed. In learning to live whole, they develop a new understanding and begin to ensure that every decision and action they make is in service of their core values. Confident in who they are, they are enabled to support their people to be the same. When all people at all levels across the organization can capitalize on their strengths while declaring and overcoming their limitations, it will have a powerful and positive impact. It will transform work environments, creating a mindset of collective support and collaboration in support of the greater good. A sense of community will be established, and teams of strength assimilated, complete with experts and thought leaders with complementary knowledge and skill sets, enabling achievement of results without limits. Diversity will be embraced in a whole new way, seeking, and supporting individual and unique differences. Whether it be culture, race, personal interests or talents, people will embrace compassion to understand and support others with a collective view of acceptance; attracting a collection of self-confident individuals, striving for excellence while evolving as their individual best selves.

Individual growth promotes a sense of achievement and personal fulfillment. Where culture is built on a foundation of personal development with a philosophy of being your best self and living your best life and an objective of being in service to others (peers, subordinates, and superiors alike), people will thrive. Development should not be confined to a course, a project, a mentor, or static event, but rather redefined as an organizational way of being (how operations are run, projects are managed, and feedback is given), where people collaborate, support others, and where trust and autonomy prevail. In fostering people's passions and achievement of personal goals through a focus on their potential rather than their limitations, leaders gain trust and loyalty by enabling and inspiring them to rise to their best. When people feel supported and valued, they contribute discretionary effort and become vested in the pursuit of team and company goals. When everyone at every level is empowered to bring their whole self to work, engagement will flourish, teamwork will thrive, and results will tell the story of success.

TAKE ACTION

Be brave, speak your truth and celebrate your greatness. Choose courage over fear and start each morning with assuredness and a steadfast belief in yourself to conquer the day with fury and passion. Life will continue to present new challenges. Equip yourself with the ability to overcome each encounter by acknowledging you are capable and worthy. When you learn to confidently embrace your individuality, the way you see the world and live your life will be transformed in a positive and remarkable way, creating a much-deserved opportunity to live big with no regrets. When you are confidently unafraid, you act only from a good-natured, well-intended place. When you show up authentically with no hidden agendas, you can just be; present with others, connected to them from an authentic, genuine place with a focus on what you can give versus what you can get. When you transform fear into courage, you liberate others to do the same. As a role model living into your own possibility, you give others permission to do the same. In doing so you will start to move the world to a place where people live with compassion in the spirit of serving others, transcending self-interest, and working to a greater good.

Embrace the journey to vividly live out your legacy. When you allow yourself to live your best life as your truest self, you will make the world an abundant, more meaningful place for all to not just live but to THRIVE. Start the movement - believe in yourself, change your life, change the world.

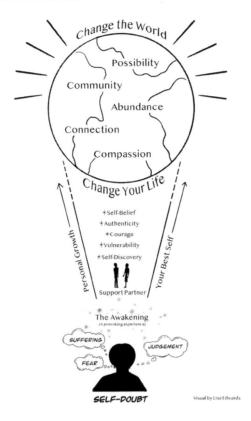

Visual by Lisa Edwards

Take Action in Ten Simple Steps:

1. Identify three challenges you are fearful of approaching.
2. Identify three self-limiting beliefs that are creating these fears.
3. Write down three negative impacts this avoidance is having.
4. Write down three positive outcomes from making forward movement on these challenges.
5. Write down one thing you will commit to do in the next thirty days to challenge yourself to moving forward.
6. Name one person who can support you in holding this commitment to yourself.
7. Record how you feel before and after taking that action.
8. Record the outcomes of taking that action (include what you learned about yourself).
9. Celebrate embracing courage to overcome your fears.
10. Do it again!

Sandra Wrycraft, Certified Coach Practitioner

Strategy & Talent Consultant, Executive Coach

With two decades of leadership experience across a broad range of environments, one thing remains constant; people are what make great organizations successful. My passion is in supporting others' growth and development; inspiring them to overcome barriers, particularly self-limiting thoughts, and behaviors in order to live life to its fullest potential. My aspiration is to change the world one self-believer at a time.

I am committed to becoming my best self and to live as a role model to my bright and brave son, Luke whose youth represents a future of limitless possibility. I believe it is our obligation to leave this world a better, brighter place for the next generation and in living into that vision and creating a community of support, we will individually realize our undiscovered possibilities in order to live our best life.

Connect with Sandra:
www.findinc.ca
sandra@findinc.ca
www.twitter.com/swrycraft
www.linkedin.com/in/sandrawrycraft/

Conclusion

As you've learned from the stories and philosophies included in this book, there is no shortage of the types of adversity these authors encountered. In your life, if you haven't experienced challenges, *you will*. Life *is* suffering. Be it from mental or physical health challenges, the loss of a loved one, the loss of a job, or the loss of innocence. We will all face something that will shake the foundations of our world.

With the DNA of 20,000 generations, you are not only a survivor, but when you keep going, you will adapt. While we may be here for a short and sometimes confusing time, we can be better for it.

After reading this book, we hope you embrace the concept that no matter what the challenge is that you are facing, that there are many ways to not only survive but to thrive beyond it. Your opportunity is to get through the hardship and then extract the lesson the adversity offered.

Now it's time for you to record your story. Not necessarily as the authors have in this book, but in your way. It may be for your children and family, it may be for a broader audience, or it may be for yourself. Regardless of who gets to hear or read your story, you will know that you can face any adversity and adapt.

The Certified Coaches Federation
Making the World a Better Place through Coaching

BECOMING A CCF COACH

COULD YOU BE A COACH?

If you are an empathetic person who wants to make the world a better place and enjoy helping people become their best, becoming a CCF coach may be right for you.

THE CERTIFIED COACHES FEDERATION'S DEFINITION OF COACHING

Coaching is a professional relationship that helps people break through their limitations to achieve extraordinary results in their lives, careers, businesses, or organizations.

The process of coaching encourages clients to deepen their learning, improve their performance, and enhance their quality of life through self-discovery and self-empowerment. In each meeting, the client chooses the focus of conversation, while the coach listens and contributes with observations and questions. This collaboration creates clarity and moves the client into action.

Coaching accelerates the client's progress by providing greater focus and awareness of choice. Coaching concentrates on discovering and clarifying goals and eliciting strategies and solutions to get the client on track to achieve their future goals at a pace that is achievable for the client.

CCF coaches recognize that results depend on the client's intentions, choices, and actions, supported by the coach's efforts and application of the coaching process.

• • • • •

Contact us today by visiting our website at www. CertifiedCoachesFederation.com, sending an email to Support@ CertifiedCoachesFederation.com, or calling us at 1-866-455-2155 (North America) or 011-705-738-1256 (Internationally).

Printed in the United States
By Bookmasters